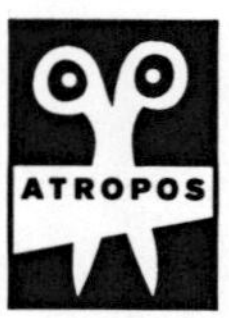

ATROPOS PRESS
new york • dresden

Facticity, Poverty and Clones:
On Kazuo Ishiguro's *Never Let Me Go*

Brian Willems

Think Media EGS Series is supported by the European Graduate School

ATROPOS PRESS
New York • Dresden

151 First Avenue # 14, New York, N.Y. 10003

cover image: Nancy Jones, "cactuseyes" (detail) (2008)
cover design: Hannes Charen

ISBN 978-0-9825309-7-9

to my mother

Contents

Acknowledgments

I would first like to thank, once again, Avital Ronell for making so much seem possible. I am also very grateful to Wolfgang Schirmacher and all those at the European Graduate School. Special acknowledgement must also be given to Mirjana Bonačić for her careful reading and great patience. Thanks to Dave and Jes for doing what they do, how they do it. To Nancy Jones for her image. And also, without question, to Mela.

Introduction

This book delineates and analyzes the philosophical ramifications of the rhetorical strategies and semantic thematizations of death, poverty and clones in Kazuo Ishiguro's 2005 novel *Never Let Me Go*. My central argument is that by repositioning an awareness of one's own death into beings that are other-than-human Ishiguro's novel becomes an allegory of the so-called "human condition." What this allegory shows is that the poverty of awareness usually ascribed to the animal is itself what is most human about "humanity." This argument unfolds through a tripartite structure: (1) the thematic centrality of an awareness of one's own death (facticity) is developed in Ishiguro's novel, which tells the story of a number of clones raised as organ hosts. Then a reading of facticity as a human-only trait is advanced, a reading which is disrupted by the uncanny proximity the clones have towards the non-cloned. Similar rhetorical structures of proximity and difference, such as antanaclasis, are shown to be paramount to the formal construction of the text; (2) the ability to make the poverty of the non-human visible as what is actually most human is developed. A rereading of both the "everyday" and "boredom" locates this making-visible, reflexively, within poverty itself. This rereading is developed through recursive notions of both memory and the autobiographical narration of self; (3) making poverty visible involves, because of its reflexive nature, an experience of being-towards-poverty. This reading is developed through the ability of the visceral body to formulate a tropism of an experience of facticity which can only develop from the non-rational "poverty" of the corpus. It is argued that the body's physical paroxysms are not to be read as an antitropism to "rational thinking" but rather as a foregrounding of the processes of deterritorialization and reterritorialization. The development of this movement is not an argument for an expanded self as much as a renewal to the self we tend to forget we are.

The first chapter analyses the experience of one's own death, or facticity, in *Never Let Me Go*. The chapter is titled "The Familiarity of Strangeness in Death" because a sheltering of both closeness and difference is traced through a number of rhetorical and semantic strategies. However, before providing an overview of a number of main points covered in this chapter, a brief introduction to Ishiguro's novel is appropriate.

Never Let Me Go is a novel told in the first person by Kathy H., who introduces herself at the outset as a somewhat privileged "carer" who is soon to give up this position and become a "donor." While these terms are ambiguous at first, their meaning slowly develops over the first part of the novel which tells the story of Kathy's days at a boarding school called Hailsham. There we are introduced to the other main characters, fellow students Tommy and Ruth, and a number of guardians from the school, including Miss Lucy, Miss Emily, and Madame, the latter being a rather elusive figure who appears at the school to take the artwork the children make away to what is known as "the Gallery." However, soon the mystery of who the students really are is revealed: Hailsham is a facility for clones who are being raised as organ donors for the "normals" of Britain. Upon leaving Hailsham, Kathy, Tommy and Ruth take up residency at the Cottages, a sort of half-way house the clones occupy before becoming "carers," meaning those who would provide care for clones undergoing their donations. Eventually, however, all "carers" become donors, and Kathy is writing her memories of her and her friends during her last days as a carer, leading up to her becoming a donor, like those before her.

The argument of my first chapter focuses on the thought surrounding facticity and the manner with which it is dealt in *Never Let Me Go*. Facticity is developed in its role as a human-only trait by centering on Martin Heidegger and readers of Heidegger; the main thrust of this traditional reading of facticity is that whereas both animals and humans die, it is only humans that can know their own death "as such," and thus incorporate a dying-within-life. Ishiguro's novel re-schedules such a facticity into the clones of the novel who are, actually, very much and even more-than human, exhibiting the same emotions, concerns and joys that are usually attributed to "normals." However, because of the homodiegetic nature of the first-person narration, the narratee of the novel is also "assumed" to be a clone. This second-person address, which is too blatantly not actually written for a clone, then interrupts accepted notions of the position of the implied reader. As such, the novel becomes an allegory of "the human condition" which disrupts one of the coordinates of the allegory itself – the human condition on which it is based. The structure of this representation and disruption is developed on a rhetorical level through an exegesis of what will just briefly be referred to here as Freud's treatment of the *fort/da*, antanaclasis and the over-explicit apostrophe of the narratee; on a thematic level these structures are developed through a discussion of lying, the "perverse," and "non-relation."

The aim of the second chapter is to develop how this disruption is made visible. My reading begins with the notion of the "everyday" and "idle talk" and their relationship to interpretation. The impetus for this reading begins in the "flat" narrational tone of Kathy, the character-narrator of the novel. A reevaluation of boredom as a fundamental attunement accompanies an assessment of the ability of poverty, or the flat-everyday, to awaken an experience of temporality and profound comportment. This thought is then expanded through readings of poverty and experience centering on the work of Walter Benjamin. From this a theory of allegory which foregrounds the difficulties of reading itself is posited, beginning with Paul de Man and Avital Ronell. It is seen that a "double-bind" of being arises through the self-reflexivity of a philosophical poverty, which is structurally and thematically related to the "*fort/da*" argument from the first chapter. This self-reflexivity is then shown to be what is actually *most* human through a discussion of memory and the autobiographical self.

The third and final chapter traces the transition from making poverty visible to *being poverty*. This discussion begins with the body as a location of experience, which begins with the thought of Charles Darwin on emotions and the autonomic nervous system. The main figure from *Never Let Me Go* for this chapter is Tommy, who is able to experience facticity not only through explicit linguistic revelation but also via the paroxysms of his visceral body. Tommy's position between expression and experience is then read along with the thought of Gilles Deleuze and Félix Guattari on the dual-movement of deterritorialization and reterritorialization. This doubled-structure is then used to explore the relation between light and shadow in the novel in which light is used not to dispel shadow but to make shadow visible. A constant renewal of the relationship with this new visibility of poverty is then explored along with Ronell's work on recursiveness and the test which foregrounds the emptiness of the structure of the test that Kathy and Tommy undergo at the end of the novel, a test to prove their love in order to obtain a temporary deferral from donating their organs, which they find was only a rumor.

All three chapters aim to show the philosophical implications of the rhetorical and thematic structures of recursiveness and poverty which are seen not as antithetical to a human condition but rather as ways of making what is most human visible, and thus possible.

1. The Familiarity of Strangeness in Death

Where death waits for us is uncertain; let us look for him everywhere.
-Michel de Montaigne[1]

Ishiguro has stated that when reading a review of one of his novels, after seeing whether it is favorable or not, what he is most interested in is how his work has been summarized: "Have they actually summarized the book in the way that I wanted the book to come over?" he asks; "For a long time, at the beginning of my career, I would actually get favorable reviews that praised me for a book that I didn't mean to write. They were emphasizing all the wrong things and praising me for a book that I didn't intend to write."[2] Keeping this in mind, the centrality of an experience of death in *Never Let Me Go*, which is indicated by the title of this chapter, has been clearly stated by Ishiguro himself: "My subject matter wasn't going to be the triumph of the human spirit. I was interested in the *human capacity* to accept what must seem like a limited and cruel fate."[3] In addition, Ishiguro has asked: "What really matters if you know that [death] is going to happen to you?" He continues: "What are the things you hold on to, what are the things you want to set right before you go? What do you regret? What are the consolations? What are the things you feel you have to do before

---

[1] De Montaigne, Michel, "That to Study Philosophy is to Learn to Die," *The Works of Montaigne*, ed. William Hazlitt (London: John Templeman, 1842), 29.

[2] Allan Vorda and Kim Herzinger, "An Interview with Kazuo Ishiguro," *Conversations with Kazuo Ishiguro*, ed. Brian Shaffer and Cynthia Wong (Jackson: University Press of Mississippi, 2008), 83. Interviews are quoted from this volume when possible.

[3] Moore, Michael Scott and Michael Sontheimer, "*Spiegel* Interview with Kazuo Ishiguro," *Spiegel Online*, Internet: http://www.spiegel.de, accessed March 24, 2009 (emphasis added).

you go? And also the question is, what is all the education and culture for if you are going to check out?"[4]

Actually, *Never Let Me Go* troubles the idea of what Ishiguro calls "human capacity" by telling the story of a group of young students, who are really human clones, becoming aware of the inevitability of death. As Louis Menand puts it: "Their lives are short; they know that they are doomed."[5] The "limited and cruel fate" Ishiguro refers to is that these students are raised as organ donors for the public at large. The clones die in their early thirties, with no one surviving their "fourth donation"[6] of an organ,[7] because after that a donor always "completes"

---

[4] John Freeman, "Never Let Me Go: A Profile of Kazuo Ishiguro," *Conversations with Kazuo Ishiguro*, ed. Brian Shaffer and Cynthia Wong (Jackson: University Press of Mississippi, 2008), 195.

[5] Louis Menand, "There's Something about Kathy: Ishiguro's Quasi-Science-Fiction Novel," *New Yorker* 81.6 (2005), 78.

[6] Kazuo Ishiguro, *Never Let Me Go* (London: Faber and Faber, 2005), 3. Further references will be given parenthetically.

[7] In the report "Cloning Human Beings," made by National Bioethics Advisory Commission for the U.S. President in 1997, spurned by the cloning of the sheep Dolly, the commission discusses the "Potential Therapeutic Applications of Nuclear Transfer Cloning," including the "Potential Applications in Organ and Tissue Transplantation," the commission differentiates between vital and non-vital organs for removal, although details on which organs are donated are never given in *Never Let Me Go*. "Many human diseases, when they are severe enough, are treated effectively by organ or tissue transplantation, including some leukemias, liver failure, heart and kidney disease. In some instances the organ required is non-vital, that is, it can be taken from the donor without great risk (e.g., bone marrow, blood, kidney). In other cases, the organ is obviously vital and required for the survival of the individual, such as the heart. All transplantation is imperfect, with the exception of that which occurs between identical twins, because transplantation of organs between individuals requires genetic compatibility," Available on the Internet:http://bioethics.georgetown.edu, accessed March 24, 2009. The commission then unilaterally condemns any form of human cloning for the purpose of organ donation: "In principle, the application of nuclear transfer cloning to humans could provide a potential source of organs or tissues of a predetermined genetic background. The notion of using human cloning to produce individuals for use solely as organ donors is repugnant, almost unimaginable, and morally unacceptable. A morally more acceptable and potentially feasible approach is to direct differentiation along a specific path to produce specific tissues (e.g., muscle or nerve) for therapeutic transplantation rather than to produce an entire individual. Given current uncertainties about the feasibility of this, however, much research would be needed in animal systems before it would be scientifically sound, and therefore potentially morally acceptable, to go forward with this approach," ibid.

(*NLMG* 203).[8] The literariness of the novel comes forth in Ishiguro's statement regarding the novel's subject matter being that of the problematic notion of the "human condition"; it will be shown that because the clones function as an *allegory* of the human condition they actually foreground a familiarity-in-strangeness within the idea of this so-called human condition itself. In other words, the familiarity-in-strangeness of what is human disrupts anterior notions of what the "human condition" is in the first place. While the notion of allegory is developed in chapter three, at the moment it is important to keep in mind Avital Ronell's reading of the work Walter Benjamin did on the way allegory disrupts anteriority. Ronell argues that "Disfiguring itself even as it unfolds, the allegorical attacks understanding as it profiles a power to defy comprehension. It defies the comprehension – indeed, the comprehensiveness – promised by the symbol, which offers an image of organic totality. By contrast, the allegorical dessicates the organic unity of the world potentiated by the symbol."[9]

The idea of connecting a disruption of unity with clones may at first seem anomalous because, by definition, clones are copies. The word "clone" comes from the Greek *klon*, meaning a branch or twig, referring to the process by which a plant cutting can grow into an adult version of itself. For animals, monozygotic twins, whether created naturally or artificially, are the closest of copies, sharing all mitochondrial DNA from the same egg.[10] However, in order for the clones to function as an allegory, there also needs to be some difference between the clones and their antecedents. On the one hand it can be said that the clones in the novel are at least *treated* differently than "normal" humans, most tragically through their role as organ hosts. However, in almost every other respect, they are human in

---

[8] Leona Toker and Daniel Chertoff argue that "The term 'complete' in Ishiguro's novel suggests that one has accomplished one's mission in life; it also evades the notion of 'death,'" "Reader Response and the Recycling of Topoi in Kazuo Ishiguro's *Never Let Me Go*," *Partial Answers: Journal of Literature and the History of Ideas* 6.1 (2008), 164.

[9] Avital Ronell, *Stupidity* (Urbana; Chicago: University of Illinois Press, 2002), 107.

[10] John Harris, *On Cloning* (New York: Routledge, 2004), 2-3.

their emotions and intelligence.[11] So the clones do not occupy a clear position of difference *or* similarity to "normal humanity." While the kind of difference the clones foreground is developed as allegorical because it is temporal by looking at the work on allegory by Paul de Man,[12] at the moment it can be stated that *Never Let Me Go* is not a novel about delineating the line between humans and beings that are other-than-human, but rather about scrambling an ability to comfortably draw those lines in the first place. What the novel does do, however, is to open up a space for difference from within similarity. As such, it recalls one of de Man's claims for what rhetoric itself does, which is: "Rhetoric radically suspends logic and opens up vertiginous possibilities of referential aberration."[13] The clones occupy such a "cozy state of suspension" (*NLMG* 140) because they do something that only humans are supposed to be able to do: they are able to experience their own possibility of no-longer being.

An awareness of mortality has traditionally been used as one of the ways to close up a definition of humanity, rather than open it to vertiginous possibilities of referential aberration. However, rescheduling this awareness in a being that is different-than-human begins to form a ground from which to question the anterior assumptions of what actually constitutes "the human condition" itself. The figure of the clones will be shown to open such possibilities because the way they experience facticity is troubling in its concomitant assumptions and disruptions. For example, Brooke Allen argues that an inkling of facticity (assumption) is in fact what separates the clone children from "normals," who have no such inklings (disruption): "They differ from ordinary children only in their vague awareness of what the future holds for them and in their

[11] The one major difference is that no clone is able to reproduce, a topic taken up below.

[12] Paul de Man, *Blindness and Insight: Essays in the Rhetoric of Contemporary Criticism* (Minneapolis: University of Minnesota Press, 2006), 224-6.

[13] Paul de Man, *Allegories of Reading: Figural Language in Rousseau, Nietzsche, Rilke and Proust* (New Haven; London: Yale University Press, 1979), 10.

resignation to it."[14] This "difference" will be seen through a strong reading of the "vague" captured in Allen's quote.

Ishiguro has stated that he shortened the lives of his characters in order to make their grappling with death more intense, coupling the clones with "we" and "people," meaning assumingly non-cloned humans: "'We all face the inevitability of our lives coming to an end, or of organs failing if not being removed. People search for something that will carry on beyond death, through art or religion or love, but everyone has that same fate to accept. My interest, in this book, was in compressing that into 30-odd years of three individuals' lives.'"[15] Ishiguro's interest is in compressing "that" into the shortened lives of his characters. "That" seems to refer to a number of elements: the inevitability that "we" all face, the search for something to help create a belief in a life extending beyond that inevitability and the acceptance that "facing" such a fate implies. While all of these aspects will come under exegesis below, the focus of this chapter is a reading of the kind of experience of mortality which the clones undergo. This reading is accomplished first through the novel's development, and more importantly critique, of a *nonrelational* acceptance of death, and second through what it means for an *other-than-human being* to undergo this experience which is usually limited to humans only.

This reading is structured along issues raised by Martin Heidegger's thought on the awareness of one's own death, or *facticity* [*Faktizität*].[16] The assumption that facticity is supposedly a human-only trait is germane to the novel because the clones are, on the one hand, identical to humans both on the level of their DNA and in their emotions. However, despite, but also because of, this similarity, the clones are also treated in a tragically "non-human" fashion, meaning that they are farmed

---

[14] Brooke Allen, "The Damned and the Beautiful," *New Leader* (March/April 2005), 26.

[15] Emily Mead, "Future Present," *Publishers Weekly* (January 21 2005), 47.

[16] Which can, at this moment, be briefly, if somewhat cryptically, stated thus: "The concept of facticity implies that an 'innerworldly' being has being-in-the-world in such a way that it can understand itself as bound up in its 'destiny' with the being of those beings which it encounters within its own world," Martin Heidegger, *Being and Time*, trans. Joan Stambaugh (Albany: State University of New York Press, 1996), 52.

for their organs. As quoted in a footnote above, the US National Bioethics Advisory Commission has stated that "The notion of using human cloning to produce individuals for use solely as organ donors is repugnant, almost unimaginable, and morally unacceptable."[17] The novel, which does "imagine" this situation, is in one sense a treaty on the ethicality of human cloning by an implied author. However, and perhaps more forcefully, the novel functions as an allegory which questions what the "human condition" might be covering up in the first place. The fulcrum of difference needed for this allegory to take place rests on a reading of an awareness of one's facticity.

Heidegger states that while humans are able to come to an experience of their own finitude, the relationship that non-human beings have to facticity is vitiated; for example, while an animal's relation to finitude is not one of complete absence, it is not the same as the human's. Therefore it is a *lesser* relationship, meaning one of *poverty* [*Armut*].[18] What this differentiation means is that whether read as the ability to do philosophy or to speak a language, accessibility to the possibility of one's demise implies a second-order level of consciousness[19] that has been

---

[17] Harris states that "The creation of compatible organs through CNR [Cell Nuclear Replacement] is one of the major potential therapeutic applications of the technique, although it is currently regarded as highly speculative. Again the capacity of stem cells to form any part of the human organism would be harnessed to create 'tailor-made' organs, which, because they are formed from cells, which are clones of the intended recipient, would be compatible and immune from the body's normal mechanisms for rejecting 'foreign' tissue. The procedure would be the same described above, up to the point of harvesting ESC [Embryonic stem cells]. Ideally, ESC might be induced to *differentiate* in the laboratory, that is, to specialise into specific types of cells, and then grown until a full organ could be available for transplant. In a future scenario, this procedure would obviate the major problem of shortage of organs, as people in need of an organ could have 'their own' spare organs created by this means, and the problem of immunological rejection would be solved by cloning the cells used," *On Cloning*, 8. Harris does not address the use of humans as hosts of these organs.

[18] Martin Heidegger, *The Fundamental Concepts of Metaphysics: World, Finitude, Solitude*, trans. William McNeill and Nicholas Walker (Bloomington; Indianapolis: Indiana University Press, 1995), 192-195.

[19] "Secondness," according to Charles Peirce's well-known categories of firstness, secondness and thirdness, is the level in which the human is to be first found because it is there that reason initially makes an appearance. See Charles Peirce, *Peirce on Signs: Writings on Semiotic by Charles Sanders Peirce* (Chapel Hill: The University of North Carolina Press, 1991), 180-203.

assumed to set humanity apart from other animals, allowing human beings alone to appropriate what Heidegger calls "being-there," or "Dasein." This chapter shows how Ishiguro's novel challenges these assumptions through its interplay of implied authors and readers; as Eluned Summers-Bremner argues, while discussing J. M. Coetzee's *Disgrace* along with Ishiguro's novel, "*Disgrace* and *Never Let Me Go* show how, for humans, sex and death – the enigma of our finitude as it exceeds biological explanation – are functional impasses that are definitional but also ethically demanding of human beings."[20]

The novel's structure may be initially described as a story told in the first-person by a clone to a narratee who is a fellow clone. However, a difference develops in that the implied reader of the story is actually not a clone, and therefore the story becomes an allegory. What this allegory offers is a tale of a group of beings who, despite their many similarities, are still somehow different from humans. These beings' experience of facticity is "repugnant" to the implied reader because they never seem to rebel against their fate: they seemingly just do what they are "supposed" to do without any resistance.[21] James Butcher states that "Perhaps the most disturbing aspect of the book is the stoicism with which the clones face their fate."[22] He continues by saying that "they are brainwashed into believing that donation is the only option for them. None of them seeks to escape to avoid their fate."[23] One the one hand Butcher does take this a step further and begins to make the connection between this inability to rebel and the human condition itself: "But that is not to say that they are mindless automatons. On the contrary, these are people who are every bit as human as the members of the

[20] Eluned Summers-Bremner, "'Poor Creatures': Ishiguro's and Coetzee's Imaginary Animals," *Mosaic* 39.4 (December 2006), 147.

[21] The theme of what one is "supposed" to do resonates throughout the stories of Ishiguro's first work to be published after *Never Let Me Go*, the collection *Nocturnes*.

[22] James Butcher, "A Wonderful Donation," *Lancet* 365 (2005), 1299.

[23] Ibid. Butcher also takes this a step further and begins to make the connection between this inability to rebel and the human condition itself: "But that is not to say that they are mindless automatons. On the contrary, these are people who are every bit as human as the members of the society who created them. They love and hate and want desperately to cling onto life, but do not know the rules that govern their existence," ibid.

society who created them. They love and hate and want desperately to cling onto life, but do not know the rules that govern their existence."[24] However, he seems to be conflating two separate issues: an acceptance of facticity and an instrumentality which presumably shortens the clones' natural lifespans. This chapter argues that even with instrumentality "removed," the story of these beings accepting their fate is disturbing in itself because it raises questions about the ability of the implied reader to experience facticity at all. In fact, this allegory functions as a mirror reflecting the impossibility of a factically aware human condition in the first place, which is a reflection of the position Heidegger describes as poverty.

Heidegger's location of poverty in the non-human animal indicates too bold a demarcation line for *Never Let Me Go*, which is a story of blurred thresholds rather than deep cuts. What is not intended here is that the clones are somehow "treated as animals" in the novel. As Daniel Vorhaus argues, it is important that by the time we find out the main protagonists are clones, it's "too late" to think of them as anything but human: "his clones have already established themselves as ordinary people. They laugh, cry, squabble, reconcile, grow older and, ultimately, they fall in love. While Ishiguro's tale has an unmistakable air of science fiction to it, it is difficult for the reader to view its protagonists as anything other than remarkably *normal.*"[25] However, a discussion of animals, or of "the animal," has historically been one of the primary locations of a definition and questioning of what constitutes being "human," which is an admittedly and profoundly problematic notion. *Never Let Me Go* blurs the line between a human and other kinds of being not through modes of what-something-is-not but rather through incorporation and contamination. Looking at Ishiguro's representation of facticity not only questions assumptions made by Heidegger regarding non-humans, but more importantly it provides a discussion of applying *poverty* to the human situation itself. Summers-Bremner sees questioning the role of facticity

---

[24] Ibid.

[25] Daniel Vorhaus, "Review of Kazuo Ishiguro, *Never Let Me Go*," *The American Journal of Bioethics* 7.2 (2007), 99.

within the human itself as one of the central contributions of *Never Let Me Go*:

> the title also signals the novel's central problem. It is a problem arising within the theory and practice of the posthuman that I find registered less by [N. Katherine] Hayles than by the readerly encounter set up by Ishiguro's novel. Hayles presents the concept of posthumanity as a domain "in which constraints act in dynamic conjunction with metaphoric language to articulate the rich possibilities of distributed cognitive systems [...] includ[ing] human and nonhuman actors" [...] But she does not address the fact that the posthuman is itself the product of a crucial impasse within the human being: the unimaginable fact of death. To the extent that posthumanity proceeds without a structurally generated address to this, its irreducible historical cause – a matter of limit or the pre-given unthinkability of the end of human life from within the bounds of reason, rather than a matter of imagined content – it is doomed to be forever wishful.[26]

While in no way aiming to resuscitate "the posthuman" per se, Summers-Bremner's call for an incorporation of poverty within a re-thinking of the human itself needs to be addressed. One of the main points being argued here is that the poverty of being that has been philosophically ascribed to animals is in fact the coordinates of what is most human. Or, as David Farrell Krell words it: "Appropriate Dasein, rapt to the ownmost possibility of its existence, is an animal."[27] In a re-vamping of Heideggerian terminology, humans are not being-towards-death, but *being-towards-poverty*.

---

[26] Summers-Bremner, "'Poor Creatures,'" 154.

[27] David Farrell Krell, "Spiriting Heidegger," *Of Derrida, Heidegger, and Spirit*, ed. David Wood (Evanston: Northwestern University Press, 1993), 22.

1.1 Being-towards-death

Although it may not be clear what is happening at the time, the novel opens with Kathy H. dryly stating an awareness of her own death: "My name is Kathy H. I'm thirty-one years old, and I've been a carer now for over eleven years. That sounds long enough, I know, but actually they want me to go on for another eight months, until the end of this year" (*NLMG* 3). The reason for any difficulty in understanding these opening lines as a statement of facticity is because of the homodiegetic nature of the narrator[28] which assumes that the narratee has knowledge regarding the referents of "carer" and "long enough." This confusion leads Claire Messud to state that: "we 'naturally' assume she's at work in Britain's healthcare system, tending to the elderly or infirm. That this is an insufficient understanding is, within the paragraph, abundantly clear [...]"[29] Initially it would seem that such confusion in the novel would force its readers, as Deborah Britzman states, to "become slow readers, caught between our anticipations and the consequences of the signifier. We lose our place. It can feel as if the book is reading us, turning our pages."[30] However, the withholding of information which turns readers into "slow readers" is actually a

[28] Meaning a narrator who is "obliged to justify [...] the information he gives about the scenes from which 'he' was absent as a character [...]"Gérard Genette, *Narrative Discourse Revisited*, trans. Jane Lewin (Ithaca: Cornell University Press, 1988), 78. For a strong reading of the interplay of multiple levels of narration in Ishiguro, especially in *Remains of the Day*, see Claire Pégon, *L'Art de la Fugue chez K. Ishiguro* (Toulouse: Presses Universitaires du Mirail, 2004), esp. 33-57.

[29] Claire Messud, "Love's Body," *The Nation* (May 16 2005), 30. Bruce Robbins argues that in the opening sentence there is another kind of estrangement in operation: "If the word 'carer' seems a bit mysterious, it's because the congenial everyday verb has been absorbed into an official-sounding occupational category," Bruce Robbins, *Upward Mobility and the Common Good: Toward a Literary History of the Welfare State* (Princeton: Princeton University Press, 2007), 199.

[30] Deborah Britzman, "On Being a Slow Reader: Psychoanalytic Reading Problems in Ishiguro's *Never Let Me Go*," *Changing English* 13.3 (December 2006), 307. See Ronell on the potentiality of "close reading," which is not just necessarily slow but can also be fitful and anxiety-ridden, in *The ÜberReader*, ed. Diane Davis (Urbana; Chicago: University of Illinois Press, 2008), 210-11.

standard literary technique, especially prevalent in thrillers. In fact, this technique actually makes readers read on, becoming "fast readers" who want to know what happens next. What the opening of the novel does entail is the presentation a number of conflicting elements which, as the analysis of the novel progresses, will be seen not to resolve but rather to make visible their own ambiguity (although this could be dubbed a "fast ambiguity").

At the outset *Never Let Me Go* presents a seemingly straightforward introductory statement which is at the same time semantically confusing; the novel begins with an interruption of the implied reader's understanding of events, a pause, which is then a motivation to solve a puzzle, the clearly shaped missing pieces of which makes searching the box of tiles for a match all the more urgent. Interruption in given understanding coupled with a desire to assimilate that interruption back into an organic whole is what the beginning of any text does. In other words, the novel opens with the game of *fort* [gone]/*da* [there] that Freud describes in *Beyond the Pleasure Principle*,[31] although with a difference; for although Freud allows for a number of interpretations to come forth from a game his grandson is playing, throwing a toy and having it brought back again (renunciation of desire and entry into the symbolic, revenge on a parent for leaving or because of an unpleasant situation in general), the structural movement of "from me to the other" remains, or it is at least played at. *Never Let Me Go* develops a different movement by not letting the *fort* go into the *da*. As such, it is similar to Derrida's reading of the *fort/da* in *The Postcard* in which he opens with a description of the relation of one side of the structure to the other: "The serious play of the *fort/da* couples absence and presence in the *re-* of returning [*revenir*]. It overlaps them, it institutes repetition as their relation, relating them the one and the other, the one to the other, the one over or under the other."[32]

---

[31] Sigmund Freud, *Beyond the Pleasure Principle*, trans. James Strachey (New York; London: W. W. Norton and Company, 1989), 13-17.

[32] Jacques Derrida, *The Postcard: From Socrates to Freud and Beyond*, trans. Alan Bass (Chicago; London: The University of Chicago Press, 1987), 320. Alan Aycock develops a thorough reading of Derrida's use of Freud in this

However, the initial interest-generating confusion of the novel eventually dissipates when, about a third of the way through, it is learned that (1) Kathy is one of many clones who have been manufactured as organ-hosts for humans who live in the public domain and that (2) each of the clones must first assume the role of "carer," meaning that they travel around the country looking after those going through the process of donating their organs, a role which actually awaits every carer. "Carer" is narrator Kathy's position throughout the novel. However, being a carer usually lasts only a few years, and every carer, no matter how long they serve, eventually becomes a donor. Although the reader might not immediately understand that Kathy is talking about her death at this point, she is: "though I'll miss being a carer, it feels just about right to be finishing at last come the end of the year" (*NLMG* 4). Kathy, in her "extended" role as carer, exceeds the norms of her position, although she has not quite been incorporated into the next stage of donor; Kathy is also between, for the moment, the *fort* and the *da*.

The first third of *Never Let Me Go* is the story of the young clones' growing awareness of the finitude of their existence; on one level character-narrator Kathy displays a calm and almost given acceptance of her fate on the opening pages, which assumes that she has therefore accepted her eventual nonexistence. This calm can be seen when Kathy, discussing the recovery center where her close if difficult friend Ruth is recuperating from her donations, says that the center would not be such a bad place to expire: "The centre Ruth was in at that time, it's one of my favourites, and I wouldn't mind at all if that's where I ended up" (*NLMG* 17). However, Cynthia Wong questions this seemingly smooth surface when she observes: "Each stage [meaning that of "carer" and then "donor"] is a

---

context, arguing that "The play of fort-da, then, occupies much the same analytical space in Derrida's writings as the play of *differance*, because it substitutes the centrifugality of uncertainty for the centripetality of the Western quest for a transcendental signified," "Derrida/Fort-Da: Deconstructing Play," *Postmodern Culture* 3.2 (1993), Internet: http://www.iath.virginia.edu/pmc/text-only/issue.193/aycock.193, accessed March 24, 2009.

perverse rehearsal and reminder of each and another person's imminent end."[33]

Wong's quote raises a number of important issues regarding where such a reminder of one's end comes from and how another's death can relate to one's own. However, perhaps the first question to be taken up is: why is the rehearsal of each stage of the clones' development *perverse*? Etymologically, "perverse" derives from the Latin *perversus*, meaning "to turn away,"[34] usually from what is right, good, or the law. So what is it that Wong sees the clones turning away from in both roles as carers and donors? Wong states that the rehearsal of one's own death, along with another's, is perverse. This rehearsal is perverse because it is a turning away from a forgetting of one's facticity, of mortality.

Although Wong does not follow up on the use of "perverse" in her chapter, further on she seems to support my reading by seeing the movement of turning away from, which is a type of pause from joining, as unfortunate: "As one unfortunate appropriation of what is to come for herself [meaning death-by-donation], Kathy pauses momentarily,"[35] before realizing that there is nothing she can do, except, in the last lines of the novel, "drive off to wherever it was I was supposed to be" (*NLMG* 282), meaning to start her shortened life of a donor. But why is such introspection construed as negative by Wong, why is it an "unfortunate appropriation"?[36] Wong sees Kathy's driving off and doing what she is "supposed to do" as a consequence of her accepting her facticity, or of her appropriating what she is to become, meaning one of "those left unguarded, unguided, and unhinged in the world."[37] Just as Kathy's rehearsal and reminder

---

[33] Cynthia Wong, *Kazuo Ishiguro, Second Edition* (Tavistock: Northcote House Publishers Ltd., 2005), 96 (emphasis added). While Wong's work was originally published in 2000, the second edition has a supplemental chapter on *When We Were Orphans* and *Never Let Me Go*.

[34] Friedrichsen, R. W. Burchfield and C. T. Onions, *The Oxford Dictionary of English Etymology* (Oxford: Oxford University Press, 1966), 672.

[35] Wong, *Kazuo Ishiguro*, 102.

[36] In an assumingly unintentional connection, "appropriation" is often the preferred translation of Heidegger's "*Ereignis*," or that which brings something into its own.

[37] Ibid., 103.

of her fate is perverse, so is the appropriation of that fate. What Wong is actually constructing as perverse is a turning away from a *forgetting* of facticity. What Wong is describing as an "unfortunate appropriation" is not the pause necessarily but *that* the pause causes Kathy to realize that there is nothing but for her to die. For Wong, what is perverse and unfortunate is a rehearsal, a reminder, an appropriation of facticity.

In a 2006 interview with Wong and Grace Crummett, Ishiguro states the importance of parents instilling this "forgetting" of mortality in their children. In the following quote Ishiguro speaks about how near the end of *Never Let Me Go* Kathy and her then-boyfriend Tommy confront former guardians of their now-defunct boarding school. In this scene, Ishiguro says, "we're presented with an idea that in order to have a proper childhood, an element of deception must be used. If they had known they would die in the way they do, would they have embraced this arts education? They might say, 'What's the point? Why are we making all this effort'? […] To make this childhood work, you have to deceive them into believing it's all worth while."[38] However, in order to deceive, there has to be something to hide. Hence what is needed is to occupy the place of the lie, of the secret; this is the location of the told and not told which is structured by the forward thrust coupled with a holding-back which is present in the opening homodiegetic lines of the novel.

A similar structure is stated more explicitly near the end of the novel, when Miss Emily tells Tommy the reasons Miss Lucy was dismissed from Hailsham. Miss Lucy wanted the students to know exactly who they were and why they had been created. But Miss Emily says that "what she wanted to do, it was too *theoretical*" (*NLMG* 262). Instead what was needed was a lie:

> "Lucy Wainright was idealistic, nothing wrong with that. But she had no grasp of practicalities. You see, we were able to give you something, something which even now no one will ever take from you, and we were able to do that

---

[38] Cynthia Wong and Grace Crummett, "A Conversation about Life and Art with Kazuo Ishiguro," *Conversations with Kazuo Ishiguro*, ed. Brian Shaffer and Cynthia Wong (Jackson: University Press of Mississippi, 2008), 218.

> principally by *sheltering* you. Hailsham would not have been Hailsham if we hadn't. Very well, sometimes that meant we kept things from you, lied to you. Yes, in many ways we *fooled* you. I suppose you could even call it that." (263)

Miss Emily argues, much as Ishiguro in the interview quoted above, that a gift, the gift of a promising future, was passed on to the children through the form of a lie. This structure is developed in the next chapter along the lines of allegory. At this point in the novel, however, Tommy, who will form the locus of another experience of facticity, dryly sides with the theoretical approach of Miss Lucy instead: "'I think Miss Lucy was right. Not Miss Emily'" (268).

A forgetting of facticity is necessary according to Ishiguro, and also implicitly for Wong, who says that a turning away from such a forgetting is perverse. However, Ishiguro also states that in the clones' gradual learning of their fate as mortals they become "better humans." However, in the novel's representation of the becoming-aware of facticity what is actually disturbed is the assumption that humans posses this ability to "lie" about facticity.

In the same interview quoted above, Ishiguro describes the trick necessary to get beings over the hump of becoming aware of the possibility of their own non-being. He says that the teachers at the "school" at which the clones find themselves

> deceive the students [regarding their fate], but they gave them something better, not to be better donors, but to be better humans. [...] In order to persuade people to make the effort to learn and actually face what is often a difficult and complicated procedure – how to conduct human relationships and not mind getting hurt and upset – we have to be tricked to think there is a payoff.[39]

Ishiguro directly correlates being a better human with a forgetting of facticity. In a profile for *The Observer* Ishiguro

[39] Wong and Crummett, "A Conversation about Life and Art with Kazuo Ishiguro," 219.

continues this line of thought when he says: "'Hailsham is like a physical manifestation of what we have to do to all children [...] It is a protected world. To some extent at least you have to shield children from what you know and drip-feed information to them. Sometimes that is kindly meant, and sometimes not.'"[40] Humanity is drip-fed, "Like a patient etherised upon a table."[41] What Ishiguro seems to be saying here is that what is necessary for child rearing to successfully take place is a forgetting of facticity, a shield from the consequences of fate. Initially this seems a reversal of Heidegger's claims that an awareness of facticity is what makes humans human. However, *Never Let Me Go* shows how it is a *struggle* with this experience of coming to grips with one's fate that is "most" human. This struggle is implicit in the fooling, lies and drip-feeding that humanity undergoes in the process of becoming aware of facticity, although whether that process actually ever ends with a captured awareness of one's own death is indeed in doubt.

1.2 Facticity and Humanity

In order to understand what an ambiguous experience of facticity might mean, it is important to pay attention to how Heidegger argues that facticity is a human-only trait, since it is a key way to differentiate human and non-human beings. However, the clones in *Never Let Me Go* are not non-human animals or androids, and in fact Ishiguro's comments on the novel show how he thinks of them either as human or better than human. In addition, as Myra Seaman argues: "By focusing the novel on the experiences and feelings of the clones – represented

---

[40] Tim Adams, "'For Me, England is a Mythical Place,'" *The Observer* (Feb 20 2005), 17. Ishiguro continues, "'When you become a parent, or a teacher, you turn into a manager of this whole system. You become the person controlling the bubble of innocence around a child, regulating it. All children have to be deceived if they are to grow up without trauma,'" ibid.

[41] T. S. Eliot, "The Love Song of J. Alfred Prufrock," *Collected Poems: 1902-1963* (Orlando: Harcourt, Brace and Company, 1991), 3.

through Kathy's narration of her memories and experiences, especially with her closest friends, Ruth and Tommy – Ishiguro makes clear that their identity is no different from that of the humans who created them, or those of us who are reading their story [...]"[42] However, there are differences in the novel between clones and non-clones. These differences, hinted at above under the aegis of poverty, will best come forth by developing the arguments Heidegger, and those after Heidegger, have made which center around the human/animal divide. This line can perhaps first be seen in the manner Heidegger, in *Being and Time*, uses three different terms to describe the ways humans and non-humans die. According to Heidegger, the biological ending of all life is *perishing* [*Verenden*].[43] While it is possible for both humans and non-humans to *perish*,[44] it is also possible for humans to relate to death in their own way, which Heidegger says is *to demise* [*Ableben*].[45] To demise, a being must first find itself "*face to face* with the 'nothing' of the possible impossibility of its existence."[46] In other words, the being must be able to experience the potential of its own nonexistence. This experience forms the third term: "Let the term *dying* [*Tode*] stand for that *way of Being* in which Dasein *is towards* its death."[47] For Heidegger, the ability to demise is reserved for humans, or, as Stuart Elden puts it in his article "Heidegger's Animals": "humans, in their being, realize that their being is in issue."[48] However, what Heidegger is interested in is not so much the event of death itself (*perishing*), but rather the *experience* of being-towards-death [*Sein-zum-Tode*],[49] or of how the *awareness* of one's being is an issue. As Angelos Mouzakits

---

[42] Myra Seaman, "Becoming More (than) Human: Affective Posthumanisms, Past and Future," *Journal of Narrative Theory* 37.2 (2007), 265. However, this equating characters and actual readers is problematized below.

[43] Heidegger, *Being and Time*, 291.

[44] "Dasein too 'has' its death, of the kind appropriate to anything that lives [...]" (ibid.).

[45] Ibid.

[46] Ibid., 310.

[47] Ibid., 291.

[48] Stuart Elden, "Heidegger's Animals," *Continental Philosophy Review* 39 (2006), 276.

[49] See Havi Carel, *Life and Death in Freud and Heidegger* (Amsterdam: Rodopi, 2006), 75.

argues: "Indeed it seems that the idea of 'finitude' does not refer primarily to the unavoidable occurrence of death (since this has been thought from time immemorial) but that it rather indicates the *horizon* wherefrom Being and being-human can and should be thought if our thoughts are to be illuminating and productive [...]"[50]

The horizon of an experience, or an awareness, of one's own death is the ability to engage in "the study of philosophy" of the title of de Montaigne's essay, a quote from which is used for the epigraph of this chapter. The title of the essay is: "That to Study Philosophy is to Learn to Die," and in it de Montaigne's thought is not based so much on Plato's *Phaedo*, where Socrates states that "the one aim of those who practise philosophy in the proper manner is to practise for dying and death,"[51] but rather it is based on Cicero's Latinization of the text.[52] Cicero translated Socrates' practicing of death [*μελέτη θανάτου*] as "*commentatio*," meaning "*a reflecting upon death*, i.e. continued meditation upon this subject."[53]

The reason that the turn towards reflection is important for this discussion is that reflection, or a second-order level of consciousness, is seen by Heidegger as the "horizon" of being-towards-death, or as a definition of what the non-human animal is unable to do to the same degree as the human. The strategy of the structure of *Never Let Me Go* is to engage in the thrust towards that horizon (*fort*) without privileging the arrival (*da*). This position of being in a position of having but not having will be developed below; however it should be remembered that these challenges to Heidegger's thought are not necessarily or

[50] Angelos Mouzakits, "Radical Finitude Meets Infinity: Levinas's Gestures to Heidegger's Fundamental Ontology," *Thesis Eleven* 90.1 (2007), 65.

[51] Plato, *Phaedo*, trans. G. M. A. Grube (Indianapolis: Hackett Publishing Company, Inc., 1977), 12.

[52] De Montaigne opens his essay with a call to Cicero.

[53] Cicero, *On the Immortality of the Soul, or* Quaestinonum Tusculanarum, *volume I* (Annover: Flagg, Gould, and Newman, 1833), 142n97. On the preference of Seneca, St Jerome and others for *meditatio* rather than *commentatio*, especially in relation to a "good madness" that comes from the practice of dying, see M. A. Screech, "Good Madness in Christendom," *The Anatomy of Madness: Essays in the History of Psychiatry, volume 1, People and Ideas*, ed. W. F. Bynum, Roy Porter and Michael Shepherd (Oxford: Taylor and Francis, 2004), 29-30.

only made against Heidegger, but more profoundly *through* Heidegger's thought on what will be developed as a *nonrelational* experience of death.

The importance of raising these questions about the location of finitude has been summarized by Matthew Calarco:

> What would happen to the distinction between mortal and animal if *mortals* were unable to experience death as such? Or, conversely, if the inability to speak did not preclude an experience of death as such? Or if the ability to name death did not guarantee access to death as such? What if death refused any and every testimony or attestation, refused any "as such"? And what would be the consequences for Heidegger's existential analytic in *Being and Time* if the distinction between dying and perishing could no longer be sharply or definitively drawn? What status might the existential analytic have once these questions were raised for thought? These are the questions that motivate Derrida's analysis of death in *Aporias*, and the point of posing them is perhaps this: we can no longer continue in good conscience – and it is nothing less than an unthinking form of good conscience that has prevented these questions from being raised – to grant Heidegger's existential analytic the fundamental status it currently has in contemporary thought without, at the very least, raising these questions *as* questions. And if it is indeed the case that thinking through these questions leads us to understand that the distinctions between man and animal, and dying and perishing, no longer hold – or fail to hold absolutely, or perhaps hold otherwise, or are more complicated than we tend to believe – then the various conceptual systems and institutions (ethical, political, religious, economic, etc.) based on such seemingly indivisible borders should also come into question.[54]

[54] Calarco, "On the Borders of Language and Death," 21.

1.3 The Nonrelation of Heidegger's Facticity

As argued above, the question of undergoing an experience of facticity is at the heart of *Never Let Me Go*. The older Kathy, who is narrating the story and nearing the end of her life, seems "to have had" this experience. The first third of the novel is about how she, and other clones, come about this experience. In one sense this knowledge comes from "above," meaning that the teachers, or "guardians" of the school, explicitly tell the children their "purpose." This can be seen when one of them – the too theoretical Miss Lucy – eventually revolts by publicly saying what is usually left unsaid. However, in a structure related to the position of poverty, this "unsaid" is also given space in the story, because the students have always already known, somehow, what is going to happen to them, although this knowing is scanty. This undercurrent of foreknowledge can be seen when Kathy and Tommy discuss an early interaction Tommy had with Miss Lucy, before she provides her explicit revelation. Miss Lucy was obviously struggling to hold herself back from telling Tommy about the fate in store for him:

> "There's something else," [Tommy] went on. "Something else she said I can't quite figure out. I was going to ask you about it. She said we weren't being taught enough, something like that."
>
> [Kathy responds] "Taught enough? You mean she thinks we should be studying even harder than we are?"
>
> "No, I don't think she meant that. What she was talking about was, you know, about *us*. What's going to happen to us one day. Donations and all that."
>
> "But we *have* been taught about all that," I said, "I wonder what she meant. Does she think there are things we haven't been told yet?" (*NLMG* 29)

Kathy and Tommy know the word "donation," but they are not yet able to experience its "proper" meaning, which is indicated by both Tommy, and then Kathy, referring to "all that"; there is no real experience contained within the generality of the "all that." Although Kathy and Tommy have been given the word "donation," its meaning is still grouped together with other "stuff" they would just rather not talk about. But at the same time they *are* aware of something else out there; there is, as seen below, a "whisper" of their fate which is hard to name. Ishiguro has stated that "'If information does trickle gradually it's because the children themselves do not realise who they are. The reader is on a sort of parallel journey, but it is not a mystery story. My focus is elsewhere.'"[55] Toker and Chertoff argue that "The novel subtly explores the educational techniques that have conditioned them to accept their predicament. These techniques are, to some extent, re-enacted by the narrative structure which affects the reader in parallel to the intellectual development of the characters."[56] However, the story's homodeigetic nature does not really allow for such an easy reading of a parallel journey; in addition, it will be seen that "the reader" is not such a solid entity as one might assume. Instead it is more accurate to say that "It is *as if* they have known this crucial fact all along but *without knowing* that they knew."[57] The reason it can be said that this statement, also made by Toker and Chertoff, is "more accurate" is because it more closely follows the structure of the opening lines of the novel; the "as if" recalls Wong's "rehearsal," and "without knowing" Wong's "reminding" – this later statement by Toker and Chertoff begins to develop a reading of the meaning of the book following its structure of a spinning around in the *fort/da*.

The experience of facticity is poetic, in the sense that Charles Simic gives when he says that "The labor of poetry is finding ways through language to point to what cannot be put into words."[58] This poetic experience of facticity is actually the labor of the clones: they have not been explicitly told what will happen to them, and they have to chase down their inkling of the "all that." In addition, the structure of told/not told is not limited

---

[55] Qtd. in Nicholas Wroe, "Profile: Living Memories: Kazuo Ishiguro," *The Guardian Saturday Pages* (Feb 19 2005), 20.

[56] Toker and Chertoff, "Reader Response and the Recycling of Topoi in Kazuo Ishiguro's *Never Let Me Go*," 166.

[57] Ibid., 167 (emphasis added).

[58] Charles Simic, "Notes on Poetry and Philosophy," *New Literary History* 21.1 (1989), 218.

to the opening pages of the novel. To put one more example in play, when Ruth lets on that she has been shown special treatment by one of the guardians who supposedly gave her a pencil case, Kathy says: "Still, I hated it when Ruth hinted in this way. I was never sure, of course, if she was telling the truth, but since she wasn't actually 'telling it', only hinting, it was never possible to challenge her" (*NLMG* 57).

This "double-bind" of the clones' experience of facticity has been a focus point, if not always developed, in the literature surrounding the novel. Allen states that: "They have merely the very vaguest ideas about this future and are diffident about inquiring into it too aggressively."[59] Michiko Kakutani includes the role of non-verbal knowledge within linguistic revelation when reading the moment of the students being explicitly told about their fate as a moment also containing "intimations" of their mortality. Kakutani argues that the novel is "an oblique and elegiac meditation on mortality and lost innocence: a portrait of adolescence as that *hinge moment* in life when self-knowledge brings *intimations* of one's destiny, when the shedding of childhood dreams can lead to disillusionment, rebellion, newfound resolve or an ambivalent acceptance of a preordained fate."[60]

One manner of beginning to think how Kathy and Tommy's *intimations* of facticity can also be part of an explicit *hinge moment* of revelation is through a reading of Heideggerian *nonrelation.* In order to develop this concept, first Heidegger argues that the reason that an awareness of one's own death is important is that it causes a sense of anxiety [*Angst*] which is an essential mood [*Stummung*] through which there can be an experience of Dasein.[61] Then Heidegger argues that the reason

---

[59] Allen, "The Damned and the Beautiful," 25.

[60] Michiko Kakutani, "Sealed in a World That's Not As It Seems," *New York Times* Section E (April 4 2005), 1, (emphasis added). Similarily, Antonio Munno states that "They know they are being prepared for a life as 'carers' and 'donors' but although they recognise the words they don't fully understand what this means," "*Never Let Me Go,*" *General Practitioner* (February 2007), 69.

[61] "*Angst* as a mode of attunement first discloses the *world as world,*" Heidegger, *Being and Time*, 175. Or, as de Montaigne describes: "The end of our race is death; 'tis the necessary object of our aim, which, if it fright us, how is it possible to advance a step without a fit of ague? The remedy the vulgar use is not

that anxiety is different from fear (which all animals experience[62]) is that anxiety is not being fearful of something in particular, but rather it is the indefinite experience of fear itself: "The threat does not have the character of a definite detrimentality which concerns what is threatened with a definite

---

to think on't; but from what brutish stupidity can they derive so gross a blindness? They must bridle the ass by the tail," "That to Study Philosophy is to Learn to Die," 27. On the other hand, there is the Epicurean symmetry argument which states that since our pre-natal state of non-being was (1) not fearful at the time, and (2) is it not fearful to us now in life, therefore *post mortem* non-being should also create no anxiety for us. This argument is developed, with special attention given to (2), in James Warren, *Facing Death: Epicurus and His Critics* (Oxford: Clarendon Press, 2004), 57-108.

[62] In *The Expression of the Emotions in Man and Animals* Darwin argues that fear is common to both human and non-human animals: "I have seen a dog much terrified at a band of musicians who were playing loudly outside the house, with every muscle of his body trembling, with his heart palpitating so quickly that the beats could hardly be counted, and panting for breath with widely open mouth, in the same manner as a terrified man does," Charles Darwin, *From So Simple a Beginning: The Four Great Books of Charles Darwin*, ed. Edward Wilson (New York: W. W. Norton & Co., Inc., 2006), 1330. Stanley Giannet argues that "We have grossly underestimated and minimized animal abilities and cognitive-emotional processes. Mental experiences are very real and vital to humans and in so far as they occur in animals, they must also be vital and meaningful to them. The weight of the neuropsychological, cognitive, ethological, and sociobiological evidence suggests that animals, in varying degrees, have the ability to formulate concepts, feel and experience emotions, understand causality, quantify, and demonstrate object permanence, intentionality, planning, self-recognition and awareness... Furthermore, evidence suggests that animals have perceptual consciousness abilities and even dream (as evidenced by Rapid Eye Movement / REM sleep), empathize, and deceive in a way that is remarkably similar to humans. Let's not forget their ability to communicate via a panoply of rudimentary language processes. Scientists claim, however, that the cardinal difference between animals and humans is that humans have a capacity for moral judgments and thought. [...] We are ethical sentient beings whereas animals are only sentient beings," "The Human-Animal Divide: Interdisciplinary Ethical Reflections," *Journal of Evolutionary Psychology* 24 (2003), 9. John Deigh argues that while a theory of emotions must deal with the fact that emotions are common to both humans and non-human animals, that does not mean that they experience the *same* emotions: "On the contrary, the set to which humans are liable is much greater than the set to which beasts are liable. Shame over a moral failing, for instance, is an emotion to which humans are liable and beasts are not. It is to say, though, that some emotions are common to both sets. These are, in many cases, what I will call primitive emotions," *Emotions, Values, and the Law* (Oxford: Oxford University Press, 2008), 18.

regard to a particular factical potentiality for being. What *Angst* is about is completely indefinite."[63] The apparent indefiniteness of anxiety is the nonrelational experience of Dasein. On the one hand, anxiety's nonrelationality is important for being because it is what allows being to question being.[64] As Heidegger states in a course of University of Freiberg lectures from 1923, published as *Ontology: The Hermeneutics of Facticity*, "fundamental *questionableness*" is "relucent in all characteristics of being – *ontic questionableness*: *caring*, unrest, anxiety, *temporality*."[65] However, on the other hand Heidegger then asks, "How is the problem of death related to this?"[66] For Heidegger, it is in hermeneutics that a questioning can be found which does not a priori assume "the traditional idea of man."[67] The reason that hermeneutics is the connection between death and anxiety is that hermeneutics is also a mood of nonrelation: hermeneutics is not about the interpretation of a specific object but rather "a doctrine about the conditions, the objects, the means, and the communication and practical application of interpretation."[68] As Eric Nelson argues, what is most "natural" to Dasein is not belonging to something, but rather the nonrelation of nonbelonging: "Dasein is primordially strange and foreign, we do not even know what 'man' is […] and we remain strangers to ourselves […] Singularity and difference are constitutive of Dasein through its openness as well as its uncanniness and questionability such that Dasein is each time a question to itself." [69] The clones of *Never Let Me Go* seem to occupy such a

---

[63] Heidegger, *Being and Time*, 174.

[64] De Montaigne's admirer Blaise Pascal places the argument on a grand scale: "But even if the universe were to crush him, man would still be nobler than his slayer, because he knows that he is dying and the advantage the universe has over him. The universe knows nothing of this," *Pensées*, trans. A. J. Krailsheimer (London: Penguin, 1966), 95.

[65] Martin Heidegger, *Ontology: The Hermeneutics of Facticity*, trans. John van Buren (Bloomington: Indiana University Press, 1999), 13.

[66] Ibid.

[67] Ibid.

[68] Ibid., 10.

[69] Eric Nelson, "Heidegger and the Ethics of Facticity," *Rethinking Facticity*, ed. François Raffoul and Eric Nelson (Albany: State University of New York Press, 2008), 137.

position of nonrelation, holding open a question even within being the answer to that question themselves.

1.4 Nonrelation as Coexistence

Development on a substantial level of the relation-filled "hinge moment" of recognition of non-human difference for the clones will assist in delineating aspects of the way the novel works on a rhetorical level. This moment of recognition occurs when a number of clones come out from behind a corner to surprise "Madame," a seldom-seen authority figure at Hailsham. Martin Puchner argues that that this is actually a kind of primal scene: "It is a scene that promises to reconstruct the origin, within her [Kathy's] consciousness, of her status as a mere double of the human."[70] However, an exegesis of this scene will put into question a number of choices Puchner has made in order to paraphrase the situation: the words "origin," "mere" and "double" are more problematic than Puchner allows. However, the passage in question does work as a "primal scene" on a rhetorical level: what has been tentatively called the "*fort/da*" structure of the novel is an expression of the trope of antanaclasis, or the repetition of a single word but with different meanings each time. Or, as Derrida words such a doubling in *The Postcard*: "if the game is called complete on one side and the other, we have to envisage an eminently symbolic completion which itself would be formed by these two completions, and which therefore would be incomplete in each of its pieces, and consequently would be completely incomplete when the two incompletions, related and joined the one to the other, start to multiply themselves, supplementing each other without completing each other."[71]

The background to this scene is that the students routinely make artwork, some of which is taken by Madame to be placed

---

[70] Martin Puchner, "When We Were Clones: On Kazuo Ishiguro," *Raritan* XXVII (Spring 2008), 38.

[71] Derrida, *The Postcard*, 320.

in "the Gallery." Part of the mystery surrounding Madame comes from the suspicion that she is somehow afraid of the student clones. Kathy, her friend Ruth and some others decide to put this suspicion to the test. They wait for Madame's arrival to Hailsham and they pop out from around a corner to see her reaction:

> she just froze and waited for us to pass by. She didn't shriek, or even let out a gasp. [...] And I can still see it now, the shudder she seemed to be suppressing, the real dread that one of us would accidentally brush against her. And though we just kept on walking, we all felt it; it was like we'd walked from the sun right into chilly shade. Ruth had been right: Madame *was* afraid of us. But she was afraid of us in the same way someone might be afraid of spiders. We hadn't been ready for that. It had never occurred to us to wonder how *we* would feel, being seen like that, being the spiders. (*NLMG* 35)

In a very important sense Kathy's description of the event fits into a "primal scene" moment of a hinge-moment revelation. She says that "We hadn't been ready for that" and that "It had never occurred to us to wonder [...]" The primal scene is reported as if "this experiment demonstrates to the narrator and her friends, *perhaps for the first time*, how deeply the humans feel their difference from the clones, a difference that the clones then internalize and accept as unquestioned fact."[72] However, there is an apparent conflict in this reading that surfaces through the trope of antanaclasis which is used in the last sentence: "It had never occurred to us to wonder how we would feel, *being* seen like that, *being* the spiders" (emphasis added). While the word "being" appears twice, it takes on a different role in each use. In the first instance, "being" is a part of the progressive passive construction of "being seen." In the second instance, "being" as a static verb shows how the clones now occupy the state held by spiders for those who are afraid of them. The reason this trope is important for a reading of this scene is that

[72] Puchner, "When We Were Clones," 38 (emphasis added).

while on one level this is a primal scene in which Kathy, and presumably the other clones involved, first see themselves as different from uncloned humanity. However, the underpinning of antanaclasis opens up the rhetorical possibilities for the signifier of "being": in the midst of this revelation there is, on the one hand, a doubling back through the synchronic being/being couple. Such a doubling-back is the point of antanaclasis, which comes from the Greek for reflection or bending back [ἀντανάκλασις]. However, on the other hand there is a diachronic relationship; it is *because* of being seen that they are being spiders. So there is both a bending back and a bending forward contained within Kathy's statement. There is both the whisper of the nonrelational and the explicit revelation of causality.

In addition, when Kathy continues to reflect on the event, she reinforces this dual structure by not only describing the moment of explicit revelation but by also opening up the space for a "whisper" of the nonrelational. This whisper comes from a part of her has always been waiting for this moment to happen:

> All the same, some of it must go in somewhere. It must go in, because by the time a moment like that comes along, there's a part of you that's been waiting. Maybe from as early as when you're five or six, there's been a whisper going on at the back of your head, saying: "One day, maybe not so long from now, you'll get to know how it feels." So you're waiting, *even if you don't quite know it*, waiting for the moment when you realize that you really are different to them; that there are people out there, like Madame, who don't hate you or wish you any harm, but who nevertheless shudder at the very thought of you – of how you were brought into this world and why – and who dread the idea of your hand brushing against theirs. The first time you glimpse yourself through the eyes of a person like that, it's a cold moment. It's like walking past a mirror you've walked past every day of your life, and suddenly it shows you something else, something troubling and strange. (*NLMG* 36, emphasis added)

In this quote both the always already and the hinge moment are both present. The always already can be seen in the "whisper" that has been going on at the back of Kathy's head all along, while the hinge moment can be seen in the "first time you glimpse yourself through the eyes" of someone who is scared of you, and in the image of walking past a familiar mirror and suddenly seeing "something troubling and strange." In one sense this passage stresses the temporality of experience, that there is first a whisper and then the cold moment of experience. However, there is a strength in the textual coexistence in which the *process* of belonging to an experience of facticity is kept in play. This process is akin to Heidegger's reading of nonrelation, which is about delaying the grounds that allow for interpreting rather than the interpretation.

However, such a positive reading of copresence is not shared by Earl Ingersoll, for example, who argues that the nonrelational aspect of this moment shows an unwillingness rather than an openness, stating that "the 'truth' that the students are all clones is hardly one they relish confronting. That unwillingness to acknowledge their origins helps in part to explain how long this narrative must go on before the truth can finally be 'outed,' primarily because it operates in that psychological closet of truths we all would prefer not to open."[73] Ingersoll seems to side solely with the moments of linguistic revelation: "Undoubtedly, the most interesting 'revelations' are those provided by Miss Emily."[74] What is important to note in the reading presented here is not the negation of one type of experience in favor of the other, but rather the incorporation of both into the same passage. This incorporation, or textual coexistence, can be seen both on the rhetorical level of the antanaclasis and on the semantic level of a copresencing of whisper and explicitness. This combination will form the coordinates of the uncanny in the next section.

Before proceeding, however, one more example may be examined. A nonrelational experience of knowledge can also be seen in the novel's first scene of explicit revelation, when Miss

---

[73] Earl Ingersoll, "Taking Off into the Realm of Metaphor: Kazuo Ishiguro's *Never Let Me Go*," *Studies in the Humanities* 34.1 (2007), 49.

[74] Ibid., 50.

Lucy tells the clones directly what their purpose is and how they are different from "normal" human beings:

> "If you're going to have decent lives, then you've got to know and know properly. None of you will go to America, none of you will be film stars. And none of you will be working in supermarkets as I heard some of you planning the other day. Your lives are set out for you. You'll become adults, then before you're old, before you're even middle-aged, you'll start to donate your vital organs. That's what each of you was created to do [...] You were brought into this world for a purpose, and your futures, all of them, have been decided [...] You'll be leaving Hailsham before long, and it's not so far off, the day you'll be preparing for your first donations. You need to remember that. If you're to have decent lives, you have to know who you are and what lies ahead of you, every one of you." (*NLMG* 79-80)

The students who are gathered around Miss Lucy for this dissemination have nothing to say, and they do not talk about it amongst themselves afterwards. This leads Kathy to admit that the knowledge was always already there, somewhere, vaguely: "it feels like I *always* knew about donations in some vague way, even as early as six or seven" (81). Kathy being Kathy, she wants to locate the source of the whisper. She finds it another domain in which semantic stability is troublesome, sex: "when the guardians first started giving us proper lectures about sex, they tended to run them together with talk about the donations. [...] it's possible the guardians managed to smuggle into our heads a lot of the basic facts about our futures" (ibid.). Discussions of sex are excellent vehicles for smuggling, at least as long as Judith Butler's reading of the constructedness of sexuality is kept in mind. Butler argues that it would be a mistake to side completely either with essentialism or constructivism in regard to sexuality: "For sexuality cannot be summarily made or unmade, and it would be a mistake to associate 'constructivism' with 'the freedom of a subject to form her/his sexuality as s/he pleases."[75] Similar to the potentiality within the everyday of poverty, Butler sees the impetus for the performativity of gender within constraint itself: "Performativity is neither free play nor theatrical self-presentation; nor can it be simply equated with performance. Moreover, constraint is not necessarily that which sets a limit to performativity; constraint is, rather, that which impels and sustains performativity."[76] Kathy traces the whisper of non-explicit experience to discourses on sex which, as seen in Butler's reading, is another instantiation of foregrounding middle rather than the endpoints of *fort/da*, much as with antanaclasis.

1.5 Difference and Fear

One important aspect of the "spider episode" is the feeling of fear that Madame experienced upon being surprised by the clones. As Kathy says, "Madame *was* afraid of us. But she was afraid of us in the same way someone might be afraid of spiders" (*NLMG* 35). What kind of fear is being delineated here? There seems to be a division between fearing human beings, and fearing non-human beings. This does not mean that Madame in any way saw the clones as animals, or that a spider is somehow uncannily close to being human. Rather, Madame's response points towards the coordinates of a debate about difference and incorporation, of where the natures of human and non-human animals lie.

Later in the novel Kathy provides some explanation of Madame's response: "there are people out there, like Madame, who don't hate you or wish you any harm, but who nevertheless shudder at the very thought of you – of how you were brought into this world and why – and who dread the idea of your hand brushing against theirs" (36). This fear is not hatred. In fact, to

[75] Judith Butler, *Bodies That Matter: On the Discursive Limits of "Sex"* (New York; London: Routledge, 1993), 94.

[76] Ibid., 95.

actually *hate* spiders could be pathologic.[77] What Kathy sees as the root of Madame's fear is that within the extreme similarity of humans and clones there remains some sort of difference. In fact, difference is what separates fear from metaphor, in that "Fear is the result of a possible discrepancy between the outer and the inner properties of entities,"[78] while metaphor "is precisely the figure that depends on a certain degree of correspondence between 'inside' and 'outside' properties."[79] The question is, how can Heidegger's division of being help in an understanding of the copresencing of difference and closeness being delineated here? And more importantly, what do the passages in Ishiguro have to say about Heidegger's theory? The answer is found by looking at how Heidegger's notion of the *fearsome* relates to the presence of both difference and closeness in Freud's reading of the uncanny, a reading which is based on a literary scene of organ donation from E. T. A. Hoffmann's story "The Sandman" in section 1.6.

For the Heidegger of *Being and Time*, in order for there to be a feeling of the fearsome [*das Furchtbare*] there has to be the presence of *difference*, of something queer [*geheuer*] that is also actually *within range*. The relative closeness of this difference is important. If it is too far away, there is no generation of the fearsome. What is fearsome is something that is approaching, something that may possibly touch: "it can reach us, and yet it may not."[80] Key here is the coexistence of two elements, that which is different and that which has the possibility to touch.

What is frightening about the clones for Madame is that the difference is so small, in fact this difference is very close, it lies in side us. The clones are *just only* different than other humans;

---

[77] Or, perhaps Kathy would be happy to be elevated to a being that it would be possible to hate in the sense that hate would at least be confirmation of personhood. See Brian Willems, "The Hyperreal Territory of Animals," *Poiesis* 10 (Summer 2008).

[78] De Man, *Allegories of Reading*, 150.

[79] Ibid.

[80] Heidegger, *Being and Time*, 180. In other words: "Death can also be the nearness in distance," Jari Kauppinen, "Death as Limit of Phenomenology: The Notion of Death from Husserl to Derrida," *Analecta Husserliana* 66 (2000), 338. For a relation between Heidegger's reading of fear and the attunement of anxiety see Brian Willems, *Hopkins and Heidegger* (London; New York: Continuum, 2009), 38-41.

the clones are creatures that embody a clinamen of difference which is so small that it is scary. In what is now a rather well-known formulation, Masahiro Mori has developed a reading of the fear generated from this minimal difference in regard to humans and their different-than-human counterparts – human-like dolls, robots and other artificial creatures – calling the location of this fear the "uncanny valley."[81] If a human sees an industrial robot or a DVD player they do not seem particularly scary, however, when that creation gets *closer* to a human shape, but is yet *still somehow different*, identification suddenly drops off, and fear sets in. This sudden drop-off is Mori's uncanny valley, and it is a problem for many CGI representations of human beings.

The uncanny valley is first set about through proximity: a representation to be close to the human image in order for fear to take place. Tzvetan Todorov describes what is uncanny about such proximity through his differentiation of the uncanny from the marvelous in *The Fantastic: A Structural Approach to a Literary Genre*. Here the uncanny encompasses proximity in that it allows the reader, upon finishing a novel from the genre of the fantastic, to make sense of what happened using established laws, while the marvelous requires a restructuring of dynamics of the world in order to come to such an understanding:

> The fantastic, we have seen, lasts only as long as a certain hesitation: a hesitation common to reader and character, who must decide whether or not what they perceive derives from "reality" as it exists in the common opinion. At the story's end, the reader makes a decision even if the character does not; he opts for one solution or the other, and thereby emerges from the fantastic. If he decides that the laws of reality remain intact and permit an explanation of the phenomena described, we say that the work belongs to another genre: the uncanny. If, on the contrary, he decides

[81] This term was first put forth in English in Masahiro Mori, "The Uncanny Valley," trans. Karl MacDorman and Takashi Minato, *Energy* 7.4 (1970), 33-35.

> that new laws of nature must be entertained to account for the phenomena, we enter the genre of the marvelous.[82]

Todorov's differentiation is structurally reminiscent of Butler's insistence on a location of the impetus of performativity from within constructedness. Difference-within-familiarity (or proximity) can also be seen in Kathy's description of the landscape surrounding the Cottages which the clones move into after their time at Hailsham: "We could see hills in the distance that reminded us of the ones in the distance at Hailsham, but they seemed to us oddly crooked, like when you draw a picture of a friend and it's almost right but not quite, and the face on the sheet gives you the creeps" (*NLMG* 116). In this quote a number of near-far pairs are collated: the hills at the Cottages are similar to those at Hailsham, although they both lie in the distance; the drawing of a close friend is not what is remembered, and the face of the person from life now rests on a sheet of paper. The strangeness of similarity can also be seen when Kathy, after the time in the Cottages and when she is with Tommy, looking for a deferral, sees Madame again after so many years: "'It was really spooky,' I said, 'because she looked exactly the same'" (239).

However, no matter how human the clones may be, there is a level of difference presented which allows for them to function in a literary fashion. Difference is the second element of the uncanny valley. Difference in the spider scene is represented by the clones being looked upon through the antanaclasis of "being." Because of this commingling of difference and similarity I believe that the word "uncanny" may be apt to this situation. An example of what such a reading could look like has been provided by Krell, who sees the structure of Freud's uncanny (and of holding open the question of the *fort/da*), which is the focus of the next section, underpinning Heidegger's thought on being in the face of the fearful, or being-towards-death:

> Is it only fear of death, this feeling of being ill at ease or uncanny, this unhomey sensation – whatever fine distinc-

[82] Tzvetan Todorov, *The Fantastic: A Structural Approach to a Literary Genre*, trans. Richard Howard (Ithaca: Cornell University Press, 1975), 41.

tions or sweeping claims Heidegger may try to make? It is more like a pervasive, indeterminate anxiety, a fundamental or founding mood that Heidegger at other times also reads as joy, melancholy, and profound boredom. In the face of *what* are we anxious, joyous, melancholy, or deeply bored? Everything. Beings as a whole. Nothing. No thing at all. An impersonal yet thoroughgoing alienation marks Heidegger's thought about who we are. In his inaugural lecture of 1929, "What Is Metaphysics?" he finds an appropriately impersonal phrase for it: *Es wird einem unheimlich*, literally, it becomes uncanny for one; more loosely, one begins to feel uncannily not at home, one looks at no one in particular and for no particular reason says, "It's getting strange."[83]

1.6 The Uncanniness of Organ Removal

Freud's essay "The Uncanny," first published in 1919, begins by stating that the uncanny [*das unheimlich*] "is undoubtedly related to what is frightening – to what arouses dread and horror [...]"[84] However, Freud's essay also differentiates the uncanny from other things fearful. Initially Freud examines the word "uncanny" through the lens of various dictionaries in a number of languages. This is to illustrate how the uncanny is both "that class of the frightening which leads back to what is known of old and long familiar"[85] and also how it is frightening "because it is *not* known and familiar."[86] Rather than trying to smooth over this difference, Freud attempts to find out what it is about the uncanny that allows it to couch such a contradiction, much in the

[83] David Farrell Krell, "*Das Unheimliche:* Architectural Sections of Heidegger and Freud," *Research in Phenomenology* 22 (1992), 45.

[84] Sigmund Freud, "The Uncanny," *Art and Literature*, ed. Albert Dickenson (London: Penguin, 1990), 339.

[85] Ibid., 340.

[86] Ibid., 341.

same way that an explicit experience of facticity can perhaps or even must hold the whisper of the nonrelational within.

To facilitate his discovery Freud reads Hoffmann's short story "The Sandman" along with Ernst Jentsch's 1906 interpretation of its uncanniness. In order to allow for readers to catch up, Freud offers a nearly three-page summary of Hoffmann's story about a college student who falls in love with his professor's daughter, Olympia, who turns out to be an automaton. Freud's extensive summary is itself uncanny in that it is precisely in its "too much of the same," or over-retelling, that difference makes an appearance. As Nicholas Royle comments in his book *The Uncanny*: "what is bizarre is that Freud seems completely oblivious to the fact that his 'short summary' is fundamentally *his own* 'short story' [...] Freud himself seems robbed of the sense that telling or retelling a story is always, in some sense, something new, another story. His summary inevitably differs in various ways from Jentsch's or indeed anyone else's."[87]

Freud's summary of the story includes his single criticism of Jentsch. Freud quotes Jentsch arguing that what is uncanny about Hoffmann's story is that the reader is left in suspense regarding whether Olympia is actually a human or not,[88] thus bringing forth Jentsch's central thesis on the uncanny, which is that "the word suggests that a *lack of orientation* is bound up with the impression of the uncanniness of a thing or incident."[89] However, for Freud the question of whether Olympia is a human is not where the uncanny is really located in the story, much as for *Never Let Me Go* the status of the clones as human is not central to the debate. Instead, and in a literal sense, for both Freud and Ishiguro the uncanny is to be found in the theme of organ removal. Freud says: "The main theme of the story is, on the contrary, something different [than the undecided nature of Olympia's being], something which gives it its name, and which is always re-introduced at critical moments: it is the theme of the

---

[87] Nicholas Royle, *The Uncanny* (Manchester: Manchester University Press, 2003), 40.

[88] Freud, "The Uncanny," 347-8.

[89] Ernst Jentsch, "On the Psychology of the Uncanny," *Angelaki: A New Journal in Philosophy, Literature, and the Social Sciences* 2.1 (1996), 8.

'Sand-Man' who tears out children's eyes."[90] This deed is done in order to feed children on a "half-moon."

Indeed, when re-visiting Hoffmann's story post-Freud, the eyes do appear much more frightening than any suspense as to the ontology of Olympia. The Sandman "'throws handfuls of sand in their [the children who will not go to sleep] eyes, so that they jump out of their heads all bloody; and he puts them into a bag and takes them to the half-moon as food for his little ones; and they sit there in the nest and have hooked beaks like owls, and they pick naughty little boys' and girls' eyes out with them.'"[91] What is uncanny about this image from Hoffmann's story is on one hand similarity: eyes are being taken from one group of children to feed another group of children. However, these "other children" are also different; they are in a different place, residing on a "half" moon, and they are partly non-human. *Never Let Me Go*, in a sense, could then be seen as a reversal of Hoffmann's story; instead of organs from humans being used to keep alive partially non-human beings, the opposite is happening – organs from beings different-than-humans are harvested to keep the "possibles," or "normal" humans alive beyond their "natural" lifespan. Both stories revolve around the structure of the familiarity-in-strangeness of the uncanny; the difference developed below is that what is uncanny in Hoffmann is *them*, and what is uncanny in Ishiguro, through the allegory the implied author develops, is *us*.

Samuel Weber, in a 1973 essay later incorporated into *The Legend of Freud*, provides a reading of Freud's uncanny that locates it within certain rhetorical strategies of literature. Weber states that "the words 'heimlich' and 'unheimlich' are not simply opposites, but that heimlich itself is the repository of ambivalent meanings, signifying on the one hand, the familiar and domestic, on the other and simultaneously the concealed and the hidden."[92] Thus the uncanny follows the structure of the doubled, the rehearsal, of repetition. Weber states: "first, since the uncanny is

---

[90] Freud, "The Uncanny," 348.

[91] E. T. A. Hoffman, "The Sandman," *The Best Tales of Hoffman*, ed. E. F. Bleiler (New York: Dover, 1967), 185.

[92] Samuel Weber, *The Legend of Freud, Expanded Edition* (Stanford: Stanford University Press, 2000), 209.

a form of anxiety, and since anxiety in general is produced by the mechanism of repression, the uncanny must involve some form of the return of the repressed."[93] He continues: "Second, this explains why the word *Heimlich* includes its opposite, *unheimlich*, since the latter is nothing new but only something originally familiar, which has been repressed."[94]

However, what Weber focuses on is the rhetorical structure of repetition in the uncanny. This structure comes forth in a change of thought in Freud which can be seen, as Weber shows, after the 1926 paper "Inhibition, Symptom and Anxiety."[95] It is here that Freud flips his original thesis of repression producing anxiety over to its opposite, that of anxiety producing repression.[96] The reason this flip is essential is that it puts anxiety, more specifically castration-anxiety, at the heart of Freud's thought.[97] In other words, this flip places non-identification at the center of becoming:

> For what the child "discovers" – that is, interprets – as "castration" is neither nothing nor simply something, at least in the sense in which the child expects and desires it to be: what is "discovered" is the absence of the maternal phallus, a kind of negative perception, whose object or referent – perceptum – is ultimately nothing but a difference, although no simple one, since it does not refer to anything, least of all to itself, but instead *refers itself indefinitely*.[98]

---

[93] Ibid., 211.

[94] Ibid. Freud makes a similar statement in *Beyond the Pleasure Principle*, written around the same time as "The Uncanny": "The patient cannot remember the whole of what is repressed in him, and what he cannot remember may be precisely the essential part of it. Thus he acquires no sense of conviction of the correctness of the construction that has been communicated to him. He is obliged to *repeat* the repressed material as a contemporary experience instead of, as the physician would prefer to see, *remembering* it as something belonging to the past," 18-9.

[95] Weber, *The Legend of Freud*, 214.

[96] Ibid., 214-5.

[97] Ibid., 215.

[98] Ibid., 215-6. Hélène Cixous describes the rhetorical structure of Freud's essay in a similar manner: "Nothing turns out less reassuring for the reader than this niggling, cautious, yet wily and interminable pursuit (of something – be it a domain, an emotional movement, a concept, impossible to determine yet variable in its form, intensity, quality, and content). Nor does anything prove to be more

What emerges from the uncanny is "neither nothing nor simply something." Instead it is an experience of indefinite referral, of reflection, or of the process of identity formation as apposed to identity arrival. Later in the essay Weber reformulates this point:

> What should have remained concealed and what has nonetheless, in a certain manner, emerged, engenders the uncanny because its very appearance eludes perception, its being is not to be had, because it side-steps and side-tracks – and not just Freud – by repeating, doubling, splitting and reflecting. The uncanny is thus bound up with a *crisis* of perception and of phenomenality, but concomitantly with a mortal danger to the subject, to the "integrity" of its body and thus to its very identity, which – if we accept the psychoanalytic theory of narcissism – is based upon this body-image as its model.[99]

Weber's reading of the uncanny develops one of the rhetorical tropes also used in *Never Let Me Go*, which is that of a holding open the possibilities opened through "repeating, doubling [clones], splitting [genes] and reflecting [Cicero]."[100]

---

fleeing than this search whose movement constitutes the labyrinth which instigates it; the sense of strangeness imposes its secret necessity everywhere. The ensuing unfolding whose operation is contradictory is accomplished by the author's double: Hesitation. We are faced, then, with a text and its hesitating shadow, and their double escapade," "Fiction and Its Phantoms: A Reading of Freud's *Das Unheimliche* (The 'Uncanny')," *New Literary History* 7.3 (Spring 1976), 525.

[99] Weber, *The Legend of Freud*, 233.

[100] In an interview which took place just before and after September 11, 2001, Weber hones in on the necessity of uncanny in relation to repetition: "Nietzsche – who, together with Kierkegaard, placed the question of repetition, recurrence, *Wiederkeher* on the agenda – writes somewhere that with passing years one finds oneself returning to certain questions that seem to change very little over time. These questions, which function as a kind of bedrock of identity, are more difficult to 'lose' than to retain. Whether this 'bedrock' becomes a source of strength and discovery or a prison depends on how those questions 'return': whether they primarily only 'determine,' in the simply restrictive sense of setting limits, or whether the limits they trace gesture toward a space not simply contained within the area they demarcate. This is one of the reasons why a sense of the 'uncanny' – indeed, an openness to it – is indispensable, if one is to avoid

The relationship between facticity and the uncanny is that they both follow a similar logic: death is what removes us from life, and with an incorporation of death within life there is a removal-from-home within the home-ness of life itself: "since death is that which would radically deprive us of being at home, since it would deprive us of our being in general, it is uncanny."[101]

Philippe Lacoue-Labarthe, in his discussion of the uncanny in *Poetry as Experience*, aligns it against the artificiality of an over-presumed facticity in a reading of Paul Celan's "The Meridian" speech. Lacoue-Labarthe argues that this speech is a response to how "For Heidegger, art and the work of art are equally *unheimlich* [...]."[102] However, Lacoue-Labarthe also warns that "this kind of determination is not enough; it assigns art too easily, appropriates the *Umheimliche* too rapidly"[103] because it immediately sides the uncanny with "marionettes, robots, and artificial bombast [...]"[104] What Celan teaches is that the uncanny is not aligned with non-humanity, but is rather its opposite, namely "the natural."[105] The clones, with "enough" difference to function as an allegory of the human condition, enact both a reflection and destabilizing of the human referent. The uncanny is not so easily displaced upon the strangeness of the non-human: *it is within – it is at the heart of the human itself.*

This is a different functionality than that which appears in Ishiguro's *The Remains of the Day*, for example, in which there

---

the kind of entropy that a purely obsessive recurrence would entail," Samuel Weber, "Stages and Plots: Theatricality after September 11, 2001, a Discussion with Simon Morgan Wortham and Gary Hall," *Theatricality as Medium* (New York: Fordham University Press, 2004), 338.

[101] Steven Davis, "The Path of a Thinking, Poetizing Building: The Strange Uncanniness of Human Being on Earth," *Heidegger and the Earth: Issues in Environmental Philosophy*, ed. Ladelle McWhorter (Kirksville: Truman State University Press, 1992), 44.

[102] Philippe Lacoue-Labarthe, *Poetry as Experience*, trans. Andrea Tarnowski (Stanford: Stanford University Press, 1999), 45.

[103] Ibid.

[104] Ibid., 46.

[105] Ibid. This is a similar theory to what Theodor Adorno presents on "natural beauty" in *Aesthetic Theory*: "The identity of the artwork with the subject is as complete as the identity of nature with itself should some day be," trans. Robert Hullot-Kentor (Minneapolis: University of Minnesota Press, 1997), 63.

is an assumed truth running under the split identity of the narrator's "I," as Michel Terestchenko explains:

> Ishiguro's narrator refers to himself in the first-person singular, but the long monologue which structures the novel paradoxically questions the identity of the "I" (a concern that underlies many of Ishiguro's works). Indeed, *The Remains of the Day* deals with a person who, for almost all his life, has been deceiving himself in the name of a professional ethics of obedience set up as an ideal of "dignity." Returning to himself and to his past only very late in life, he uncovers this deception and the illusions it has fostered. The initial alienating split between the human being and his function is ultimately followed by the liberating split in the narrator, who suddenly becomes aware that his life has been a failure.[106]

Never Let Me Go maps a different set of coordinates; instead of a "split" that can, at least in theory, be healed, the clones are the strange-within-us; there is nothing different, more originary or escapable about the uncanny they highlight. However, *Never Let Me Go* is not the first instance of the uncanny to have been noted in Ishiguro's work. Brian Shaffer has performed a strong interpretation of Ishiguro's fourth novel, *The Unconsoled*, through the same-but-different of Freud's uncanny. Shaffer's reading of "familiarity-in-strangeness" is important because of the way it brings into focus that what is frightening in the "Madame" scene from *Never Let Me Go* is actually what has always already been there (as Kathy puts it). Quoting Freud's essay on how the uncanny is both that which is and is not familiar,[107] Shaffer gives a number of examples from *The Unconsoled*, Ishiguro's novel about an avant-garde pianist and his troubles surrounding a concert: "buses seem to wait for Ryder in order to take him precisely where he wishes to go [...]

---

[106] Michel Terestchenko, "Servility and Destructiveness in Kazuo Ishiguro's *The Remains of the Day*," *Partial Answers: Journal of Literature and the History of Ideas* 5.1 (2007), 77-8.

[107] Brian Shaffer, *Understanding Kazuo Ishiguro* (Columbia: University of South Carolina Press, 1998), 99-100.

food is served on the public buses and trams on which he rides [...] long-lost relatives appear out of nowhere."[108] What is uncanny in these examples is not that life is "marvelous," but rather that it is exactly what is wished for. The uncanny here is immediate wish fulfillment, or a matching of external and internal realities (de Man's reading of metaphor). This "exact" match only makes its difference from "normal" reality more intense. In her reading of *The Unconsoled* Katherine Stanton argues that "Reading against the grain – that is, against the notion of Ishiguro as psychological realist – we may also read it as a moment of sudden and uncomfortable proximity, when boundaries become blurred and troubles shared."[109] Natalie Reitano calls the difference that is necessary for proximity to exist the "wound" of the novel, although she defines two different kinds of wounds contained therein:

> In *The Unconsoled,* Ishiguro produces rivaling discourses of the "wound": the wound figures as both traumatic rupture and as the site where finite beings are exposed to one another at what Jean-Luc Nancy calls the "limit of community." The limit of community occurs where the myth of total community, either lost or to come, is interrupted. Called to an experience of what lies outside us, we refuse to "make operational" community as a work or work that would prescribe fulfillment in some destiny. Through the pianist Ryder and the composer Brodsky, who have been called together to save the city by commencing a new epoch through aesthetic production, Ishiguro opposes the time of melancholic repetition to that of interruption.[110]

Other examples of the uncanny in *The Unconsoled* can be found in the shifting space of the novel, which is both unfamiliar and exceedingly accommodating. For example, when the main

---

[108] Ibid., 100.

[109] Katherine Stanton, *Cosmopolitan Fictions: Ethics, Politics, and Global Change in the Words of Kazuo Ishiguro, Michael Ondaatje, Jamaica Kincaid, and J. M. Coetzee* (New York; London: Routledge, 2006), 17.

[110] Natalie Reitano, "The Good Wound: Memory and Community in *The Unconsoled,*" *Texas Studies in Literature and Language* 49.4 (Winter 2007), 362.

protagonist Ryder is in a hurry, an unusually small door not previously noticed appears which leads quickly down to the street, just where Ryder wants to go.[111] Another example is when Ryder leans against an impossibly narrow balcony so that he is "just able to peer in through the nearest window."[112] Maintaining this difficult position is rewarded by the room "growing steadily more familiar":[113] this room, it turns out, *is* the parlor of his childhood home in Manchester, although he is currently in an unnamed city in central Europe. What these examples show is that Kathy's conjunction of the familiar and the strange is not new to Ishiguro's work. Richard Robinson argues, quoting both Roland Barthes and Freud, that

> Ryder is like Oedipus getting lost in the forking paths between Thebes and Corinth, returning to an unremembered home, where he is both esteemed guest and absent husband and father, in order to find the answer to the riddle, "Who am I". Barthes pointed out, in reference to Agatha Christie's *The Murder of Roger Ackroyd*, that the first-person narrator, concealing "the profound darkness of the existent 'I'", can be the one "whodunit". The guilty narrator, encircling his own home, is also suffering from what Freud diagnosed as the *unheimlich* or uncanny – "that class of the frightening which leads back to what is known of old and long familiar."[114]

In addition, Paul Veyret sees an uncanny structure functioning in Ishiguro's first novel, *A Pale View of Hills*. After initiating a discussion of Freud's reading of the uncanny, Veyret observes:

> The novel rests on a paradox, one of a repetition and a retranscription of memories: Etsuko Sheringham appears above all, according to the law of narration, to have listened to the other protagonists of her past. However, the voice of

---

[111] Kazuo Ishiguro, *The Unconsoled* (London; Boston: Faber and Faber, 1996), 281-2.

[112] Ibid., 213.

[113] Ibid., 214.

[114] Richard Robinson, "Nowhere, in Particular: Kazuo Ishiguro's *The Unconsoled* and Central Europe," *Critical Quarterly* 48.4 (2006) 122.

> Etsuko appears fissionable, as with the atom, and melts with the other known woman from Nagasaki. "I" is an other.[115]

Etsuko's re-telling of her past life in post-atomic Nagasaki is a repetition and retranscription through which something new emerges, unsettling the reliability of Etsuko's narration; difference is located in that which is *most* familiar: the self. These coordinates of similarity and difference found throughout Ishiguro's work form the structure for reinscribing Heidegger's notion of death with an impoverished and supposedly "non-human" experience of death, a notion only seen when reflected in the "fully" human facticity experienced by the clones.

1.7 The Title of the Novel as an Instantiation of Closeness and Difference

Fear that the self is divided is one way to understand the title of *Never Let Me Go*. As argued above, the proximity of the clones to the "normals" of Britain creates a sense of fear in the novel. However, it is not only Madame who is afraid. As revealed at the end of the novel, *all* the guardians were scared. In the novel's final confrontation between an older Kathy and Tommy, joined in love and hoping for a deferral from Ms Emily and Madame from becoming donors, Kathy asks Ms Emily why Madame is afraid of them. Ms Emily responds:

> "Is she afraid of you? We're *all* afraid of you. I myself had to fight back my dread of you all almost every day I was at Hailsham. There were times I'd look down at you all from my study window and I'd feel such revulsion [...]" She stopped, then something in her eyes flashed again. "But I was determined not to let such feelings stop me doing what was right. I fought those feelings and I won." (*NLMG* 264)

[115] Paul Veyret, *Kazuo Ishiguro: L'encre de la mémorie* (Pessac: Presses Universitaires de Bordeaux, 2005), 46 (translation mine).

Giorgio Agamben argues that a fear which arises from *proximity* is actually a fear of the animal within. Agamben makes his argument quoting Walter Benjamin's *One-Way Street*:

> For Benjamin, the predominant feeling in disgust is the fear of being recognized by what repulses us. "The horror that stirs deep in man is an obscure awareness that in him something lives so akin to the animal that it might be recognized" [...] Whoever experiences disgust has in some way recognized himself in the object of his loathing and fears being recognized in turn. The man who experiences disgust recognizes himself in an alterity that cannot be assumed – that is, he subjectifies himself in an absolute desubjectification.[116]

Agamben's reading of Benjamin raises three important conjectures that relate to a reading of the title *Never Let Me Go*: (1) that there is a recognition of something strange within the self; (2) the subject then fears being recognized herself, presumably by this strangeness; and (3) a self is created from *within* an unassumable alterity. As Calarco argues, Agamben's project "entails abandoning the idea that man's relation to death and language constitutes any possibility proper to man. In contrast to Heidegger, human death and language is refigured by Agamben as radically ex-appropriating, and it is beginning from

---

[116] Giorgio Agamben, *Remnants of Auschwitz: The Witness and the Archive*, trans. Daniel Heller-Roazen (New York: Zone Books, 2002), 106-7. Elsewhere, Agamben calls readings of man/animal and inside/outside as part of the "anthropological machine" set up to defend "the human": "Insofar as the production of man through the opposition man/animal, human/inhuman, is at stake here, the machine necessarily functions by means of an exclusion (which is also always already a capturing) and an inclusion (which is also always already an exclusion). Indeed, precisely because the human is already presupposed every time, the machine actually produces a kind of state of exception, a zone of indeterminacy in which the outside is nothing but the exclusion of an inside and the inside is in turn only the inclusion of an outside," *The Open: Man and Animal*, trans. Kevin Attell (Stanford: Stanford University Press, 2004), 37.

this site of exposure that Agamben unfolds his subsequent works on human community and politics."[117]

Fear of a divided self is essential for a closer reading of the title of *Never Let Me Go*. In the book, the title comes from a fictional song from an album by "Judy Bridgewater" called *Songs after Dark*. The album was obtained by Kathy through one of the "Exchanges," where the students trade the artwork they have made for that made by other students.[118] The only song on the album that really caught Kathy's attention was "Never Let Me Go," and she listened to it in her six-person dorm room as often as she could, as long as she was able to find some privacy. Kathy would dance while listening to the song and she imagined that the lyrics which really grabbed her, "Never let me go...Oh baby, baby...Never let me go..." (*NLMG* 69) were about a mother wanting to hold her baby close to her, never wanting to part from such a close bond. This thought was reinforced by Kathy's dancing to the song while "holding an imaginary baby to my breast [...] I'd grabbed a pillow to stand in for the baby [...]" (71).

However, during one of Kathy's performances she caught Madame watching her from the doorway. Doors always had to be kept open at Hailsham, and this allowed Kathy to see Madame watching her with a tear-stained face. Kathy connects this to the way Madame looked at the students as if they were spiders, although there is a difference. This time, watching

---

[117] Calarco, "On the Borders of Language and Death," 17-8. Vilém Flusser's theory of communication is that language as a removal from nature is also a removal from death and hence a form of immortality. See Vilém Flusser, "What is Communication?" *Writings*, trans. Erik Eisel, ed. Andreas Ströhl (Minneapolis; London: University of Minnesota Press, 2002).

[118] Kathy describes the Exchanges thus: "Four times a year – spring, summer, autumn, winter – we had a kind of big exhibition-cum-sale of all the things we'd been creating in the three months since the last Exchange. Paintings, drawings, pottery; all sorts of 'sculptures' made from whatever was the craze of the day – bashed-up cans, maybe, or bottle tops stuck onto cardboard. For each thing you put in, you were paid in Exchange Tokens [...] The rule was you could only buy work done by students in your own year, but that still gave us plenty to choose from, since most of us could get pretty prolific over a three-month period," (*NLMG* 15-6). For the clones the Exchanges were a place for the creation of self through the physical products of others; Kathy says that the Exchanges "were our only means [...] of building up a collection of personal possessions" (16).

Kathy dancing, Madame looks "with that same look in her eyes she always had when she looked at us, like she was seeing something that gave her the creeps. However, this time there was something else, something extra in that look I couldn't fathom" (ibid.). Kathy fills in this something extra with a knowledge she barely knows she has: Madame is crying because she knows that the students cannot have babies (72). In one sense the intrusion of Madame does not effect a new interpretation of the title; Kathy still hopes the baby will somehow "stay." However, with the addition of the information that the clones are sterile, the title may be read as a statement of being trapped in a life you might otherwise not want to have. Being sterile is being controlled. Therefore the title of the novel might be read as: "[They] Never Let Me Go." While the anonymity of the "they" which produces, organizes and uses the clones is dealt with in the next chapter, in this version the title has changed from an imperative to a statement: Kathy is unable to escape from the world that created her. This interpretation, actually, is the opposite of what Madame tells Kathy the "real" reason was for her tears in the novel's denouement. Madame argues that Kathy was trying to hold tight the old, pre-they world that was slipping away:

> "When I watched you dancing that day, I saw something else: I saw a new world coming rapidly. More scientific, efficient, yes. More cures for the old sicknesses. Very good. But a harsh, cruel world. And I saw a little girl, her eyes tightly closed, holding to her breast the old kind world, one that she knew in her heart could not remain, and she was holding it and pleading, never to let her go. That is what I saw." (267)

While Madame's interpretation of the scene seems straightforward at first, seeing a girl longing for a kinder world that would not use her as an organ farm, it is actually ambiguous regarding the notion of facticity. First, what is the "old kind world" that Madame sees disappearing? In the context of the denouement, this world is Hailsham, an institution which was allowed to exist because a potential future dialogue was possible, one which would see the clones as "fully human," and therefore they would be privy to the same right as the "normals." However, a world which clones humans and then just lets them be is an odd notion of "kind." However, it seems that the old kind world that Madame is referring to is actually a world where human beings would not be cloned. It is this cloneless world that Madame sees Kathy holding close to herself, a world in which she would never have come into being. Kathy, as a clone, is holding on her potential non-being; in fact, she is addressing it to never let her go. Kathy is experiencing death-in-life in this scene, holding such a perverse knowledge close to her although she barely knows what she is doing.

However, perhaps this is also a misreading because the coordinates of what "child" and "parent" might mean in a world where human cloning is prevalent would be so radically different:

> Cloning, after all, seems to raise the possibility of a wholly new kind of child, one made not from sex or sexual recombination, but rather from the transfer of genetic information from a single progenitor into its offspring. But in reality, while we do not know what sort of a human being a clone would be, neither do we have any real objective purchase on the variety of new kinds of children we make through new reproductive technologies and through new social mechanisms. We may be able to determine the origins of a child's DNA, but that only begins the process of *reinventing ideas of relatedness and how relatedness conveys status and responsibility*. We have amazing new ways to make children, and think of that process in increasingly design-oriented terms.[119]

While the term "reinventing" is perhaps naïve, "rethinking" ideas of relatedness is at the heart of *Never Let Me Go* on figurative and thematic levels. This new relatedness is a reflexive repetition through which difference becomes visible, and it maps out different coordinates than do traditional notions

---

[119] Glenn McGee, "A Pragmatic Approach to Human Cloning," *The Cloning Sourcebook*, ed. Arlene Judith Klotzko (New York: Oxford University Press, 2001), 176 (emphasis added).

of "parent" and "child." Britzman's analysis of the novel hinges on the clones' removal from the complexes that develop from having parents, meaning the desires, laws and frustrations that a development along with the "other" of a parent involves: "The replica students were never born, but inexplicably, they desire, they love, they want recognition [...] How can a copy have real feelings if there is no original object, if there is no mother?"[120] Britzman points out that these children are the opposite of Melanie Klein's "object relations theory"[121] in that the children-clones do not internalize the adult others in their world, but rather the adult others, quite literally actually, internalize them and therefore the clones are removed from the normals' realm of responsibility: "Their questions are the inverse of the Kleinian child, for essentially Kathy H. and her friends will end up as the inside of the mother's body: they provide her treasures and so their curiosity, their drive to know cannot affect the Other."[122] Britzman furthers her argument:

> Ishiguro's novel severs this second chance [of the child saving the parents from themselves, following the thought of Hannah Arendt] by supposing the psychoanalytic mythology of the Oedipal conflict in reverse: rather than the child wanting to have one parent and kill the other one, it is the parents who kill the child and refuse the law of mortality and incest. There is no law. Language becomes truncated, made euphemistic: there are replicas, the normals, them and us, models, carers, doners, and no last names. With the veil of deception that is language, the desire for recognition, a relation that also saves the world, or at least offers a lifeline

---

[120] Britzman, "On Being a Slow Reader," 312. A similar argument is posed for the cyborg in Donna Haraways' "A Cyborg Manifesto: Science, Technology, and Socialist-Feminism in the Late Twentieth Century," *Simians, Cyborgs and Women: The Reinvention of Nature* (New York; Routledge, 1991).

[121] As a brief example, in *Envy and Gratitude* Klein (referring to her theory of "the good breast") sets out to describe how "Envy contributes to the infant's difficulties in building up his good object, for he feels that the gratification of which he was deprived has been kept for itself by the breast that frustrated him," Melanie Klein, *Envy and Gratitude: A Study of Unconscious Sources* (London: Routledge, 2003), 6.

[122] Britzman, "On Being a Slow Reader, 312.

between those yet to become and those already here, unravels.[123]

Standards of closeness and difference between self and other are being stood on their heads, and the first things that are discarded are what McGee called "status and responsibility." The clones, to put it succinctly, are being used. The justification for this use is to locate their bodies outside the sphere of human responsibility. As Michael Davidson argues, the difference between cloned and uncloned humans "is not only about sexual difference but about the difference between disability and normalcy, between a body that, in order to be productive, must not be *reproductive*."[124] Puchner at first seems to agree with Davidson. Puchner states that "The clones' theory about human sexuality is a mirror image of their own lives, namely as something that is determined by functionality."[125] However, for Puchner Kathy's dancing scene is the location of not so much a difference but rather the lack of one. Puchner asks: "Is this faint and submerged longing [of Kathy's for a child] a sign of the gulf that separates humans from clones?"[126] No, Puchner answers; although he does not develop his reading to the extent undertaken here, there is the beginning of an argument for reading the clones' differences from "normal" humanity as an allegory of the poverty of what constitutes what is taken for the human condition itself: "Humans, too, are the product of some sort of biological copying, and human parentage is never entirely free from doubt. We may be looking for parents lost or never known or for some other fantasy of origin and original. Reproduction and the nuclear family are not necessary attributes of the human."[127] Puchner continues, delineating the proximity of the uncanny, without developing the idea that the "fantasy of origin and original" actually refers to the lie that "we" live in order to make our short lives bearable: "The difference Ishiguro

---

123 Ibid., 315.

124 Michael Davidson, *Concerto for the Left Hand: Disability and the Defamiliar Body* (Ann Arbor: University of Michigan Press, 2008), 213. Davidson's section on *Never Let Me Go* is titled "Told and Not Told."

125 Puchner, "When We Were Clones," 42.

126 Ibid.

127 Ibid.

presents us with is fundamental at one moment, but at the next it seems to shrink before our eyes into a minor technicality, too weak to ground any ontological difference between clones and humans."[128]

Puchner's reading, while strong, does not go far enough. The minor technicality which is too weak for an ontological gap between human and clone actually points to the dismantling of a number of assumptions of what can constitute humanity. In this sense the human clones are "a literal realization of what, figuratively, his protagonists have always been."[129] It is here that Britzman's analysis proves most useful, as it continues to circle around an analysis of the human:

> It is not only that Ishiguro's novel performs its own resistance to being read, itself a version of never letting go. And it is not just that Ishiguro presents readers with a peculiar ontological difficulty in the form of a negation novel narrated by a replicate-being, whose fate as a copy is to copy and replace a human part. While both dynamics in and of themselves – the uncanny, inquisitive creatures and the fate of their illegible design – present ontological difficulties, the anxiety of reading these creatures belongs to readers.[130]

Never Let Me Go, because of its structure of coexistence, makes visible the "anxiety of reading" in its readers. However, the engine for this anxiety needs to be developed in the next section in which it will be seen that another literary level inserted between the narrator and implied reader, the narratee, is a figure of disruption.

---

[128] Ibid. Unfortunately, this is the point in Puchner's essay where he finishes his discussion of *Never Let Me Go*.

[129] Lisa Fluet, "Introduction: Antisocial Goods," *Novel* 40.3 (2007), 208. This issue of *Novel* is devoted to Ishiguro.

[130] Britzman, "On Being a Slow Reader," 308.

1.8 Re-Scheduling Facticity: Narratee as Non-Human

Never Let Me Go posits coordinates of what was above described as "nonrelation" both in the way the clones come about an experience of facticity through 1) a mix of having always known and a moment of linguistic revelation and 2) in the concomitant distance and closeness of the uncanny. These coordinates of suspension can also be seen in the opening "confusion" of the novel, where the meaning of such terms as "carer" remains unresolved. As with all of Ishiguro's work, the manner in which the narrator presents information deserves attention; the assumptions being made by the narrator are paramount. For example, as Peter Verdonk describes the opening lacunae of Ishiguro's second novel, *An Artist of the Floating World*: "a kind of second-person vacuum is created, and the reader is drawn in to fill it, and becomes positioned as a participant in the fictional world.[131] The same vacuum is in play in *Never Let Me Go*. In the opening lines of the novel it is assumed that the term "carer" is understood by the narratee. This is clear because the term is not explained, put in quotation marks, or otherwise marked. Taken as given, the term sets off the novel's "hermeneutic rhythm,"[132] meaning that from the get-go assumptions about the narratee are going to be germane to the plot of the novel, shaking the ground under the reader's feet.

What the unmarked use of "carer" does is to raise the following question: Who is the narratee supposed to be in order to be in the know? Other language in the novel's opening lines only compounds the narratee's assumed knowledge, therefore expanding the narratee's role. This can be seen, for example, when Kathy states: "That sounds long enough, I know [...]" This quote indicates assumed knowledge by the addressee in a number of ways. "That" is an anaphoric reference to the previous "over eleven years," but "over eleven years" sounds "long

[131] Peter Verdonk, *Stylistics* (Oxford: Oxford University Press, 2002), 34.

[132] Jonathan Culler, *Structuralist Poetics: Structuralism, Linguistics, and the Study of Literature* (Ithaca: Cornell University Press, 1976), 211.

enough" to whom exactly? To "us" narratees who now not only are assumed to know what a "carer" is but also the average time-frame for someone to be in this position, which seems to be for less than eleven years. As Mark Jerng argues, "This particular double mode of address interrupts the easy divide between the implicit reader as human and the 'you' as clone. Indeed, the structure of address places being a human and being a clone side-by-side, as 'you' are made to shuttle in-between the universal condition of being human and the universal condition of being a clone."[133] The "double mode of address" puts clone and human on a plane of coexistence. The rhetorical structure of this doubling foregrounds assumptions made regarding the narratee, the narration constructs an aura of authenticity for the novel by placing narrative bifurcations in the hands of a heavily voiced *discours* rather than an "objective" *historie*, and thus it naturalizes the fiction. As the novel draws attention to itself as a construction, its mode of "side-by-side" makes visible the constructed basis of the human. According to Keith McDonald, such meta-referencing functions in *Never Let Me Go* thus: "The novel draws attention to itself as a construction, strengthening the illusion that it is the narrator telling this story, and that the reader acknowledges the authenticity of the narrative, distancing Ishiguro from the writing process,"[134] which is actually a statement that is true for all first-person narration, except theoretically for autobiography.

Never Let Me Go foregrounds the nature of subjectivity via its narrative stance. The opening of the novel highlights a gap between the narratee and the implied reader. This gap was seen in Verdonk's statement regarding *Artist of the Floating World*, but it can be seen as early as Ishiguro's first novel. Mike Petry describes how in *A Pale View of Hills* the main character and narrator of this story, Etsuko, seems to tell her story in a plain fashion, but as the novel progresses the story becomes increasingly contradictory: "Etsuko is by no means always

---

[133] Mark Jerng, "Giving Form to Life: Cloning and Narrative Expectations of the Human," *Partial Answers: Journal of Literature and the History of Ideas* 6.2 (2008), 391.

[134] Keith McDonald, "Days of Past Futures: Kazuo Ishiguro's *Never Let Me Go* As 'Speculative Memoir,'" *Biography* 30.1 (Winter 2007), 79.

conscious of what she is saying or implying, and about what words she uses to communicate her stories. In fact, many of the connotations and implications of her narrative are more often than not invisible to her. The reader is meant to recognize this gap, and the major effect of it is that Etsuko 'is spoken' by her own narrative."[135] In a 1990 interview Ishiguro states that at the time of writing *A Pale View of Hills* "I was very interested in the technique of using gaps and spaces in fiction to create very powerful vacuums. That's something that I always used in my later fiction, but I think it's particularly noticeable in my first book."[136] Additionally, Wong has observed another gap functioning in Ishiguro's work, one of a gap between individuals and nations,[137] a position similar to Homi Bhabha's assessment of *The Remains of the Day*, in which "The brilliance of Ishiguro's exposition of the ideology of service lies in his linking the national and the international, the indigenous and the colonial, by focusing on the anti-semitism of the inter-war period, and thus mediating race and cultural difference through a

---

[135] Mike Petry, *Narratives of Memory and Identity: The Novels of Kazuo Ishiguro* (Frankfurt am Main: Peter Lang, 1999), 49.

[136] Don Swain, "Don Swain Interviews Kazuo Ishiguro," *Conversations with Kazuo Ishiguro*, ed. Brian Shaffer and Cynthia Wong (Jackson: University Press of Mississippi, 2008), 97.

[137] See Cynthia Wong, "The Shame of Memory: Blanchot's Self-Dispossession in Ishiguro's *A Pale View of Hills*," *CLIO* 24.2 (1995). Rob Burton offers a slightly different reading in relation to Ishiguro's first novel: "the episodes from *A Pale View of Hills* serve as an introduction to the floating world, a dominant motif in each of Ishiguro's six novels to date. In addition to referring to a specific cultural and historical phenomenon (ukiyo-e) central to Ishiguro's second novel, the floating world also refers more broadly to an elaborate web of memories and epiphanies spun by narrators who are caught between two worlds (whether moral, ideological, or geographical)," *Artists of the Floating World: Contemporary Writings between Cultures* (Lanham: University Press of America, 2007), 42. Malcolm Bradley, Ishiguro's creative writing instructor, has a similar view (although while seemingly lumping all "Japanese novels" together): "his three novels to date could well seem to have acquired their reticence from the tradition of the Japanese novel, though they owe just as much to Ishiguro's own aesthetic invention. His books too touch large historical events, but always very indirectly, and from the standpoint of chosen moments from closely perceived individual lives," *The Modern British Novel* (London: Secker and Warburg, 1993), 424.

form of difference – Jewishness – that confuses the boundaries of class and race and represents the '*insider's outsidedness*.'"[138]

On a thematic level the novel constructs an unworking of the division not between nations but between human and other-than-human: the clones "grapple with the great divide between their understanding of themselves as humans and their society's consideration of them as non-humans – as mere bodies lacking deep interior selves or souls, artificial products of a human science whose sole purpose is to extend the lives of 'genuine' humans."[139] However, it develops that "society's" viewpoint of the clones is merely a reflection of what is so difficult to see in itself. This development is reflected on the level of narrative technique in which there is a shift in *who* is spoken in this recontextualization; instead of the implied reader completing the narratee's story, *it is the narratee that is completing the implied reader's story*. As Briztman was quoted arguing above, "It can feel as if the book is reading us, turning our pages." The gap in the novel is not, as in Ishiguro's early books, one that assumed an underlying truth that the narrator is unable to grasp. Instead this is a gap found within this repositioning itself.

As an illustration of how the gap in Ishiguro's earlier work is different, the "you" that is addressed in his second novel, *An Artist of the Floating World*, is a key foil. The opening sentence of the novel provides a stark contrast to what is going on in *Never Let Me Go*: "If on a sunny day you climb the steep path leading up from the little wooden bridge still referred to around here as 'The Bridge of Hesitation', you will not have to walk far before the roof of my house becomes visible between the tops of two gingko trees."[140] Verdonk, who was quoted at the beginning of this section, argues that through the second-person address in this novel "a kind of second-person vacuum is created, and the reader is drawn in to fill it, and becomes positioned as a participant in the fictional world." It is in the "filling" of the vacuum that a difference between *An Artist of the Floating*

---

[138] Homi Bhabha, "Unpacking My Library Again," *The Journal of the Midwest Modern Language Association* 28.1 (Spring 1995), 14.

[139] Seaman, "Becoming More (than) Human," 265.

[140] Kazuo Ishiguro, *An Artist of the Floating World* (New York: Vintage, 1989), 7.

World and *Never Let Me Go* takes place. In the latter, this gap is already filled by humanity; therefore, another reading of division and difference needs to take place. In a 1999 interview with François Gallix, Ishiguro states that in *An Artist of the Floating World* "I wanted to create the effect that the reader was actually not being addressed directly by the narrator but that the reader was actually eavesdropping on this rather enclosed narrator talking to somebody he imagined [...]"[141] The difference in *Never Let Me Go* is that the narratee and narrator are the same, they are both clones; what is unsettling is not just difference but also an uncanny ipseity.

In *Never Let Me Go* the implied reader is unable to complete the work of narration that the others, meaning the narrator and narratee, have taken up; while the implied reader may refuse to be read by the text, the text still reads the implied reader. In the opening pages of *Never Let Me Go* Kathy assumes and agrees with the narratee's presumed disapproval: "I know" she says, as if she is just as ready to move on to being a donor as "we" are anxious to see her do so. Although see her move on to what? To whatever comes after being a carer: however, "we" all "already know" what that is, so there is no need to mention it.

There are other instances in the novel of this second-person address which help develop the role of the narratee. Early in the novel, Kathy, who seems to have been given certain privileges because of her skill as a carer, understands the narratee's possible resentment of her advantages: "I know carers, working now, who are just as good and don't get half the credit. If you're one of them, I can understand how you might get resentful – about my bedsit, my car, above all, the way I get to pick and choose who I look after" (*NLMG* 3). The narratee is corralled into the role of a carer. In addition, he or she must stay in something worse than where Kathy stays and they cannot choose those they look after. There are numerous other examples of such second-person address in the novel. For instance, Kathy, who is from the privileged "boarding school" of Hailsham, wonders if the narratee has undergone the same experience at

---

[141] François Gallix, "Kazuo Ishiguro: The Sorbonne Lecture," *Conversations with Kazuo Ishiguro*, ed. Brian Shaffer and Cynthia Wong (Jackson: University Press of Mississippi, 2008), 150.

their school: "I don't know how it was where you were, but at Hailsham we had to have some form of medical almost every week [...]" (13).[142] In another example, Kathy introduces the theme of "collections" in a similar manner: "I don't know if you had 'collections' where you were" (38). However, another example, which reflects the horrific alternative reality the novel envisions, takes place during a lesson about the concentration camps of the Second World War, which are described as being surrounded by electric fences. The young students do not treat the subject with the proper gravity and everyone begins "shouting and mimicking touching electric fences" (77). It is then that the guardian, Miss Lucy, days "'It's just as well the fences at Hailsham aren't electrified. You get terrible accidents sometimes'" (ibid.), providing a mere hint of what is actually happening at other institutions. Even if not exactly the same as Kathy in all respects, the role of the narratee in *Never Let Me Go* is becoming quite specific: it is that of a less-privileged clone, one that has experienced horrors beyond those described in the novel. This specificity calls into question the difficulties some reviewers of the novel have had in seeing that the narratee is a clone like Kathy.[143]

The implication being drawn out here is that "we" narratees are a part of Kathy's club, meaning that we are also clones, ready to die; automatically, the narratee is included in a world ready for death since she or he is a part of Kathy's world of "carers" and "donors"; this inclusion is illustrated by "our" impatience for her to get on with what she/we was/were made for. *Never Let Me Go* begins with the assumption that the narratees are other-than-humans that know their own death. However, it is

[142] Under the "Technical Problems" that need to be overcome for Cell Nuclear Replacement to become a reality, Harris includes: "*Illnesses of the donor*: the somatic cell from which the nucleus is taken may carry the genetic defect for which the person is being treated, although genetic engineering could in theory help to overcome this problem," *On Cloning*, 12.

[143] Another aspect of assumed complicity with the narratee is that Kathy is not the one holding herself back from entering this part of her life, but rather a never-explained "they" do, presumably those who want her to continue in her current position, although not much more information is ever given throughout the novel about "them," because we all have the same amount or lack of information about our oppressors.

important that this figure of apostrophe is *too* explicit – it cannot be taken literally – and hence an implied reader is addressed through the position of the narratee: if it is "obvious" that the implied reader is not a clone, then it is also "obvious" that the implied reader does not know their own death.

However, the narratee-as-donor reading being developed goes against a number of the readings of the novel (with Jerng, quotes above being a notable exception), where the one addressed is assumed to be one of the "normals" of Britain[144] or from a future clone-friendly public[145] - nearly anything but a clone.[146] However, the assumptions made about the narratee do clearly point to its being a clone, and the relationship between clones and "normals" developed throughout the book indicates that within the context of the story a "normal" human would probably never read a word written by a clone. This is because clones receive treatment which ranges from fatal torture to at most fearful tolerance. In addition, Ishiguro, to be sure, did not write his book in the year 2005 for a world of clones. The implied readers are "normal" humans reading his books. What the text does is to invite an intensely proximate (because given) relationship between the implied reader and narratee; in this familiarity-in-strangeness the novel sets up the coordinates of the uncanny. As Ingersoll argues, "Clearly, Ishiguro is attracted to the comforting deceptions of the familiar, a familiarity that can turn itself inside out to reveal a radical otherness."[147] What this proximity also indicates is that this radical, uncanny otherness is us.

---

[144] James Wood, "The Human Difference," *The New Republic* (May 16 2005), 37.

[145] McDonald, "Days of Past Futures: Kazuo Ishiguro's *Never Let Me Go* As 'Speculative
Memoir,'" 82.

[146] Richard Bradford comes close to the position of narratee-as-clone presented here (although still assuming the narratee is an ordinary, normal person), however without exploring it further: "We might assume that the clones will draw our sympathy, perhaps horrified empathy, but instead we find that they become the observers and we, the ordinary normal people who read novels like this, become its mute robotic subjects," *The Novel Now: Contemporary British Fiction* (Malden: Blackwell, 2007), 217.

[147] Ingersoll, "Taking Off into the Realm of Metaphor," 42.

While the coordinates of the uncanny have been developed in this chapter as the coordinates of a nonrelational experience of death, criticism of such a nonrelational experience has centered on Derrida's reading of the remnants of language to be found in Heidegger's formulation. Focusing on Derrida's criticism will help provide an understanding of the power of Ishiguro's novel recontextualization.

1.9 Divisions of Death and Divisions of Life

In order to develop a reading of Derrida's critique of the concept of nonrelation and how it relates to the repositioning of the narratee/implied reader, Heidegger's division of death into the difference between to perish, to demise and dying needs to be expanded by also taking into account his division of life.[148] As argued above, according to Heidegger the human dies in a different way than the non-human animal, and therefore the human has a different relationship to death. Moving onto Heidegger's similar divisions of life, a question that must be addressed is *how the animal's lack of understanding can ever be known.*

In §49 of *The Fundamental Concepts of Metaphysics*, Heidegger examines the question of "*Can we transpose ourselves into an animal at all?*"[149] For Heidegger this is a question of "*accessibility itself,*"[150] an accessibility to the world which differs in degree for different types of beings. Heidegger divides this question of world into three parts. These parts are structurally related to Heidegger's divisions of the concept of death: [151] both include a privileged position for the human, a

---

[148] Although this and the following section focus more on the theoretical background of the question of the non-human than its manifestation in *Never Let Me Go*, the stage is being set for the way the allegory of the human condition from *Never Let Me Go* revises some of Heidegger's concerns presented here.

[149] Heidegger, *The Fundamental Concepts of Metaphysics*, 201.

[150] Ibid.

[151] See David Farrell Krell, *Daimon Life: Heidegger and Life-Philosophy* (Bloomington; Indianapolis: Indiana University Press, 1992), 128-30.

diminished position for the animal, and a moot position for matter (the latter goes unstated in Heidegger's reading of death, for something that is never in life cannot pass into death[152]). Both structures of life and death ascribe to the animal not a lack, but rather a gradation of less. The reason both structures are developed here is that the question of whether Heidegger's concept is really one of gradation and not one of kinds is at the heart of Derrida's criticism.

Heidegger develops the three theses regarding an entity's relationship to the world thus: "[1.] The stone is worldless [*weltlos*]; [2.] The animal is poor in world [*weltarm*]; [3.] Man is world-forming [*weltbildend*]."[153] Briefly, the stone has no means with which to see or view its world, and cannot participate in it "as such"; the animal can see, hear and taste its world, but it cannot think about it *as* world (for example, a bee can sense and use a flower, but cannot separate the flower into "stamen," "petal," and so on; nor can it understand the flower's chemical properties); humankind is that which can come to understand its world in a way that actually forms that world, rather than just responds to it. As Gerard Kuperus summarizes, the animal "lacks the kind of opening up of the world that is made possible through out – specifically human – attunements."[154] What is not being attempted here is a development of a world-forming nature in animals. Instead, *Never Let Me Go* shows how Heidegger's description of the poverty of the animal is actually a description of the human. Such an analysis becomes available through Derrida's critique of Heidegger's nonrelation.

---

[152] Walter Benjamin offers strong readings of the power of the "inanimate" stemming from his readings of translation to Kafka's work. For analysis see Beatrice Hanssen, *Walter Benjamin's Other History: Of Stones, Animals, Human Beings, and Angels* (Berkeley: University of California Press, 2000).

[153] Heidegger, *The Fundamental Concepts of Metaphysics*, 184.

[154] Gerard Kuperus, "Attunement, Deprivation, and Drive: Heidegger and Animality," *Phenomenology and the Non-Human Animal*, Corinne Painter and Christian Lotz, ed. (Dordrecht: Springer, 2007), 13.

1.10 Derrida's Critique of Nonrelation

Derrida has leveled an important criticism at Heidegger's division of being. This criticism puts into focus a reading of the "weak" ground initially developed above along with Puchner's quote "The difference Ishiguro presents us with is fundamental at one moment, but at the next it seems to shrink before our eyes into a minor technicality, too weak to ground any ontological difference between clones and humans." Derrida describes the animal's situation in Heidegger as a lack of a precise definition, of how "The animal has a world in the mode of not-having, or, conversely, it is deprived of world because it *can* have a world [...] The logical contradiction between the two propositions (the animal does and does not have a world) would mean simply that we have not yet sufficiently elucidated the concept of world [...]"[155]

Heidegger's reading of world in this context is not tied only to the animal. He asking whether humankind can have access to the world of the animal (or empathy with the animal) through the three-fold prism of: "Can we transpose ourselves into an animal? Can we transpose ourselves into a stone? Can we transpose ourselves into another human being?"[156] The reason these three divisions are important for Heidegger is that they each answer the question of empathy in a different way. For transposing ourselves into an animal, we would feel that there is the ability to do so, if we could only see the world in the same way as the animal;[157] for the stone, it is a different kind of question because there is doubt as to the stone offering any possibility at all of being with it in any meaningful way;[158] as for transposing oneself into another human being, *the problem of the question itself is exposed.* The problem of the question for Heidegger is that it assumes that we are separate from each

---

[155] Derrida, *Of Spirit: Heidegger and the Question*, trans. Geoffrey Bennington and Rachel Bowlby (Chicago; London: University of Chicago Press, 1991), 50-1.

[156] Heidegger, *Fundamental Concepts*, 202.

[157] Ibid., 203-4.

[158] Ibid., 204.

other as human beings, and that a gap needs to be overcome in order to have a relation with the other, but this is not the case at all: human beings are originarily with each other always and already, and to even pose such a question shows a lack of understanding the state of being human.[159] As Heidegger states in "Hölderlin and the Essence of Poetry," humans are already in a conversation with each other: "We are a conversation, that always also signifies we are *one* conversation. The unity of a conversation consists in the fact that in the essential word there is always manifest that one and the same thing on which we agree, on the basis of which we are united and so are authentically ourselves. Conversation and its unity support our existence."[160] However, the problem with Heidegger's problem begins to become apparent in his use of conversation as what is binding for all humanity, for while the familiarity-in-strangeness structure that was developed between the narratee and implied reader already begins to indicate that within this always already being-with there is a contamination of something other-than or more-than human, Heidegger's use of conversation points to a very human language, or speech as the unitary factor. The importance of language at the threshold of self and other is the crux of Derrida's argument.

In Derrida's extensive commentary on Heidegger, *Of Spirit*, there is a seven-page footnote added after the lecture's original presentation in 1987. This footnote was prompted by a comment from Françoise Dastur about Heidegger's rethinking the importance of the question in his later work. In this footnote-response Derrida explores what happens before any question can ever be asked, arguing that:

> when we interrogate [*Anfragen*] the possibility of any question, i.e. language, we must be *already* in the element of language. [...] Language is *already* there, in advance [*im voraus*] at the moment at which any question can arise about it. In this it exceeds the question. This advance is,

---

[159] Ibid., 205.

[160] Martin Heidegger, "Hölderlin and the Essence of Poetry," in *Elucidations of Hölderlin's Poetry*, trans. Keith Hoeller (Amhurst: Humanity Books, 2000), 57.

> before any contract, a sort of promise of originary alliance to which we must have in some sense already acquiesced, already said *yes*, given a pledge [*gage*], whatever may be the negativity or problematicity of the discourse which may follow.[161]

The "originary alliance" of which Derrida speaks is why Heidegger indicates that the question of whether a human can have empathy for another is impossible: there is always already a being-with the other through this originary "yes." However, Derrida's focus is the role of language in such a human being-with. However, it should be noted her that further on in "Hölderlin and the Essence of Poetry" Heidegger does state this need for an originary yes directly when he connects language's "authentic" appearance with conversation in a simultaneous emergence of world:

> Since language has authentically come to pass as conversation, the gods have come to expression and a world has appeared. But again it is important to see that the presence of the gods and the appearance of the world are not merely a consequence of the occurrence of language; rather, they are simultaneous with it. And this to the extent that it is precisely in the naming of the gods and in the world becoming word that authentic conversation, which we ourselves are, consists.[162]

Still, what Derrida's footnote argues is that it is difficult to use the question, which is simultaneously apparent with authentic being, to put that being into question. David Farrell Krell formulates the argument in similar manner: "How *question* the structure of *Fragen* without on the one hand confirming its power and on the other begging the question?"[163] The answer Krell posits is located in the ambiguous relationship to world of the animal: "the animal is neither *Dasein* nor *Zuhandensein* [readiness-to-hand] nor *Vorhandensein* [presence-at-hand],

---

[161] Derrida, *Of Spirit*, 129n5.
[162] Heidegger, "Hölderlin and the Essence of Poetry," 57-8.
[163] Krell, "Spiriting Heidegger," 15.

because one can think animality in terms of neither *existentials* nor *categories*. [...] animal life puts the very notion of *ontological difference* at risk."[164] This putting difference at risk is the "weakness" that Puchner finds in *Never Let Me Go*. Although, again, the clones are in no way "animals," the concept of animal life, because of its ambiguous relationship to world, is able to offer a way to question the structure of the question itself. This is a departure from Heidegger's reading because instead of looking "back" from the human towards the animal and trying to decide where consciousness arose, this approach begins with animality and does not assume that unconsciousness is what necessarily precedes consciousness. This reversal, or reflection, however, is not only found in Derrida's critique of Heidegger. Maxine Sheets-Johnstone, for example, in "Consciousness: A Natural History," re-schedules the question "How does consciousness arise in matter?" to an investigation of the evolution of the animate form.[165] Quoting Paul Churchland's argument in *Matter and Consciousness*, which states that human beings need to get used to living with the fact that they are creatures of matter, Sheets-Johnstone stresses that "The problem comes not in living with that fact but in living *hermetically* with that fact."[166] The allegory of the familiarity-in-strangeness of *Never Let Me Go* is one way to begin doing just that.

Hermetic dwelling with the philosophical poverty of the animal maps the simultaneous being-close and being-distant that was developed along with a reading of Freud's uncanny. The importance of *Never Let Me Go* is that it does not negate, but rather incorporates; it foregrounds contamination from both sides. *Never Let Me Go* occupies and more importantly makes visible the philosophical middle position of the poverty of the animal. This two-fold location is what Krell calls the "double promise which in some sense precedes all questioning."[167] This "double" argument, however, is no stranger to Heidegger's concept of empathy: "The same [problem in understanding the

[164] Ibid., 24.

[165] Maxine Sheets-Johnstone, in "Consciousness: A Natural History," *Synthesis Philosophica* 44.2 (2007), 284.

[166] Ibid. (emphasis mine).

[167] Krell, "Spiriting Heidegger," 30.

nature of 'the question'] is true of the term 'empathy' which suggests that we must first 'feel our way into' the other being in order to reach it. And this implies that we are 'outside' in the first place."[168] For Heidegger, being human at all already means being this "double" being-with: "Insofar as human beings exist at all, they already find themselves transposed in their existence into other human beings, even if there are factically no other human beings in the vicinity."[169]

Perhaps at this point it is important to restate Derrida's critique of Heidegger's position. There are two main points to Derrida's discussion: 1) this originary being-with is still locked within the mode of language, and 2) in Heidegger the "double" of being-with is described, but not followed through. As Christopher Fynsk argues, "Heidegger, by introducing his concept of *Mitsein* ('being-with'), recognized the necessity of thinking Dasein in relation, but he failed to carry through this concept in any manner adequate to his own description of the facticity of Dasein."[170]

---

[168] Heidegger, *Fundamental Concepts*, 203.

[169] Ibid., 205.

[170] Christopher Fynsk, *Language and Relation...that there is language* (Stanford: Stanford University Press, 1996), 153. Much of Fynsk's work is concerned with Maurice Blanchot, who has repositioned Heidegger's thought on death in order to see how the experience of the dying of others is something we can actually experience. Blanchot offers a complex reading of what it means to be human. This can be seen, for example, in his novel *Thomas the Obscure*. For Blanchot, an intimate and profound relationship to death can be gifted from the dying to the living: "For the first time she raised the words 'give oneself' to their true meaning: she gave Anne, she gave much more than the life of Anne, she gave the ultimate gift, the death of Anne [...]," Maurice Blanchot, *Thomas the Obscure*, trans. Robert Lamberton, in *The Station Hill Blanchot Reader: Fiction and Literary Essays*, ed. George Quasha (Barrytown: Station Hill, 1999), 104. This gift, in part, seems to be a devotion to what is no longer human, to a being-other that could be read into a relationship with non-humans: "no longer a human being but simply a being, marvelously a being, among the mayflies and the falling sons, with the agonizing atoms, doomed species, wounded illnesses [...]" ibid., 105. However, further in the same novel Blanchot asserts what is human and not animal in the midst of such a gift: "I seemed to have been removed from the human condition because I had truly accomplished it [...] I was the one whose complete absence alone makes the step or the thought possible, before the beasts, beings who do not bear within them their dead double, I lost my last reason for existing. There was a tragic distance between us. A man without a trace of animal nature. I ceased to be able to express myself with my voice which

So another tactic is needed since even to ask a question of empathy already assumes an erroneous location of a gap between beings. Heidegger seems to agree, arguing that the question of empathy between humans "creates the illusion that in this being alongside one another there is initially a gap which needs to be bridged [...] as though one human being would first have to empathize their way into the other to reach them."[171] However Derrida's criticism is that this already-alongside is still a promissory "yes" of language. This is also the location of Derrida's criticism of Heidegger's divisions of death. For Derrida, Heidegger's reading of the Dasein-only ability to experience death "as such" "marks the difference *of* language, the impassable difference between the speaking being between the speaking being that *Dasein* is and any other living thing."[172]

Derrida's critique is that Heidegger's nonrelation is an experience of the "as such." This division using the "as such" is not one of gradation but kind, and, as Derrida argues, it remains "unthought" in the work of Heidegger: "Heidegger says: 'Animals cannot do this [experience death as death]. But animals cannot speak either. [*Das Tier kann aber auch nicht sprechen.*]' These two remarks are deliberately juxtaposed, without, however, Heidegger feeling authorized to go any further than indicating something like a flash in the sky concerning a link

no longer sang, no longer even spoke as the voice of a talking bird speaks [...] I proved in every way that only humanity is capable of dying," ibid., 112.

[171] Heidegger, *Fundamental Concepts*, 206. Heidegger develops this thought further on: "This illusion of a prior separation between one human being and another is reinforced by the philosophical dogma that man is initially to be understood as subject and as consciousness, that he is primarily and most indubitably given to himself as consciousness for a subject," ibid., 208.

[172] Jacques Derrida, *Aporias*, trans. Thomas Dutoit (Stanford: Stanford University Press, 1993), 35. In Ishiguro's *When We Were Orphans* the narrator, Christopher, comments on the sounds made by a man dying in an adjacent room who he thought was a man he had met before. He describes realizing they are two different men thus: "The realization that these were two different men rather chilled me. So identical were their pitiful whimpers, the way their screams gave way to desperate entreaties, then returned to screams, that the notion came to me this was what each of us would go through on our way to death – that these terrible noises were as universal as the crying of new-born babies," Kazuo Ishiguro, *When We Were Orphans* (London: Faber and Faber, 2000), 305.

between the *as such* of death and language."[173] Krell also argues that Heidegger's ontology does not address this issue: "If existential ontology always needs the question of being (*die Frage nach dem* Sein) to have been 'clarified beforehand' [...] it also always needs 'life' to have been clarified in precisely the same way."[174] This is why the complication of the "hinge moment" of linguistic revelation in *Never Let Me Go* with the "whisper" of the process of learning to experience one's own death is so important; it locates the allegory of the novel in another domain than the "as such" without denying the uniqueness of being human – this is because the experience of facticity takes place in the realm of being "'told and not told'" (*NLMG* 79). And it is from within in the hermetically sealed relationship to the "human as living thing"[175] that there can be a "reconciliation" or reflection between the apparently contradictory terms set out in the "double" of told and not told, of the uncanny. Derrida states that "if, in sum, life does not know death as such, then this axiom will allow for a

[173] Derrida, *Aporias*, 36. As Iain Thomson argues, it is at the limit of death that Derrida raises his objection: "Derrida's objection focuses on and problematizes the idea of a 'limit-line,' 'threshold,' or border separating life and death, which he argues is an aporia implicit in Heidegger's existential analytic. For Derrida, since Dasein embodies its possibilities existentially, and death is 'the possibility of an impossibility,' embodying the possibility *of an impossibility* would seem to entail embodying an impossibility," "Can I Die?: Derrida on Heidegger on Death," *Philosophy Today* 43.1 (Spring 1999), 33. Thomson goes on to criticize Derrida for not admitting Heidegger' claim that death is not an event, ibid., 34.

[174] Krell, *Daimon Life*, 217. Krell continues: "[...] Heidegger is more concerned to keep 'biologism' and 'animality' remote from what he calls *thinking* than to push the question of lifedeath [what Krell terms Freud and Nietzsche's concern with death being immanent in life]," ibid. Calarco argues: "On the one hand, Heidegger definitively denies the animal the capacity for language and an experience of death as such, but, on the other hand, he does not further authorize himself to say explicitly what the essential relation between language and death is that would separate mortal from animal in this experience. [...] We are thus confronted with the following questions: How might the possibility or the capacity for language that characterizes the mortal relate to an experience of death as such? Is there an experience of death as such outside of, or beyond, the possibility of language? And what would be the consequences for Heidegger's sharp distinction between mortal and animal here if there were no experience of death as such, even for mortals?" "On the Borders of Language and Death," 18.

[175] Derrida, *Aporias*, 37.

reconciliation of apparently contradictory statements, best exemplified, in my view, by the example of Heidegger, of course, but also by those of Freud and Levinas."[176]

If the relation between death and language is the unthought of Heidegger, then the relationship between the uncanny and what will a relation to death through poverty is perhaps the unthought of Freud's essay "The Uncanny." In discussing his theory that uncanny feelings arise from "something repressed with *recurs*,"[177] Freud turns his thought to images of the gruesome, meaning to "death and dead bodies."[178] Freud argues that what makes such images uncanny is that they raise not an awareness of our facticity but rather the impossibility of such an awareness: "It is true that the statement 'All men are mortal' is paraded in text-books of logic as an example of a general proposition; but no human being really grasps it, and our unconscious has as little use now as it ever had for the idea of its own mortality."[179] This notion, along with its rhetorical structure, is developed in the next chapter under the concept of

---

[176] Ibid.

[177] Freud, "The Uncanny," 363.

[178] Ibid., 364.

[179] Ibid. For a reading of the uncanny in Heidegger (which, however, does not address a linguistic ground), see Carel, *Life and Death in Freud and Heidegger*, 165-8. Carel's reading of being-towards-death in Heidegger firstly stresses the experience of death within life: "The first is that being-towards-death places death and finitude as structuring components within existence, thus breaking with the traditional view of life and death as mutually exclusive. Heidegger's notion of being-towards-death is a way of conceptualizing life and death, possibility and limitation, as intimately linked. Moreover, they are linked in a specific way: death influences life as a limit whose presence in life must constantly be taken into account, even within the context of everyday activities and projects," ibid., 65. However, later in the text, Carel does belittle any argument that the re-scheduling of facticity in the different-than-human is of importance: "It is inessential because some animals may be Dasein too, so their capacity to sense their finitude does not alter Heidegger's general claims. Yet Heidegger insists on a hyperseparation between Dasein and animals," ibid., 72n5. I agree with Carel in the sense that a list of human-like attributes for animals (language, tool-making, complex societies) holds little value in this context (although examples from both comparative psychology and cognitive ethology are important). However, the main argument here is not that the different-than-human can experience facticity, but that the human actually does not have access to it itself, as both Heidegger and Carel assume but Freud begins to destabilize.

the poverty of death. One path into such a criticism is by reading the re-scheduling of facticity in beings that are other-than-human. Such re-scheduling is important in *Never Let Me Go* because is provides a participation with a not-self located at the heart of the self. This participation is enacted through the gap between a narratee that can, eventually, experience factiticy and an implied reader that has trouble doing so. In order for this gap to be forded it must be forged in poverty.

2. Seeing Poverty

Consciousness without shudder is reified consciousness.

-Theodor Adorno[1]

A "day" is not simply a unit for counting; it is the turning of the world – each time singular.

-Jean-Luc Nancy[2]

One objection that seems to stand out regarding the claim that *Never Let Me Go* creates a gap or division between the narratee and the implied reader is that the tone of the novel's narrator is flat, bland and "level." Kathy's voice seems to do anything but create holes, providing instead a smooth surface over which the novel glides. The focus of this chapter is to show how the literary technique of creating this apparently unrippled surface is actually paramount for producing such reflective gaps, just as complete wish fulfillment opened up the critical apparatus of the uncanny. As seen in the previous chapter, the implied reader becomes a culprit in the story, meaning that her difference from the narratee resonates within a copresent, overwhelming similarity. This resonance was found to center around an awareness of finitude, meaning that the clones' eventual experience of facticity starts to foreground the trouble of claiming such an experience by the implied reader. Part of the

[1] Adorno, *Aesthetic Theory*, 331.

[2] Jean Luc Nancy, *Being Singular Plural*, trans. Robert Richardson and Anne O'Byrne (Stanford: Stanford University Press, 2000), 9.

technique of generating this participation-via-gap is through the over-explicit assumption, through apostrophe, that the narratee is a clone. Such an assumption is not meant to be taken literally by the implied reader, and a vacuum or gap begins to take shape in negotiating this strangeness, which is a familiar aspect of literature. However, another technique is used in the novel to generate participation from the implied reader, and this time it is used in conjunction with the narrator; this technique is the flat and "boring" tone of Kathy's narration. So both *boredom* and a question of *participation*, or being-with another, form important elements for this chapter; as Hille Haker argues regarding *Never Let Me Go*, "The ironical point of this deeply (bio-)ethical novel to the debate about clones, which (almost) progresses without recourse to such a discourse but instead to pure "facticity" [*Faktizität*], is the concern [*Sorge*] the clone-friends represent for each other [...]"[3] The reason why *boredom* and *participation* are present at the outset of a chapter entitled "Seeing Poverty" is that the coordinates of both a fundamental or profound boredom along with being-with others will be more easily found in the philosophical delineations of Heidegger's reading of the poverty of death (as experienced by animals) than in his realm of a human-only participation in facticity. This position is summarized by Krell:

> When Heidegger tries to separate Dasein from the animal, or to dig an abyss of essence between them, he causes the whole of his project to collapse back onto the congealed categories and oblivious decisions of ontotheology. Yet when he opens, if only for a brief moment, the "ring of disinhibitions" that links the animal to its limited, impoverished world, opens it up to the possibilities of *time* and *death*, a formidable contingency rises to confront his analysis. It is the chance that may well end all existential analysis and induce a different kind of meditation [...] the capacity to mark time and to die.[4]

[3] Hille Haker, "Narrative Bioethik," Ethik des biomedizinischen Erzählens," *Narrative Ethik: Das Gute und das Böse erzählen*, ed. Karen Joisten (Berlin: Akademie Verlag, 2007), 269, (translation mine).

[4] Krell, *Daimon Life*, 105.

2.1 The Everyday of Kathy's Narrative Voice

In order to develop a reading of the "everyday" tone of Kathy's narration, Heidegger's thought regarding being-towards-death [*Sein zum Tode*] should be restated. For Heidegger, being-towards-death is essential to the fundamental make-up of Dasein because with it "there is *constantly something still to be settled* [*eine ständige Unabgeschlossenheit*]."[5] This remainder is Dasein's movement to no-longer-Dasein [*Nichtmehrdasein*], meaning death,[6] and being-towards-death is the experience of this remainder from within life. This reflects, as David Gordon argues, some of the major changes in attitude towards death as reflected in poetry from the mid-to-late 20th century:

> One is a new absence of curiosity about what follows death, a subject that no longer is regarded as a part of life. Another is a shift of attention from death itself to the prospect of death, which unquestionably *is* a part of life and an important part. This shift entails a more self-conscious use of metaphor on the part of poets who now associate such images as darkness, stillness, coldness, and emptiness not with death but with the fading of consciousness. And finally, there is in these poems a quieter, less heroic tone of address, a resistance to the kind of overtly expressed consolation clinched by a meaningful, weighted conclusion. Instead, we find a cooler consolation implicit in the conduct of the voice as it shies away from conclusiveness.[7]

The quietness mentioned by Gordon here initiates a context in which a reading comes forth of how Kathy narrates her story in a flat, monotonous, pedestrian tone. The first aspect of this

---

[5] Heidegger, *Being and Time*, 279.

[6] Ibid., 281. Heidegger develops this thought by arguing "That Dasein should *be* together only when its 'not-yet' has been filled up is so far from the case that it is precisely then that Dasein is no longer. Any Dasein always exists in just such a manner that its 'not-yet' *belongs* to it," ibid., 287.

[7] David Gordon, *Imagining the End of Life in Post-Enlightenment Poetry: Voices Against the Void* (Gainesville: University Press of Florida, 2005), 92.

discussion, the presencing of being-towards-death in the everyday, is begun in this section. The second aspect, that of experiencing the death of others, takes place further in the chapter.

The tone of Kathy's narration can be seen in the opening lines of the novel: "My name is Kathy H. I'm thirty-one years old, and I've been a carer now for over eleven years" (*NLMG* 3). It is almost as if the novel could begin with "Hi," and this tone is maintained throughout the text, which ends with Kathy dryly accepting her fate as a donor: "I just waited a bit, then turned back to the car, to drive off to wherever it was I was supposed to be" (282). Kathy's matter-of-fact style has prompted James Wood to claim that "Kathy's voice is like an expository writing paper by a not very bright freshman,"[8] and in one sense this factual tone has been one of the fulcrums in discussing nearly all of Ishiguro's books. Salman Rushdie opens a critical review with the words: "The surface of Kazuo Ishiguro's novel, *The Remains of the Day*, is almost perfectly still."[9] And further on he states that "Just below the understatement of the novel's surface is a turbulence as immense as it is slow [...]"[10] A discussion of a "flatness" of tone is as prevalent in commentary on his last novel as it was for his first, *A Pale View of Hills*, in which the narrator, Etsuko, tells the story of her past in Nagasaki before moving to England. Ruth Forsythe argues that "Etsuko narrates her perception of present events in a rather dispassionate voice, but as she begins to explore her past, the reader becomes aware of how conflicted and emotionally charged Etsuko's memories are."[11] Etsuko's narrative unwittingly reveals that the story of betrayal and even perhaps murder that she tells about her friend Sachiko in Nagasaki is actually the story of herself.

Forsythe describes the tone of *A Pale View of Hills* as "dispassionate," although the apparent simplicity and clarity of

---

[8] Wood, "The Human Difference," 37.

[9] Salman Rushdie, "Kazuo Ishiguro," *Imaginary Homelands: Essays and Criticism 1981-1991* (New York; London: Penguin, 1992), 244.

[10] Ibid.

[11] Ruth Forsythe, "The Cultural Displacement and the Mother-Daughter Relationship in Kazuo Ishiguro's *A Pale View of Hills*," *The West Virginia University Philological Papers* 52 (2005), 102.

Ishiguro's prose, at least up until *Never Let Me Go*, has also been tagged as "poetic":

> More than any other late twentieth-/early twenty-first-century novelist [...] he deserves the nomenclature "poetic", and not because his style is self-consciously arch or layered with conceits: quite the opposite. Ishiguro's prose is precise, transparent, cautiously accessible. Yet his characters, his narrators, imply far more than they actually state.[12]

Ishiguro has said that this reservedness is a conscious part of his storytelling technique. Contrasting himself to Rushdie, to whom he has felt he has often been compared merely because both are "foreign" and became popular much at the same time,[13] Ishiguro says: "I'm interested in the way words hide meaning. I suppose I like to have a spare, tight structure because I don't like to have this improvised feeling remain in my work."[14] However, this aspect of his style did not come into the author's consciousness until the time of writing his third novel *Remains of the Day*.[15]

---

[12] Bradford, *The Novel Now*, 215.

[13] Rushdie won the Booker Prize for *Midnight's Children* in 1981 and Ishiguro's first novel was published the following year. Ishiguro credits the success of his first novel to the artistic climate of Britain at the time: "It was one of the few times in the recent history of British arts in which it was an actual plus to have a funny foreign name and to be writing about funny foreign places," Vorda and Herzinger, "An Interview with Kazuo Ishiguro," 69. Ishiguro sees comparisons to authors like Rushdie or Timothy Mo to be merely based on similarities of appellation rather than content: "I write so differently than someone like Rushdie. My style is almost the antithesis of Rushdie's or Mo's. Their writing tends to have these quirks where it explodes in all kinds of directions. Rushdie's language always seems to be reaching out – to express meaning that can't usually be expressed through normal language. Just structurally his books have this terrific energy. They just grow in every direction at once, and he doesn't particularly care if the branches lead nowhere. He'll let it grow anyway and leave it there, and that's the way he writes. I think he is a powerful and considerable writer," ibid., 70.

[14] Ibid., 71.

[15] Regarding *The Remains of the Day*, Stephen Connor argues that "Like Ishiguro's other novels, *A Pale View of Hills* (1982) and *An Artist of the Floating World* (1986), the narrative maintains a parallel between a present tense and a past tense that is gradually but unreliably retrieved in reminiscence as the narrative proceed," *The English Novel in History: 1950-1995* (London; New York: Routledge, 1996), 104. Connor then goes on to argue that the reserved

By that time he had read enough reviews of his own style to get him thinking.

> To a large extent, when I wrote *The Remains of the Day*, that was the first time I started to become very conscious of my own style. And, of course, quite rightly, these references that Stevens makes are also a reference to my own style. I think what happened was this. My first two novels I just wrote these sentences without really thinking about style. I was just writing in what I thought was the clearest way possible. Then I started to read review after review which talked about my understated or clipped style. It was the reviewers and the critics who actually pointed this out to me – where my style seemed to be unusually calm with all this kind of strange turmoil expressed underneath the calm. I actually started to ask myself, "Where does this style come from then?" It's not something I consciously manufactured. I had to face the possibility that this was actually indeed something to do with me. It's my natural voice.[16]

Reviewers of *Never Let Me Go*, however, have seen a change in the author's style, and have been critical of some of its aspects. On the one hand the "flat" tone of the novel has been seen as an indication of Kathy's lack of experience. Kathy has led a sheltered life bound by the walls of Hailsham, and "Ishiguro has perfected a narratorial voice capable of rendering

---

style of the novel is a comment on the troubled "dignity" of the British, ibid. 104-5.

[16] Vorda and Herzinger, "An Interview with Kazuo Ishiguro," 76-7. However, Ishiguro has also rallied against the idea of "quietness" in his work, stating that "Well, I don't try to be a quiet writer. That's really a question of technique more than anything else. There's a surface tension to my books – there aren't a lot of people getting murdered or anything like that. But for me, they're not quiet books, because they're books that deal with things that disturb me the most and questions that worry me the most. They're anything but quiet to me," Kazuo Ishiguro and Kenzaburo Oe, "The Novelist in Today's World: A Conversation," *Conversations with Kazuo Ishiguro*, ed. Brian Shaffer and Cynthia Wong (Jackson: University Press of Mississippi, 2008), 58.

this story in the most affecting way; the sheer narrowness of Kathy's experience is unmistakable in her voice and increases the pathos of her existence."[17] Tobias Hill describes the book as "almost without a descriptive surface, reflecting the hollowness and inhumanity of the world Ishiguro portrays."[18] He continues: "Meaningful though it is, the lack of description in *Never Let Me Go* is oppressive, and it is questionable whether Ishiguro intends the novel to come across quite so severely as it does. However, the novel's tone has also been treated more harshly, being seen as an even more extreme version of the clipped style of the author's earlier works."[19] Valerie Sayers writes that "In order to reflect Kathy H.'s ordinariness, Ishiguro here employs a style more matter-of-fact than in his other novels; the language flatter and more workaday,"[20] while Puchner claims that there is a reason for this change, stating that "this flatness is the point. Kathy H.'s confidences pose a challenge for the reader because they are so starkly at odds with the world they describe."[21] However, the flatness of Kathy's confidences does more than highlight the maniacal world she is a part of.

If it is true that Ishiguro's style in *Never Let Me Go* may be described as somehow more "pedestrian", although there are many indications that such "ordinary" language does not really exist,[22] it may also be pointed out how some critics have, like

---

[17] Stephen Bernstein, "*Never Let Me Go*," *The Review of Contemporary Fiction* 25.1 (2005), 139.

[18] Tobias Hill, "England's Dreaming," *The Times*, Weekend Review, Feb 26 (2005), 6.

[19] Ibid.

[20] Valerie Sayers, "Spare Parts," *Commonweal* July 15 (2005), 27. Although of course not all critics describe the tone thus. Allison Block says the novel has "taut, potent prose," "Ishiguro, Kazuo. *Never Let Me Go*," *Booklist* (Jan 1 & 15, 2005), 783, and Henry Carrigan calls attention to "Ishiguro's elegant prose and masterly ways with characterization," "Ishiguro, Kazuo. *Never Let Me Go*," *Library Journal* (January 2005), 98.

[21] Puchner, "When We Were Clones," 35.

[22] This argument has been forcefully made by Stanley Fish is his essay "How Ordinary is Ordinary Language?" in *Is There a Text in this Class?* (Cambridge: Harvard University Press, 1980). Friedrich Nietzsche, however, voiced a similar opinion as early as a course given during the 1872-73 winter semester at the University of Basel: "No such thing as an unrhetorical, 'natural' language exists that could be used as a point of reference: language is itself the result of purely rhetorical tricks and devices. [...] Language is rhetoric, for it only

Puchner, started to delineate a purpose to this style, a purpose which seems different than showing the depths bubbling underneath a dignified sheen as with his earlier works.[23] Siddhartha Deb says that "There are moments when the pace of the narration seems slow, circling back endlessly on memories and desires, but in a novel about transience, there is a point to this,"[24] although she does not indicate what that point might be. But Wood attempts to describe it, arguing that "*Never Let Me Go* is a fantasy so mundanely told, so excruciatingly ordinary in transit, its fantastic elements so smothered in the loam of the banal and so deliberately grounded, that the effect is not just of fantasy made credible or lifelike, but the real invading fantasy, bursting into its eccentricity and claiming it as normal."[25] One question Wood's statement begs is what is it about this mundane style that allows for such transformation? Or, to let Heidegger pose the question another way: "Is this questionable boredom actually supposed to be the *sought-after fundamental attunement* that must be *awakened?*"[26]

---

intends to convey a *doxa* (opinion), not an *episteme* (truth). [...] Tropes are not something that can be added or subtracted from language at will; they are its truest nature. There is no such thing as a proper meaning that can be communicated only in certain particular cases," qtd. in de Man, *Allegories of Reading*, 105-6.

[23] Most critics see a shift in Ishiguro's style after the first three books, as summed up by Richard Rorty who calls it a shift from the style of Henry James to that of Franz Kafka, "Consolation Prize," *Village Voice Literary Suppliment* (October 1995), 13.

[24] Siddhartha Deb, "Lost Corner," *New Statesman* (March 7 2007), 55.

[25] Wood, "Human Difference," 36.

[26] Heidegger, *The Fundamental Concepts of Metaphysics*, 77. In his essay "Boredom," film and cultural critic Siegfried Kracauer puts it thus: If one has "the sort of patience specific to legitimate boredom, then one experiences a kind of bliss that is almost unearthly. A landscape appears in which colorful peacocks strut about, and images of people suffused with soul come into view," "Bordom," *The Mass Ornament: Weimar Essays*, trans. Thomas Levin (Cambridge; London: Harvard University Press, 1995), 334.

2.2 The Mood of Idle Talk in the Everyday

In order to set up a discussion of the "point" of Kathy's narrative style, the hints Heidegger gives as to the possibility of attesting authentic being from within the idle talk that makes up everyday existence deserve attention. Heidegger argues, in §51 of *Being and Time*, which is entitled "Being-towards-death and the Everydayness of Dasein," that there must be a way that an authentic experience of being-towards-death "lurks" in idle talk [*Gerede*]:

> In Being-towards-death, Dasein comports itself *towards itself* as a distinctive potentiality-for-Being. But the Self of everydayness is the "they." The "they" is constituted by the way things have been publicly interpreted, which expresses itself in idle talk. Idle talk must accordingly make manifest the way in which everyday Dasein interprets for itself its Being-towards-death. The foundation of any interpretation is an act of understanding, which is always accompanied by a state-of-mind, or, in other words, which has a mood. So we must ask how Being-towards-death is disclosed by the kind of understanding which, with its state-of-mind, lurks in the idle talk of the "they." How does the "they" comport itself understandingly towards that ownmost possibility of Dasein, which is non-relational and is not to be outstripped? What state-of-mind discloses to the "they" that it has been delivered over to death, and in what way?[27]

It should be remembered that "idle talk" does not indicate a lack of proper terminology but rather of an inauthentic comportment towards a world. As Mark Wrathall illustrates in his essay "Social Constraints on Conversational Content: Heidegger on *Rede* and *Gerede*," an American automobile driver may read and understand a section from a British driver's manual dealing with roundabouts, but the American driver will not have assimilated the proper comportment to first look left instead of

[27] Heidegger, *Being and Time*, 296.

right when coming up to one.[28] In idle talk, according to Wrathall, "We gain through social, and in particular, linguistic interaction a richly articulated ability to isolate and discriminate features of the world of which we have little or no actual experience whatsoever."[29] Mood, as interpretation, is then a comportment towards the world in an authentic way which is not dependent on previous experience. Wrathall thus summarizes Heidegger's position: "Heidegger's account of language is committed, then, to no more than the unsurprising view that language cannot give one a full conversance with its subject matter – the kind of conversance necessary for articulating an authentic space of disclosedness."[30] However, what Wrathall does not address is the possibility for an access to authentic comportment through the inauthentic conversation of the everyday. A focus on such an access within the everyday is also indicative of a change within Ishiguro's work. If, in his earlier novels, Ishiguro was interested "in the capacity of human beings to mistake the prevailing discourse for the self's authentic promptings,"[31] it is with *Never Let Me Go* that authenticity is found within the prevailing discourse itself.

In Heidegger's quote above, he ends by wondering if there is something in the everyday that could give Dasein over to its own authentic comportment in relation to its facticity. Heidegger argues against a being-with-others as a possibility for this "something",[32] and eventually describes the need for a mood of anxiety [*Angst*] to be present in order to come to grips with the

---

[28] Mark Wrathall, "Social Constraints on Conversational Content: Heidegger on *Rede* and *Gerede*," in *Heidegger Reexamined: Volume 1, Dasein, Authenticity and Death*, ed. Hubert Dreyfus and Mark Wrathall (New York; London: Routledge, 2002), 301. Wrathall is writing explicitly to remove Heidegger from claims his reading of *Gerede* falls in line with social externalism.

[29] Ibid.

[30] Ibid., 302.

[31] Margaret Scanlan, "The Recuperation of History in British and Irish Fiction," *A Companion to the British and Irish Novel: 1945-2000*, ed. Brian Shaffer (Mladen: Blackwell, 2005), 150.

[32] Heidegger, *Being and Time*, 255.

potential non-potentiality of one's being.[33] However, anxiety is not the only authentic mood for facticity that Heidegger delineates. Heidegger actually develops two main moods through which an authentic experience of death may develop. The first, and more well-known, is anxiety. The second, and more fully developed, is that of a more mundane relationship to the world – boredom.

2.3 Boredom as an Experience of Temporality

Within Heidegger's thought the location of authenticity in the everyday is perhaps most readily found in his work on boredom. In the 1929-30 lectures that make up *The Fundamental Concepts of Metaphysics*, Heidegger takes boredom as a possible fundamental attunement, or mood. While Heidegger argues that there can be many kinds of fundamental attunements,[34] it is really only anxiety and boredom that ever receive any developed treatment in his work. But first it is important to develop what Heidegger means by "mood." Heidegger makes a difference between discussing, or arguing about a work, and actually being gripped [*ergriffen*] by the concepts [*Begriffe*] one is supposed to be comprehending.[35] Furthermore, Heidegger argues that an attunement [*Stimmung*][36] from which it is possible to philosophize, or *interpret*, the world is a *fundamental* attunement

---

[33] Ibid., 310. Hubert Dreyfus argues that "This is clearly a rejection of Husserl's attempt to ground all forms of intentionality in the meaning-giving activity of a detached transcendental subject, but it still has a decidedly Husserlian ring. It is as if Heidegger has substituted one absolute source for another, replacing the constituting activity of detached transcendental consciousness with the constituting activity of involved existential Dasein," *Being-in-the-world: A Commentary on Heidegger's* Being and Time, *Division I* (Cambridge: MIT Press, 1991), 141.

[34] Heidgger, *The Fundamental Concepts of Metaphysics*, 133.

[35] Ibid., 7.

[36] Heidegger can also use *Befindlichkeit*, *Gestimmtheit* and *Gestimmtsein* for "attunement."

[*Grundstimungen*].[37] What needs to be developed here is not only why boredom, for example, can function as a comportment for being, but also whether the style of Kathy's narration can in any sense be said to embody such a comportment.

First, an examination of what makes boredom a fundamental attunement. To this end, Heidegger develops the difference between "to become bored by" [*gelangweiltwerden von*] something (semi-automated tasks, for example) and "to be bored with" [*sich langweilen mit*] something, where *everything* is boring – the mood resides in the subject. For Heidegger, it is only the latter which is profound.[38] Being-bored-with is not a comportment tied to a single domain, but rather it is wide-spread. As Jean-Luc Marion argues, "Boredom does not have any interest in whatsoever may *be*, and hence has no more negative interest than positive: it never destroys, but always turns away [...]"[39] Here both Heidegger and Marion are making a nod towards Arthur Schopenhauer, who argues that when human beings are swinging on the pendulum between the suffering of existence and the evil of boredom that they will always choose suffering, by turning towards each other in social relations.[40] As Ronell argues amidst a discussion of Emma from Gustave Flaubert's *Madame Bovary*, boredom "pervades everything, and cannot be said simply to erupt. Nor does it desist of its own. It is prior to signification, yet it appears to be a

---

[37] Ibid. Dreyfus provides a useful gloss on Heidegger's use of "mood": "*Stimmung* seems to name any of the ways Dasein can be affected. Heidegger suggests that moods or attunements manifest the tone of being-there. As Heidegger uses the term, mood can refer to the *sensibility* of an age (such as romantic), the *culture* of a company (such as aggressive), the *temper* of the times (such as revolutionary), as well as the *mood* in a current situation (such as the eager mood in the classroom) and, of course, the mood of an individual. These are all ways of finding that things matter. Thus they are all ontic specifications of affectedness, the ontological existential condition that things always already matter," *Being-in-the-world*, 169.

[38] Heidegger, *The Fundamental Concepts of Metaphysics*, 127.

[39] Jean-Luc Marion, *God Without Being*, trans. Thomas Carlson (Chicago; London: University of Chicago Press, 1995), 115. However, Marion does go on to warn that "boredom in no way founds being, not even in disputing, in its own favor, its foundation; for the gaze of boredom, in disqualifying the idols of the visible, does not establish itself as ultimate idol [...]" ibid., 116.

[40] Arthur Schopenhauer, *The World as Will and Representation, vol. 1*, trans. E. F. J. Payne (Mineola: Dover, 1966), 313.

commentary on life; it is, at least for Emma, the place of deepest struggle."[41] As Ronell states, boredom "pervades everything" because it is a fundamental mood unattached to a domain, and it can affect life in general.

The reason that fundamental boredom has such a primordial position can be found in the German for "boredom," which is *Langeweile*, literally meaning "long while." This literal translation of the German indicates that boredom can disrupt one of the fundamental touchstones on which the self is based, meaning time: "We pass the *time*, in order to master it, because time becomes long in boredom. Time becomes long for us. Is it supposed to be short then? Does not each of us wish for a truly long time for ourselves?"[42] The mood of fundamental boredom is profound for Dasein because it opens an experience of temporality: "*Boredom springs from the temporality of Dasein.*"[43] Or, in the words of Ronell, "Boredom, with its temporal slowdown and edge of anguish, is also an authentic mode of being-in-the-world. Boredom inflects a sonic quality, it attunes a murmur or an attitude of voice. Infusing the whole text with its ground level of non-sense, Emma's boredom appears to exhaust a certain reserve before it has been tapped."[44]

The task then is to see whether commentary on the tone of *Never Let Me Go* fits into this reading of boredom as a

---

[41] Avital Ronell, *Crack Wars: Literature Addiction Mania* (Lincoln; London: University of Nebraska Press, 1992), 120.

[42] Heidegger, *The Fundamental Concepts of Metaphysics*, 80. Boredom leaves one in a state of being left empty [*Leergelassenheit*]. *Lassen* in German can connote a *letting be* that is essential for Heidegger's concept of the fundamental attunement of thinking *Gelassenheit* (often translated at "letting be"). However, Schopenhauer relates the feeling of boredom to the cause of suicide in convicts, *The World as Will and Representation*, 313.

[43] Ibid., 127.

[44] Ronell, *Crack Wars*, 120. Kuperus summarizes Heidegger's different-tiation between the poverty of the animal and boredom: "Heidegger describes the existence of *Dasein* as it is captivated in the everyday, and how its loss of captivation in the form of profound boredom relates to the poverty in world and to the captivation of the animal. The guiding questions in this regard are how Heidegger distinguishes our everyday captivation from the captivation of the animal, and how the deprivation experienced in fundamental boredom differs from the deprivation of the non-human animal," "Heidegger and Animality," 17. Perhaps then the difference between the human and the animal is not poverty but rather the potentiality for a fundamental attunement within poverty.

fundamental comportment. In order to do this, it is worth while revisiting some of the language used by critics above to describe the tone of the novel. Four quotations from critics were provided. The first was from Wood who said that "Kathy's voice is like an expository writing paper by a not very bright freshman." Although there is no "exact" way to discern what Wood means by his terms, by qualifying what can be assumed to be the inexperience of a freshman with a lack of intelligence, and pouring that into a required and perhaps uninspired Comp 101 paper, a picture begins to form. However, perhaps a more detailed analysis may be ventured by looking at Wood's comments on a term that is also used by the next critic that was quoted. Sayers states that "In order to reflect Kathy H.'s ordinariness, Ishiguro here employs a style more matter-of-fact than in his other novels; the language flatter and more workaday." One word that jumps out from a literary critic's point of view is "flatter." The term "flat" came into literary prominence with E. M. Forster's 1927 *Aspects of the Novel.* Although describing the processes of characterization in particular, Forster's comments have been influential in describing style in general. According to Forster, flat characters are "constructed round a single idea or quality"[45] and they "can be expressed in one sentence such as 'I never will desert Mr. Micawber,'"[46] a reference to the maxim Emma Micawber lives by in Charles Dickens' *David Copperfield.* However, what is of interest here is Wood's critique of Foster's concept. Wood argues that "if by flatness we mean a character, often but not always a minor one, often but not always comic, who serves to illuminate an essential human truth or characteristic, then many of the most interesting characters are flat."[47] Instead of an author needing to avoid "flatness" and to fulfill the requirements of its companion "roundness," Wood suggests that "subtlety" is a more useful concept: "It is subtlety that matters – subtlety of analysis, of inquiry, of concern, of felt pressure – and for subtlety a very

[45] E. M. Forster, *Aspects of the Novel* (Orlando: Harcourt, 1985), 67.

[46] Ibid., 68.

[47] James Wood, *How Fiction Works* (New York: Farrar, Straus and Giroux, 2008), 128.

small point of entry will do."[48] If two extrapolations may be ventured at this point, then it is possible to say that the "freshman" aspect of the style of *Never Let Me Go* indicates a lack of subtlety. This lack of subtlety can then be said to be described by Sayers' terms "matter-of-fact," "flatter," and "workaday." All of these make reference to a style that is too easy to grasp. However, in another statement Wood makes about the style of the text, this lack of difficulty is actually seen as proactive.

As a reminder, the second quote from Wood about the style of *Never Let Me Go* states that "*Never Let Me Go* is a fantasy so mundanely told, so excruciatingly ordinary in transit, its fantastic elements so smothered in the loam of the banal and so deliberately grounded, that the effect is not just of fantasy made credible or lifelike, but the real invading fantasy, bursting into its eccentricity and claiming it as normal."[49] In this quote Wood is making a correlation of cause and effect. The novel is "so mundanely told," "so excruciatingly ordinary," *that* its effect is of the real "bursting" into the fantastic and making it ordinary. However, this is a common element in "fantastic" literature, as Rosemary Jackson argues: "Fantastic literature transforms the 'real' through this kind of dis-covery [of the uncanny]. It does not introduce novelty, so much as uncover all that needs to remain hidden if the world is to be comfortably 'known'. Its uncanny effects reveal an obscure, occluded region which lies behind the homely (*heimlich*) and native (*heimisch*)."[50] In the quote from Wood the engine of the "that" is a standard literary technique even outside the genre of the fantastic, that of the tendency of a discourse, as Culler puts it, to "naturalize its signs."[51] Culler's analysis is developed out of his reading of Roland Barthes' *The Fashion System* which, despite being criticized for its failure on the level of distributional analysis,[52] can provide the basis for a pertinent rhetorical discussion. Culler

[48] Ibid.

[49] Ronell reminds us that the fundamental concept of boredom is not "bursting into" anywhere, but is always already there, *Crack Wars*, 120.

[50] Rosemary Jackson, *Fantasy: The Literature of Subversion* (London: Routledge, 2001), 65.

[51] Culler, *Structuralist Poetics*, 39.

[52] Ibid., 37.

argues that fashion not only normalizes itself by making its supplemental products practical, as in "*A linen coat for cool summer evenings*"[53] for example, but other syntactic strategies can be used such as present and future tenses to make things seems like they do or will exist, or reflexive verbs to make the products their own agents. In this sense "fashionableness lies in the description rather than in the object itself."[54] Kathy's narrative can be said not just to normalize the signs of fantasy through her pedestrian narration but also to normalize the problematic "real."

At least two rhetorical strategies can be found in *Never Let Me Go* for normalization. The first, developed in the previous chapter, is a second-person address which assumes knowledge that only a clone can have, thereby claiming the narratee is a clone (and thus, through its over-explicitness, addressing the implied reader and creating an allegory of the human condition). The second strategy could be defined as a limited world view typical to first-person narratives. In Kathy's representation, non-clone society is virtually unknown, as is the science behind the cloning process itself. "The only coercive force ever named in the book is 'society,'"[55] which is denoted by the purposefully ambiguous pronoun "they" which can be seen, for example, in Tommy's report of Miss Lucy's talk about Tommy wanting to find out the "truth" about why the clones exist. You can look, she says, however, "'They won't make it easy for you, but if you want to, really want to, you might find out'" (*NLMG* 106). Another example can be seen when Ruth is disappointed that a "possible" model she was cloned after, a woman who works in an office, turns out to be a false lead. "'I didn't want to say when you first told me about this. But look, it was never on. They don't ever, *ever*, use people like that woman. Think about it.

---

53 Ibid., 38.

54 Ibid., 39.

55 Burley, "A Braver, Newer World," 427. The word "society" actually only appears once in the novel, and not in the context Burley suggests, although her general contention is correct. This single usage takes place at the end of the novel, when Miss Emily is explaining why they, and Hailsham, existed: "But a generation of created children who'd take their place in society? Children demonstrably *superior* to the rest of us? Oh no. That frightened people. They recoiled from that" (*NLMG* 259).

Why would she want to?" (164).[56] With this strategy normalization is accomplished through both the narrator and narratee lacking the terms through which what Michel Foucault describes as a "reverse" discourse could develop.[57] In addition, this ambiguity also questions the definitiveness of explicitly stated origins.

However, it is only with the fourth quote regarding the style of *Never Let Me Go* that a philosophical notion of boredom really takes hold because now the issue of time is raised. Deb points out that the *slowness* of the novel, at points, has a function in a story about facticity: "There are moments when the pace of the narration seems slow, circling back endlessly on memories and desires, but in a novel about transience, there is a point to this." In order to understand this statement, first the temporal relation between death and boredom needs to be restated. Then, the connection between boredom and the style of the novel will need to be continued, with an emphasis put on the connection between boredom and the opening of a gap which allows for an allegory of the human condition to take place.

First, as argued above, Heidegger claims that when boredom is experienced as a fundamental attunement one is in the mood of "being-gripped" by the world. This being-gripped is having the proper comportment towards one's world, meaning, for example, in the somewhat light-hearted illustration previously provided, being an American driver at home on the roads of England. Boredom allows for this kind of comportment to be present because it shows humanity's habitat as time,

---

[56] Another example of the "they" can be found when the students arrive at the cottages. Kathy says: "We certainly didn't think much about our lives beyond the Cottages, or about who ran them, or how they fitted into the larger world. None of us thought like that in those days" (114). Additionally, later when Ruth, Tommy and Cathy are talking about how Chrissie completed after her second donation, Kathy says "'Sometimes it happens. It was really sad about Chrissie. But that's not common. They're really careful these days'" (221). Ruth replies: "'That's one reason why they keep moving us around between donations'" (ibid.) meaning so that rumors will not spread so quickly among the donors.

[57] Michel Foucault, *The History of Sexuality, Vol. 1: An Introduction*, trans. Robert Hurley (New York: Vintage Books, 1978), 101. With this concept Foucault is describing how an increase of medical disqualification of homosexuality in the 19th century also brought forth the terminology that homosexuals could then "reverse" and use to "speak in its own behalf," ibid.

meaning that through such boredom the place where one dwells becomes palpable since a human in it is not trying to escape it through distraction. In other words, Dasein interprets life for itself, or according to Schopenhauer, is suffering. In a similar manner, it could be put forward that an awareness of death also makes life palpable in the sense that facticity is seen as being tied to a second-order level of consciousness.

Second, it should be emphasized that what is not being constructed here is an argument along the lines of the novel as somehow being boring, or as causing a kind of boredom in the implied or actual reader. A more fruitful perspective is to follow through with the argument, taking a cue from Wood's comments, which reads boredom as a lack of subtlety. This perspective can be brought into focus by looking at a "turn" in Wood's criticism of Ishiguro's works. Wood seems most comfortable with the "unreliable" narrators of Ishiguro's first three novels. Narrators like the Butler Stevens from *The Remains of the Day* are what Wood constructs as being reliably unreliable,[58] meaning that there is a structure to the confusion, or in other words something to figure out: "A process of authorial flagging is going on; the novel teaches us how to read its narrator."[59] However, this structure too easily assumes "something to figure out" underneath the unreliability.[60]

This reliably unreliable narrative structure remained basically constant in Ishiguro's work until his fourth novel, *The Unconsoled*, which was used in the previous chapter as an example of the uncanny. The reason that *The Unconsoled* functioned not necessarily as the first and only example of the uncanny in Ishiguro's work but rather as one of the best is that

[58] Wood, *How Fiction Works*, 5-6.

[59] Ibid., 5. Del Ivan Janik says that "*The Remains of the Day* brings to perfection what Ishiguro had attempted in his previous novels, *A Pale View of Hills* (1982) and *An Artist of the Floating World* (1986)," "No End of History: Evidence from the Contemporary English Novel," *Twentieth Century Literature* 41.2 (Summer 1995), 166.

[60] However, Ishiguro's first novel *A Pale View of Hills* provides a looser fit between the unreliable parts in the figure of the drowned kittens, which then open up the question of whether Etsuko/Satchiko actually murdered her daughter. Lewis indicates but does not follow up on this "slippage," *Kazuo Ishiguro*, 34.

instead of flagging the implied reader to content escaping the knowledge of the narrator, everything is on the surface (all of Ryder's wishes are fulfilled). What is odd about the novel is that what is usually hidden and interior is pushed into the foreground and what is strange and unknown remains so, for everyone involved, even at the end. There is no "deeper" meaning here: "Ishiguro's insistence on how Ryder's disconnection from people and places is 'unendurable to reason' (Steiner) persists until the novel's very end,"[61] or as Ronell stated above, fundamental boredom can infuse "the whole text with its ground level of non-sense [...]" However, Wood's review of *The Unconsoled* stated that it was "empty" and that it "invents its own category of badness."[62] Although Wood later states that Ishiguro's next novel, *When We Were Orphans*, "invents its own category of goodness,"[63] he is never quite as praiseful of the surface uncanny of Ishiguro's later work. What is being put forth here by bringing together a number of these disperse comments is that what perhaps causes Wood to distance himself from Ishiugro's later work is its apparent lack of subtlety. This lack of subtlety has been connected to the flat, workaday style of *Never Let Me Go*. However, it is this shift in style that is necessary for a shift in the location of the gap found in Ishiguro's work. Instead of finding a gap between person and past, person and role, or person and country as found in his earlier books, Ishiguro has needed to flatten the screen of this novel in order to project this gap onto the human condition itself; this gap which is opened by the flatness boredom is that of finitude, which can be seen in boredom's making-temporality-visible, as Lilian Alweiss argues: "The novelty of Heidegger's position is that he shows that time does not find its meaning in eternity but that time finds its meaning in death. Time 'is' only for a being that lives with an awareness of its own mortality."[64]

---

[61] Wong, *Kazuo Ishiguro*, 67.

[62] James Wood, "Ishiguro in the Underworld," *Guardian* May 5 (1995), 5. Lewis, who also quotes this well-known passage, says Wood's comment "invents its own category of scathingness," *Kazuo Ishiguro*, 142.

[63] James Wood, "The Unconsoled: *When We Were Orphans* by Kazuo Ishiguro," *The New Republic*, Oct 16 (2000), 44.

[64] Lilian Alweiss, "Heidegger and 'the Concept of Time,'" *History of the Human Sciences* 15.117 (2002), 118.

However, this "recent" tonal shift in Ishiguro's work has actually been a goal from the start. He has stated that no matter where his novels have been set, that he has wanted them to take off into the realm of metaphors, of an allegory of the human condition, stating that "whenever I try to think of a new book, it is this whole question about how to make a particular setting actually take off into the realm of metaphors so that people don't think it is just about Japan or Britain, but also give it that sort of ability to take off as metaphor and parable."[65] *Never Let Me Go* presents a powerful engine for the kind of metaphorical take-off Ishiguro describes, and that is in the unsubtle style of Kathy's narration: "I've been praised in the past for my unreliable, self-deceiving, emotionally restrained narrators [...] But *Never Let Me Go* isn't concerned with that kind of self-deception. So I needed my narrator to be different. An unreliable narrator here would just have got in the way."[66] The question is, *would have got in the way of what*? The answer being developed is *a*

---

[65] Vorda and Herzinger, "An Interview with Kazuo Ishiguro," 75. Ishiguro continues, "Because ultimately I'm not that interested in saying things about specific societies; and, if I were, I think I'd prefer to do it through nonfiction and follow all the proper disciplines such as to actually produce evidence and argument. I wouldn't do it by creating emotional manipulation," ibid. Marc Poreé says: "Ishiguro is, and remains, an eye-witness (albeit with a sharp eye), one who refers to both the Japanese and the British as 'they.' Detached, he has no axe to grind – even though he always manages to get away with murder," *Kazuo Ishiguro: The Remains of the Day* (Paris: CNED - Didier Érudition, 1999), 13.

[66] *RandomHouse.com*, "A Conversation with Kazuo Ishiguro," (2005), Internet: http://www.randomhouse.com, accessed March 24, 2009. Ishiguro continues, "As for the more vernacular style, well, she's someone narrating in contemporary England, so I had to have her talk appropriately. These are technical things, like actors doing accents. The challenge isn't so much achieving a voice that's more vernacular, or more formal, it's getting one that properly presents that narrator's character. It's finding a voice that allows a reader to respond to a character not just through what he or she does in the story, but also through how he/she speaks and thinks," ibid. David Kippen, however, seems resistant to this difference, calling Kathy's detachment "not altogether trustworthy": "A young woman referred to only as Kath H. narrates the novel. Like Stevens in 'Remains of the Day,' and most if not all of Ishiguro's previous first-person voices, she exudes a not altogether trustworthy detachment, reserved and yet minutely observant," "Ishiguro Imagines Love among Clones," *San Francisco Chronicle* Apr 14 (2005), E1. In addition, Jerng still sees Kathy as another one of Ishiguro's unreliable narrators, "Giving Form to Life," 385.

profound mood of boredom in the gap between narratee and implied reader.

2.4 Making Poverty Visible

One term that has been repeatedly connected with "flatness" and "boredom" has been "poverty." What is being referred to is a philosophical poverty, or a poverty of experience. This philosophical approach to poverty can be found in the work of Walter Benjamin, perhaps most powerfully concentrated in his 1933 essay "Experience and Poverty." Benjamin opens this essay with a fable telling of the wisdom a father, who is on his deathbed, passes on to his children. The father "fooled his sons into believing that there was treasure buried in the vineyard. They would only have to dig. They dug, but found no treasure. When autumn came, however, the vineyard bore fruit like no other in the whole land."[67] Once again it is through a lie that experience is passed down. Benjamin sees this experience as a "precious ring"[68] to be passed down from generation to generation in the form of fable and story in order to illustrate how seeing experience in this way has been lost, destroyed by the monstrous events enlarged and enabled by the technology of the First World War. Soldiers, Benjamin argues, return from the fronts not with experience but silence. This is because "strategic experience has been contravened by positional warfare; economic experience, by the inflation; physical experience, by hunger; moral experiences, by the ruling powers."[69] It is

---

[67] Walter Benjamin, "Experience and Poverty," trans. Rodney Livingstone, *Selected Writings: Volume 2, 1927-1934*, ed. Michael Jennings, Howard Eiland and Gary Smith (Cambridge; London: The Belknap Press of Harvard University Press, 1999), 734.

[68] Ibid.

[69] Ibid., 732. In "The Storyteller" Benjamin states that "With the [First] World War a process began to become apparent which has not halted since then. Was it not noticeable at the end of the war that men returned from the battlefield grown silent – not richer, but poorer in communicable experience? What ten years later was poured out in the flood of war books was anything but experience

impossible to come to grips with experiencing the "force field of destructive torrents and explosions"[70] that the war perpetrated on all sides. Another collocation that could be added to Benjamin's list might be poetry; shell shock. As Friedrich Kittler argues in a discussion of Ernst Jünger's undergoing of the same war, "For media-technological reasons, poetry comes to an end in the trenches, those 'pure brainmills' [...] says a fellow officer and friend of Jünger whose 'intellectual faculties, in the daily rhythm between watch duty and sleep, gradually dwindle toward zero.'"[71] Put in the language of Heidegger's reading of being-in-the-world, a proper comportment cannot be found for this overwhelmingly physical experience. Or, as Benjamin words it, "For what is the value of all our culture if it is divorced from experience?"[72] Although Agamben points out that there can be a more everyday cause for such a separation: "Today, however,

---

that goes from mouth to mouth. And there was nothing remarkable about that. For never has experience been contradicted more thoroughly than strategic experience by tactical warfare, economic experience by inflation, bodily experience by mechanical warfare, moral experience by those in power. A generation that had gone to school on a horse-drawn streetcar now stood under the open sky in a countryside in which nothing remained unchanged but the clouds, and beneath these clouds, in a field of force of destructive torrents and explosions, was the tiny, fragile human body," Walter Benjamin, "The Storyteller: Reflections on the Works of Nikolai Leskov," *Illuminations: Essays and Reflections*, trans. Harry Zohn, ed. Hannah Arendt (New York: Schocken Books, 1969), 84.

70 Benjamin, "Experience and Poverty," 732.

71 Friedrich Kittler, *Gramophone, Film, Typewriter*, trans. Geoffrey Winthrop-Young and Michael Wutz (Stanford: Stanford University Press, 1999), 130. In the British tradition a great poetry was born from the war, as seen in the works of Wilfred Owen and Siegfried Sassoon, for example. In a side note, Jünger was also interested in the ability of drugs to bring one as close as possible to the experience of death without crossing over. This can be seen in comments made by the "inventor" of LSD, Albert Hofmann, who devotes a chapter in his *LSD: My Problem Child* (1979) to his admiration for and experiences with Jünger, noting that once he was able to give Jünger a strong enough dose, "The next and last thrust into the inner universe together with Ernst Jünger, this time again using LSD, led us very far from everyday consciousness. We came close to the ultimate door. Of course this door, according to Ernst Jünger, will in fact only open for us in the great transition from life into the hereafter," Albert Hofmann, *LSD: My Problem Child* (Sarasota: Multidiciplinary Association for Psychedelic Studies, 2005), 174. On drugs and literature, see Ronell, *Crack Wars*.

72 Benjamin, "Experience and Poverty," 732.

we know that the destruction of experience no longer necessitates a catastrophe, and that humdrum daily life in any city will suffice. For modern man's average day contains virtually nothing that can still be translated into experience."[73] What is most important to the discussion here is that Benjamin locates a proper comportment towards being *within* poverty itself.

> Indeed (let's admit it), our poverty of experience is not merely poverty on the personal level, but poverty of human experience in general. Hence, a new kind of barbarism [...] We say this in order to introduce a new, positive concept of barbarism. For what does the poverty of experience do for the barbarian? It forces him to start from scratch; to make a new start; to make a little go a long way; to begin with a little and build up further, looking neither left nor right.[74]

Benjamin is describing a more fundamental kind of comportment than one that would allow, in a curious coincidence of phrasing, for a person to look left (when crossing the road) in Britain but right in America. For Benjamin there is a starting over that moves straight ahead, being involved neither in left nor right comportments. This is Benjamin's "from scratch," which is, however, different from Heidegger's nonrelation because Benjamin locates the from-scratch within barbarism itself. Therefore, it is at this point that Heidegger begins to prove less useful. Even though both in his lecture of 1945 on "Poverty" (not published until 1994, and translated into French for the first time in 2004 by Philippe Lacoue-Labarthe)[75] and two years later in his "Letter on Humanism,"[76] Heidegger begins to indicate an alternative to the "less-than" model of poverty he develops in his

---

[73] Giorgio Agamben, "Infancy and History: An Essay on the Destruction of Experience," trans. Liz Heron, *Infancy and History: The Destruction of Experience* (London; New York: Verso, 2007), 15.

[74] Benjamin, "Experience and Poverty," 732.

[75] Martin Heidegger, "Die Armut," *Heidegger Studies* 10 (1994), 5-11; Martin Heidegger, *La Pauvreté (Die Armut)*, trans. Philippe Lacoue-Labarthe (Strasbourg Cedex: Presses Universitaires de Strasbourg, 2004).

[76] Martin Heidegger, "Letter on Humanism," *Basic Writings*, ed. David Farrell Krell (New York: HarperCollins, 1993).

1929/30 lectures on boredom and the animal, there is never a fully developed positive model of poverty in Heidegger's work. That is why Benjamin's thought is so important here. Benjamin's work on poverty provides powerful leverage for lifting off from Heidegger in that Benjamin provides a proactive reading of poverty. Although Benjamin presumably did not have any traffic-related issues in mind, his calling to look "neither left nor right" does indicate another kind of comportment, one perhaps "more" fundamental in that it involves a kind of starting from scratch from within the poverty of the everyday. Benjamin is conjuring "the naked man of the contemporary world who lies screaming like a newborn babe in the dirty diapers of the present,"[77] a messy person who will actually need to speak in a different language. Referencing the turn-of-the-century German writer of fantastic literature Paul Scheerbart, Benjamin elicits the need for a strange, *constructed* language to be a part of this being's coming-forth. This language seems to carry a similar flatness to that which was found in critics' readings of Kathy's narrative voice: "Scheerbart is interested in inquiring how our telescopes, our airplanes, our rockets can transform human beings as they have been up to now into completely new, lovable, and interesting creatures. Moreover, these creatures talk in a completely new language. And what is crucial about this language is its arbitrary, constructed nature, in contrast to organic language."[78]

For Benjamin there seems to be a reflexiveness in poverty; what is emancipatory about poverty is that it somehow *makes visible* a wide-ranging comportment that was otherwise hidden. In Benjamin's examples both the hiddenness and its revealing are abetted by technology (the latter can be seen in his reference to Scheerbart). Poverty's ability to make visible also lies at the heat of Hannah Arendt's thought on the subject. In Arendt's letter

---

[77] Benjamin, "Experience and Poverty," 733.

[78] Ibid. Benjamin is discussing Scheerbart's novel *The Gray Cloth*, a fantasy novel about class architecture. As an example of the need for a workaday and flat style in order for something new to come forth, in the novel, clothes, women's especially, must be drab and grey so that the colorful prisms of the glass architecture can shine forth: it is "better to have a colorful house than colorful clothing," Paul Scheerbart, *The Gray Cloth*, trans. John Stewart (Cambridge: MIT Press, 2001), 86.

to political philosopher Eric Voegelin regarding his criticism of her *The Origins of Totalitarianism*, Arendt says that to write about sociological poverty without getting angry about it is not to be in the proper comportment towards the subject: "The natural human reaction to such conditions is one of anger and indignation because these conditions are against the dignity of man. If I describe these conditions without permitting my indignation to interfere, I have lifted this particular phenomenon out of its context in human society and have thereby robbed it of part of its nature."[79] The part of the nature of poverty that is robbed is actually the self-reflexive ability of poverty to make itself visible: "For to arouse indignation is one of the qualities of excessive poverty insofar as poverty occurs among human beings."[80] One of the key aspects of poverty, then, is actually one of the key claims for its Heideggerian opposite, authenticity, or second-order consciousness. As Rafael Winkler words it in the opening to "Heidegger and the Question of Man's Poverty in World":

> Who or what is man? What is the essence of man such that to raise the question concerning his essence, concerning what or who man is, is an unavoidable issue for man? There is a doubtless something peculiar, peculiarly circular or reflexive, to the "essence" of man if, as it seems, he alone among the rest of living things can raise the question concerning his essence, can call his essence into question.[81]

Therefore, as Alexander García Düttmann argues in a philosophical sense, "the worst poverty would be to not see poverty,"[82] as stated in his "Making Poverty Visible – Three Theses." Actually, Düttmann's essay closes by combining his thought on poverty in Arendt, Benjamin and Heidegger (among others) with a focus on reflexivity, as seen in his third thesis

---

[79] Hannah Arendt, "A Reply to Eric Voegelin," *The Portable Hannah Arendt*, ed. Peter Baehr (London: Penguin, 2003), 159.

[80] Ibid.

[81] Rafael Winkler, "Heidegger and the Question of Man's Poverty in World," *International Journal of Philosophical Studies* 15.4 (2007), 522.

[82] Alexander García Düttmann, "Making Poverty Visible – Three Theses," *Parrhesia* 4 (2008), 1.

which is "The making visible of poverty lies within poverty's complicated relation to itself."[83] This relation to itself is the focus of the next section, which comes back to the fable Benjamin started his essay with in order to comment upon an often unnoticed aspect of it, and that is the *lie* the father needed to tell his sons in order to accomplish the passing-on of experience.[84] This reading is taken up along with Patrick Greaney's reading of Benjamin's thought on poverty, which is then expanded by showing how the gap opened in *Never Let Me Go* is also self-reflexive, not between the narrator and her past in analepsis, but rather between the narratee and implied reader.[85]

2.5 Benjamin's Fable and the Power of Poverty

As indicated in the previous section, one aspect of Benjamin's essay "Experience and Poverty" that deserves rereading is the role of insincerity in the passing-on of experience. This was seen in the way that the father "fooled his sons into believing that there was treasure buried in the vineyard." If the "experience" had been passed on in the form of explicit knowledge, such as the father telling his sons that "aerating the land increases crop production," the effect would not have been the same; the sons would not have gained the experience the father had wanted to pass on. The difference between gaining and not gaining experience lies in difference itself, meaning that the reason Benjamin's fable is effective is that there is a difference created between the story (buried treasure) and reality (aerating the land) from which a lesson, or allegory, can develop.[86]

[83] Ibid., 8.

[84] Although whether the father's statement is a lie at all is contentious. He seems to be truthful (intention) while not telling the truth (factual). For elaboration of lying, see Alenka Zupančić, *Ethics of the Real: Kant, Lacan* (London; New York: Verso, 2000), 43-63.

[85] For an analysis regarding heterodiegetic and homodiegetic analepsis in *The Remains of the Day* see Porée, *Kazuo Ishiguro*, 42-47.

[86] In a sense this difference is indicative of Badiou's "'right to differences'" through which he aims to elaborate how there are only differences, for "Infinite

As shown in the previous chapter in conjunction with the difference between the narratee and the implied reader in *Never Let Me Go*, the notion of difference is also central to allegory, as can be seen in how allegory is different from the symbol. For Benjamin, the symbol is tied too closely to reality: "As a symbolic construct, the beautiful is supposed to merge with the divine in an unbroken whole."[87] In other words, "The Same (the fact that I am 'absolutely identical' to myself leads to a loss of identity"[88] although such an absolute sameness can have a more libratory power, as seen in some aspects of the uncanny and also Benjamin's work on reproduction. Paul de Man is a key figure who sees an uncanny similarity residing within the symbolic: "In the world of the symbol it would be possible for the image to coincide with the substance, since the substance and its representation do not differ in their being but only in their extension: they are part and whole of the same set of categories."[89] However, allegory is literary because it contains difference, as can be seen in Benjamin's discussion of how "evil" can be an allegory: "Allegory goes away empty-handed. Evil as such, which it cherished as enduring profundity, exists only in allegory, is nothing other than allegory, and means something different from what it is. It means precisely the non-existence of what it presents."[90] In other words, in the story of the fable the meaning of the story of buried treasure is located in the structure of the lie, for meaning lies in a non-existent part of the story – a lesson in agriculture and work ethics. According to de Man allegory implies difference, and hence temporality: "this relationship between signs necessarily contains a constitutive temporal element; it remains necessary, if there is to be allegory,

---

alterity is quite simply *what there is*," Alain Badiou, *Ethics: An Essay on the Understanding of Evil*, trans. Peter Hallward (London; New York: Verso, 2001), 24. Badiou continues: "There are as many differences, say, between a Chinese peasant and a young Norwegian professional as between myself and anybody at all, including myself," ibid., 26

[87] Walter Benjamin, *The Origin of German Tragic Drama*, trans. John Osborne (London; New York: Verso, 1998), 160.

[88] Zupančić, *Ethics of the Real*, 226.

[89] De Man, *Blindness and Insight*, 207.

[90] Benjamin, *The Origin of German Tragic Drama*, 233.

that the allegorical sign refer to another sign that precedes it."[91] Or, as he asks in a delineation of the definitions of allegory, "Why is it that the furthest-reaching truths about ourselves and the world have to be stated in such a lopsided, referentially indirect mode? Or, to be more specific, why is it that texts that attempt the articulation of epistemology with persuasion turn out to be inconclusive about their own intelligibility in the same manner and for the same reasons that produce allegory?"[92] A potential answer to these queries can be found in the role *folding-back* takes in de Man's definition of allegory. De Man argues that the structures of allegory "take into account the fact that the resulting narratives can be folded back upon themselves and become self-referential."[93] Such structures "tell the story of the failure to read,"[94] and as such stories they are "perverse,"[95] a word that conjures Wong's statements developed in the previous chapter.

Put into the language of the previous section, the difference needed in order for allegory to teach comes out of perverse reflexivity which has no room to develop in the collapsed symbol; this collapse, for example, can be instigated by the overwhelming weight of technology because technology, in Benjamin's reading, is too immediate. Technology is an empty stomach, a disintegrating economy, a soldier in the line of fire. There is no space within this immediate pressure in which the difference of a lie can take place. There is no room for the "We do not know. We can only imagine."[96] The difference that is needed in allegory is usurped by the overabundance of reality technology foregrounds. This difference between allegory and symbol has been well summarized by Deleuze, who makes a connection between allegory and time that is similar to that developed in relation to boredom:

---

[91] De Man, *Blindness and Insight*, 207.

[92] Paul de Man, *Aesthetic Ideology*, ed. Andzrej Warminski (Minneapolis: University of Minnesota Press, 1997), 52.

[93] De Man, *Allegories of Reading*, 205.

[94] Ibid.

[95] Ibid.

[96] Vincent Crapanzano, *Imaginative Horizons: An Essay in Literary-Philosophical Anthropology* (Chicago; London: The University of Chicago Press, 2004), 25.

> Walter Benjamin made a decisive step forward in our understanding of the Baroque when he showed that allegory was not a failed symbol, or an abstract personification, but a power of figuration entirely different from that of the symbol: the latter combines the eternal and the momentary, nearly at the center of the world, but allegory uncovers nature and history according to the order of time. It produces a history from nature and transforms history into nature in a world that no longer has its center.[97]

The "eternal and momentary" that Deleuze connects with the symbol could describe the butler Stevens in *The Remains of the Day*. At first this may seem contradictory: Stevens offers a sense of difference between the world as he tells it and the larger historical context which he seems to miss. However, this is actually a construction of the too-similar because these are two worlds that actually fit too neatly together in a reliable unreliability. *Never Let Me Go*, which in a sense is another kind of sameness in the flat every of Kathy's voice, actually instantiates difference in the disturbing equality between narratee and implied reader. The novel does not offer the plugable gap of an unreliable narrator to infuse the destabilization of the novel with a center of truth that is just out of reach.

At this point it is possible to formulate the role that the lie played in the passing-on of an experience of facticity in *Never Let Me Go*. As Ishiguro was shown to argue in the first chapter, a parent is obliged to lie to their child regarding facticity, or in the language of the novel, guardians are obliged to deceive the students: "[the guardians] gave [the students] something better, not to be better donors, but to be better humans [...] In order to persuade people to make the effort to learn and actually face what is often a difficult and complicated procedure – how to conduct human relationships and not mind getting hurt and upset – we have to be tricked to think there is a payoff."[98] Part of

---

[97] Gilles Deleuze, *The Fold: Leibniz and the Baroque*, trans. Tom Conley (Minneapolis: University of Minnesota Press, 1993), 125.

[98] Wong and Crummett, "A Conversation about Life and Art with Kazuo Ishiguro," 218. McGee asks about kind of stories will we tell the children that are

being a better human is *not* understanding. Ronell, as quoted above, argues that Benjamin's reading of allegory shows how allegory "profiles a power to defy comprehension."[99] Comprehension, in this reading, is rendered by the "organic unity of the world potentiated by the symbol."[100] The power of difference profiled by allegory is poverty and its ability to "make visible" from within the everyday.

This "power" of allegory rests, at least in part, in its refusal to be a part of unifying comprehension. The saying "no" to telling the students about the truth of their existence allows them, as Ishiguro states, "to be better humans." Patrick Greaney traces the sources of the power of the "no" in poverty throughout his book *Untimely Beggar: Poverty and Power from Baudelaire to Benjamin.* For Greaney, the power of poverty's self-reflexive making-itself-visible lies in the "non" of its "nonenactment":

> The 'non-' of a capability's nonenactment is not a negation of its actuality but a specific mode of privation that belongs to the capability, and the "urgent" demand of this privation and the consequences for understanding power may be what make the appearance of the poor in the nineteenth century so compelling. Only in our coming to terms with the incapacity of beggars and the most destitute does the full understanding of the power of the poor become possible,

---

clones: "But what story can one tell a clone? Already we have noted that human cloning is unprecedented in the natural history of mammals. Twins are the closest existing phenomenon, and they are separated by at most a few hours. The stories of parental roles in cloning in the media are frightening in almost all cases. One has parents replicating a child who has died early due to an accident. Another has an infertile woman seeking a genetic link to her recently deceased husband through a clone from a tissue sample she happens to have lying around. Still a third has the parent raising a clone of his wife to realize his dream of seeing his wife as a child. The point of discussing children's stories is twofold. First, it is clear that whatever progress we make in infertility technologies, an important part of realizing the potential of such technology to satisfy the felt need of adults is an account of what the technology will mean for the child. More, such family relationships are heavily textured by their social and institutional histories. Being tolerant of new kinds of family will have to begin with existing technologies and move out slowly and experimentally toward the margins," "A Pragmatic Approach to Human Cloning," 180.

[99] Ronell, *Stupidity*, 107.

[100] Ibid.

because in these figures the implication of power and impotence becomes apparent and allows us to understand the kind of actuality specific to power.[101]

Although Greaney does not always differentiate whether he is discussing poverty in a social or philosophical context, here we can bring his description of social nonengagement into the philosophical discussion in the sense that in part of his development of the actual power of privation Greaney examines the "non-" within "everyday" language, as was done at the beginning of this chapter. Greaney, sounding like Stanley Fish, argues that "if poetic language does not leave communicative language behind, this is because communicative language always includes something other than communication."[102] In addition, Agamben has also constructed the possibility of power which rests in a saying "no" from within a Benjaminian absence of experience. Agamben's argument can not only in his well-known work on Herman Melville's "Bartleby the Scrivener,"[103] but also in his thought on Benjamin and experience: "When humankind is deprived of effective experience and becomes subjected to the imposition of a form of experience as controlled and manipulated as a laboratory maze for rats – in other words, when the only possible experience is horror or lies – then the rejection of experience can provisionally embody a legitimate defence."[104] Agamben, Benjamin and Greaney are all attempting to delineate a new kind of barbarism.

While Agamben is describing a "different" kind of lying than is being developed here (perhaps his could be described as a "lying of non-comportment"), it is important to attempt to specify what kind of power poverty might have, even if it is only provisional. Greaney devotes the last chapter of his book to Benjamin's reading of poverty and experience, and he argues that the power of poverty in Benjamin's writings lies in "a kind

---

[101] Patrick Greaney, *Untimely Beggar: Poverty and Power from Baudelaire to Benjamin* (Minneapolis; London: University of Minnesota Press, 2008), 7.

[102] Ibid., 51.

[103] Giorgio Agamben, "Bartleby, or On Contingency," *Potentialities: Collected Essays in Philosophy*, trans. Daniel Heller-Roazen (Stanford: Stanford University Press, 1999).

[104] Agamben, "Infancy and History," 18.

of doubleness"[105] throughout. The power of this doubleness is that it constructs the coordinates of difference; or, in other words, the emergence of difference is the power of poverty, and this difference is powerful because, as Ronell argues, it can be reinscribed to disrupt and reflexively redefine the two "original" sides that make up what is being differentiated.[106] What this means in the case of *Never Let Me Go* is that the poverty of language that Kathy "uses,"[107] and the poverty of experience that the students undergo in relation to facticity, both allow for an allegory of the human condition to develop in the space that opens between the narratee, who is a clone like the narrator, and the implied reader, a non-cloned human. However, as Greaney warns, occupying this space is hazardous: "It is impossible to live in the midst of poverty because the wounds of poverty cannot be covered up."[108] Poverty creates difference, because of its doubleness (like the doubling of the wish fulfillment of the uncanny), and this difference allows for allegory to take place. This allegory is not only meant to be read, but it reads. It reads us: "To understand poverty, we must persistently read this naked surface just as it reads and wounds us."[109] What this means is that the power of allegory lies in its ability to disassemble that which it allegorizes. In this sense it is quite true that "the birth of the reader must be at the cost of the death of the Author,"[110] or put in the language being developed here, the birth of allegory must be at the death of the symbol. This redefining of sides was true for Benjamin's fable in which the passing-on of experience was only possible by redefining the identities of the sons from

---

[105] Greaney, *Untimely Beggar*, 165.

[106] Ronell, *Stupidity*, 107. Elsewhere, Greaney states: "Formlessness cannot and must be present in forms," "Language and Form: Hölderlin's Errancy," *MLN* 113.3 (1998), 540.

[107] For a compelling reading of Heidegger's concept of "usage" [*brauchen*] and how it related to authentic human being see Christopher Fynsk, *Language and Relation: ...that there is language* (Stanford: Stanford University Press, 1996), 104-19. For further commentary see Christopher Fynsk, *Infant Figures: The Death of the "Infans" and Other Scenes of Origin* (Stanford: Stanford University Press, 2000), 35-7.

[108] Greaney, *Untimely Beggar*, 168.

[109] Ibid.

[110] Roland Barthes, "The Death of the Author," *Image, Music, Text*, trans. Stephan Heath (New York: Hill and Wang, 1999), 148.

money-scroungers to competent farmers, the agent of which was the difference created by the lie. This is also true for the ability of *Never Let Me Go* to allegorize the human condition by creating a moment of difference, wielded out of the too obvious nonconformity of narratee and implied reader, which then begins to disassemble that which it actually allegorizes – us.

2.6 Making the Possibles Visible

One of the strongest instances of "making visible" in *Never Let Me Go* has to do with the clones' relation to their own doublings, or "possibles," meaning the "original" humans from which they were copied.[111] While non-cloned humans are in evidence at Hailsham in the form of the guardians and Madame, the clones actually have no information regarding either the "original" from whence they came or of the eventual hosts for their donated organs. However, speculation as to who might be on the other end of the donations is rampant, especially once the clones graduate from Hailsham and move to the Cottages, a sort of in-between place where they slowly get acclimatized to the outside world, eventually learning to drive and move about the United Kingdom as carers who travel from recovery center to recovery center. As the actual role of carer becomes more and more real, so does speculation regarding from whom the clones were copied:

> The basic idea behind the possibles theory was simple, and didn't provoke much dispute. It went something like this. Since each of us was copied at some point from a normal person, there must be, for each of us, somewhere out there, a model getting on with his or her life. This meant, at least

[111] Harris argues that mimesis may actually be one of the motivators for the development of human cloning, *On Cloning*, 26-7. For an expanded discussion of the topic, see Rebecca Schneider, "Hello Dolly Well Hello Dolly: The Double and its Theatre," *Psychoanalysis and Performance*, ed. Patrick Campbell and Adrian Kear (New York: Routledge, 2001).

> in theory, you'd be able to find the person you were modelled from. That's why, when you were out there yourself – in the towns, shopping centres, transport cafés – you kept an eye out for "possibles" – the people who might have been the models for you and your friends. (*NLMG* 137)

The topic of possibles gained importance when a potential model was found for Ruth by one of the older clones at the Cottages who had traveled to the Norfolk coast. However, not much was known regarding what kind of person the model might be. "Some students thought you should be looking for a person twenty to thirty years older than yourself – the sort of age a normal parent would be," while others thought "they'd use for models people at the peak of their health, and that's why they were likely to be 'normal parent' age" (ibid.). Kathy, on the other hand, looks for her possible elsewhere, because of her sexual desires which she describes thus to Ruth: "'Maybe it's just me anyway. There might be something not quite right with me, down there. Because something I just really, really need to do'" (126). Kathy's worry about her desires lead her to search for possibles in the porn magazines lying about the Cottages (132; 178-80). No matter what form it takes, the topic of possibles is loaded with lack of comprehension, from not knowing who they might be to having the models being copied by the once-again unspecified "they." In general, like the clones' facticity, these questions were not probed too deeply by the clones because of the other questions that would then be raised. For example, "Then there were those questions about why we wanted to track down our models at all. One big idea behind finding your model was that when you did, you'd glimpse your future" (ibid.). As Britzman argues, "An odd reversal occurs, for the students believe their parents would hold the key to what might have been their future."[112]

In addition, the location of Ruth's possible in the "real life" seaside city of Cromer in Norfolk is also a place of uncertainty. Back at Hailsham, Miss Emily would give the students lessons

---

[112] Britzman, "On Being a Slow Reader," 316.

on the geography of England, probably in order to facilitate their visits to various recovery centers. These lessons were given by Miss Emily, who would talk about the different counties along with placing calendar pictures of each on an easel. However, "there was a gap in Miss Emily's calendar collection: none of them had a single picture of Norfolk" (*NLMG* 65). Eventually Miss Emily explained why this gap existed. Norfolk, she contended, is "'not on the way to anywhere. People going north and south [...] they bypass it altogether. For that reason, it's a peaceful corner of England, rather nice. But it's also something of a lost corner'" (ibid.). "A *lost corner*," Kathy emphasizes, "Somehow this idea caught on and soon had become accepted fact virtually throughout our entire year" (ibid.). In a novel where "The larger world remains a distant, blurred backdrop,"[113] Norfolk, because it is unpictured and unknown, comes to represent a place where answers can be found, although this proposition is proven both true and untrue. Norfolk is a location of difference thematically folded upon itself because through its ambiguity it becomes a receptacle for lost things – it is through not being there that it can be found. Norfolk is the home of Ruth's potential possible, "an attractive, professional woman who lives out Ruth's aspiration to work in an office, rather than end her life as a 'donor,'"[114] who turns out to be a false positive. However, something else is found, something not initially looked for, a copy of Judy Bridgewater's *Songs After Dark*, which Kathy had previously lost and which she and Tommy found together in Norfolk, also finding an attraction to each other they had both denied since he started going with Ruth.

Looking at this scene more closely, however, it is seen that the loss of Ruth's possible is coupled with another situation. The clones have followed the possible into a picture shop where they end up getting much too close to her, and their illusion about her being a possible for Ruth is ruined: "But now, in that gallery, the woman was too close, much closer than we'd ever really wanted. And the more we heard her and looked at her, the less she seemed like Ruth" (*NLMG* 161). Immediately after this loss of the possible, the owner of the gallery addresses the students,

---

[113] Deb, "Lost Corner," 55.

[114] Ingersoll, "Taking Off into the Realm of Metaphor," 49.

having no idea that they are clones: "'Are you art students?'" the woman working at the gallery asks: "'Not exactly,'" Kathy answers, "'We're just, well, keen'" (ibid.). What is not being set up here is a polarity that needs to be reconciled between original and copy; instead, the clones are it, there is no deeper level to be found. Ruth's possible is "lost" because the clones have gotten, or become, too close to her. Immediately after this, for the first and only time, a normal mistakes the clones for a not-clone. This is not a symbol that has a flip side to be discovered. This scene can be read literally: there are no possibles, the normals are the strange ones, the clones. The loss of the model is a paramount aspect of allegory, just as the poverty of the animal in Heidegger's thought can be reread into his vision of Dasein. In relation to what is different from them, namely the normals, Kathy and the other clones occupy a "cozy state of suspension" (140).

Upon being denied knowledge of not only who but what her possible might be, Ruth has an outburst, which at first seems to contradict this "literal" reading, claiming that "'They don't ever, *ever*, use people like that woman. Think about it. Why would she want to? We all know it, so why don't we all face it. We're not modelled from that sort [...]?" (164). Ruth continues, "'We all know it. We're modelled from *trash*. Junkies, prostitutes, winos, tramps. Convicts, maybe, just so long as they aren't psychos. That's what we came from. We all know it, so why don't we say it? [...] If you want to look for possibles, if you want to do it properly, then you look in the gutter. You look in rubbish bins. Look down the toilet, that's where you'll find where we all came from'" (ibid.). On the one hand this scene, as Ingersoll argues in an admittedly rather tongue-in-cheek manner perhaps meant to illustrate Ruth's point of view, begins to confront the ethical issues of allowing clones to be harvested for organs:

> How *could* the better established social strata be induced to allow themselves to be cloned and then be expected to live with the horror of knowing their body-doubles were going to be sliced up for transplantable organs? Better to mine society's inevitable "garbage heaps" of irredeemable human

> specimens who might be induced through offers of money or other forms of 'candy' to participate in such a grisly business.[115]

However, Ruth's address can be read in another way. The models she mentions are taken from the domain of poverty, winos and tramps, the "trash" of society. At the same time, this is a direct address to the implied reader, for the models for the clones in the novel are "normal" people. The models for the clones are us.[116] At the same time, the models for the clones are lost, they quite literally cannot be found. The loss of a model mirrors the opening epigraph of George Eliot's novel *Daniel Deronda*, which is important because it is the book Kathy is reading during her time at the Cottages. The epigraph to the first chapter, written by Eliot (Mary Ann Evans) herself, begins with the words "Men can do nothing without the make-believe of a beginning."[117] These words are useful because they foreground the reason that the models are being relegated to the domain of poverty; it is because there are no "normal" models for the clones, the copy has repositioned the original. In order to cover this lack of difference, the "make-believe" difference of a lie is necessary, which is actually the structure of allegory. This dissembling of the model is also related to facticity, as can be seen in Derrida's reading of Heidegger' concept of death:

---

[115] Ingersoll, "Taking Off into the Realm of Metaphor," 49. For an overview of ethical questions regarding human cloning, see Rollin Bernard, "Keeping Up with the Cloneses: Issues in Human Cloning," *The Journal of Ethics* 3 (1999). Bernard's central thesis is that the lacuna opened by the absence of an ethical discussion coming forth from the informed scientists who actually participate in cloning themselves is filled by "sensationalistic, simplistic, emotionally-based slogans which dominate social thought and whose intuitive appeal make them difficult to dislodge," ibid., 53.

[116] Ingersoll argues that "Ishiguro offers in Kathy and the other students something closer to the reality of our own everyday lives in which we know, yet ignore, the inevitability, say, of our own deaths, a reaction that might well seem 'obtuse' to wiser visitors to our planet from other worlds. Paradoxically, by inviting his readers into the bizarre metaphor of the clone engineered to provide others with body parts, Ishiguro allows us to explore an otherness that in the end may serve as a reflection of our innermost experiences as 'normal' human beings," ibid., 55.

[117] George Eliot, *Daniel Deronda* (London: Penguin, 2003), 7.

> Against, or without, Heidegger, one could point to a thousand signs that show that animals also *die*. Although the unnumerable structural differences that separate one "species" from another should make us vigilant about any discourse on animality or beastiality *in general*, one can say that animals have a very significant relation to death, to murder and to war (hence, to borders), to mourning and to hospitality, and so forth, even if they have neither a relation to death nor to the "name" of death as such, nor, by the same token, to the other as such, to the purity as such of the alterity of the other as such. But neither does man, that is precisely the point! Nor does even man as *Dasein*. Who will guarantee that the name, the ability to name death (like that of naming the other, and it is the same) does not participate as much in the dissimulation of the "as such" of death as in its revelation, and that language is not precisely the origin of the nontruth of death, and of the other?[118]

Derrida's argument is the argument of allegory: it is the dissimulation within the "name" of death as such that brings about the reflexive visibility of this lack. The role of visibility is also key at the end of the novel, when Kathy and Tommy find a retired Miss Emily and they get the chance to ask her about the school, and their past. Miss Emily explains, "with morbid politeness,"[119] the ethics of harvesting organs from human clones, or so-called "therapeutic cloning,":[120] "'However uncomfortable people were about your existence,'" she says, "'their overwhelming concern was that their own children, their spouses, their parents, their friends, did not die from cancer, motor neurone disease, heart disease. So for a long time you were kept in the shadows, and people did their best not to think about you. And if they did, they tried to convince themselves

[118] Derrida, *Aporias*, 75-6. Derrida's quote here seems to contradict Winkler's claim that Derrida's reading locates *logos* at the heart of the poverty of the animal, but not of finitude, "Heidegger and Man's Poverty in World," 523. For an example of a reading of Heidegger that fits Winkler's claim, see Akira Mizuta Lippit, *Electric Animal: Toward a Rhetoric of Wildlife* (Minneapolis: University of Minnesota Press, 2000), 58.

[119] Bradford, *The Novel Now*, 216.

[120] Harris, *On Cloning*, 16.

you weren't really like us. That you were less than human, so it didn't matter'" (*NLMG* 258). The role of Hailsham, then, was to lift the students out of the shadows, to make them visible to the "normals" of Britain. However, Hailsham was soon closed, and the experiment of visibility was put to an end. Miss Emily explains: "'The world didn't want to be reminded how the donation programme really worked. They didn't want to think about you students, or about the conditions you were brought up in. In other words, my dears, they wanted you back in the shadows. Back in the shadows where you'd been before the likes of Marie-Claude [Madame] and myself ever came along'" (ibid.).[121] Or, as Bruce Sterling has argued in a discussion of the biot, or of someone who is "in a position to micromanage and design the processes that shape his own anatomy":[122] "The ultimate consumer item is the Consumer. There is no metahistory we find more utterly compelling than our personal metahistory. The world has many forms of reward and gratification, but being alive and healthy underwrites all the rest of them."[123] Wolfgang Schirmacher has developed a similar concept with his *homo generator*, who "does not have to settle for what is given; he works, instead, without any restrictions, with the fundamental building blocks of life. Consequently, *homo generator* is ready for tailor-made evolution."[124] However, there is one important difference between the two, and that is that for Schirmacher the coordinates of *homo generator* are not depended upon but merely foregrounded by what is made

---

[121] Toker and Chertoff argue that "Miss Emily's helplessness is also the helplessness of the reader, who is made to feel complicit with the social structure that the novel conjures up," "Reader Response and the Recycling of Topoi in Kazuo Ishiguro's *Never Let Me Go*," 177.

[122] Bruce Sterling, *Shaping Things* (Cambridge: MIT Press, 2005), 135.

[123] Ibid., 137. Sterling continues: "As a **Biot** you cannot go back, for you had already outlived any human lifespan; you cannot be overthrown by the previous order, because your new capacities are simply too great for reactionaries to combat. You are no longer human. Not that this lets you off the hook in any way; you have a wide variety of interesting, challenging problems. It's just that none of them are human ones," ibid.

[124] Wolfgang Schirmacher, "*Homo Generator: The Challenge of Gene Technology*," *Technology and Responsibility*, ed. Paul Durbin (Dordrecht; Boston: D. Reidel Publishing Company, 1987), 204-5.

possible by gene technology.[125] This positive and even compassionate reading of the "new" human by Sterling and Schirmacher is echoed in the more "positive" reading of "shadows" which has been provided by Jun'ichirō Tanizaki, for example.[126] In defining the gap between the narratee being kept in the shadows with Kathy, and the implied reader living in out in broad daylight.

2.7 Projection

At the heart of making visible is the concept of projection. Poverty's self-reflexive ability to make itself visible, thereby

---

[125] Ibid., 204.

[126] In the long essay *In Praise of Shadows* Tanizaki argues for the value of Japanese darkness in contrast to the light of the West, as can be seen in his discussion of the presentation of food: "In the cuisine of any country efforts no doubt are made to have the food harmonize with the tableware and the walls; but with Japanese food, a brightly lighted room and shining tableware cut the appetite in half... A glistening black lacquer rice cask set off in a dark corner is both beautiful to behold and a powerful stimulus to the appetite. Then the lid is briskly lifted, and this pure white freshly boiled food, heaped in its black container, each and every grain gleaming like a pearl, sends forth billows of warm steam -- here is a sight no Japanese can fail to be moved by. Our cooking depends upon shadows and is inseparable from darkness," Jun'ichirō Tanizaki, *In Praise of Shadows*, trans. Thomas Harper and Edward Seidensticker (Stony Creek: Leete's Island Books, 1977), 16-7. At the end of his essay Tanizaki calls out to literature to be a bastion for the shadows that are being lost: "I have written all this because I have thought that there might still be somewhere, possibly in literature or the arts, where something could be saved. I would call back at least for literature this world of shadows we are losing," ibid., 42. Ishiguro has claimed Tanizaki as an influence, although he gives greater stress to Western sources, Gregory Mason, "An Interview with Kazuo Ishiguro," *Conversations with Kazuo Ishiguro*, ed. Brian Shaffer and Cynthia Wong (Jackson: University Press of Mississippi, 2008), 4. In addition, although there may not be any direct correlation, in Tanizaki's book *The Makioka Sisters* two of the main protagonists share names with the main characters of Ishigruo's first novel, *A Pale View of Hills*. Etsuko and Sachiko. See Jun'ichirō Tanizaki, *The Makioka Sisters*, trans. Edward Seidensticker (New York: Grosset and Dunlap, 1966). In Tanizaki's novel Etsuko is the daughter of Sachiko, while in Ishigruo's novel Sachiko is the projected self of Etsuko. Tanizaki and shadows are taken up again in the next chapter.

short-circuiting the "model" needed for the "copy" to be possible, can also be read as the ability to motivate an exceptional understanding, or fundamental comportment. Heidegger argues that a fundamental comportment like profound boredom [*tiefe Langeweile*] can bring about an experience of *exceptional understanding*,[127] meaning a removal from being subsumed in the phenomenological input from the world, like moths continually drawn to a flame. Another term for this kind of exceptional understanding is *projection* [*Entwurf*] and it is one of the key terms for Heidegger regarding what makes humans human. For Heidegger, "the essence of man, the Dasein in him, is determined by this *projective character*."[128] Projection is that which makes up the authentic way in which humans relate to world, meaning they are in a relation of world-formation rather than the animal's poverty. However, as developed in the first chapter, not only does the concept of a human-only being-in-the-world face criticisms regarding nonrelation, but so does being-towards-death. The two are being brought together here because they both follow a similar structure: "this projecting is nothing other than dasein's factical way of being-in-the-world."[129] What was important about Derrida's criticism of nonrelation and death in particular was the way he focused on rereading an unthought linguistic element. As Hugh Rayment-Pickard argues in *Impossible God: Derrida's Theology*:

> Heidegger's metaphysical humanism depends upon the existential analysis of *Dasein* as a living entity within a proper mode of death. In turn, the proper field of operation for the existential analysis of *Dasein* is established once the regional life sciences of biology, anthropology, psychology and the rest have been assigned their subordinate place [...] A distinct economy of life and death undergirds Heidegger's metaphysics of *Dasein*. But since *Dasein*'s metaphysical priority is established not only within a hierarchy of life, but

---

[127] Heidegger, *The Fundamental Concepts of Metaphysics*, 136.

[128] Ibid., 362.

[129] Alejandro Vallega, *Heidegger and the Issue of Space: Thinking on Exilic Grounds* (University Park: The Pennsylvania State University Press, 2003), 153.

also of death, Derrida has to resist with equal vigour Heidegger's spiritualization of the life of *Dasein* and the propriety of *Dasein*'s being-toward-death.[130]

However, what does seem essential in Heidegger's analysis is the self-reflexive nature of projection, which is actually also essential to the concept of poverty, rather than a different order of being-in-the-world:

> What is *most proper* to such activity and occurrence is what is expressed in the prefix "pro-" [*Ent*-], namely that in projecting [*Entwerfen*], this occurrence of projection *carries* whoever is projection *out and away from themselves* in a certain way. It indeed removes them into whatever has been projected, but it does not as it were deposit and abandon them there -- on the contrary: in this being removed by the projection, what occurs is precisely a peculiar *turning toward themselves on the part of whoever is projecting*...this removal that pertains to projecting has the character of *raising away into the possible* [...][131]

Projecting is essential for world-formation because projecting is connected to creation or generation in the sense of being able to create an understanding of the world beyond what is given to the immediate senses, or to be able to *react* to the world.[132] Heidegger locates the engine for this generation in a "*turning towards themselves*" that was also seen in connection to the making-visible of poverty. Additionally, Derrida traces the source of such a projection to a kind of "lie," meaning to the "fiction" that is literature. In *Geneses, Genealogies, Genres, &*

---

[130] Hugh Rayment-Pickard, *Impossible God: Derrida's Theology* (Hants; Burlington: Ashgate, 2003), 98.

[131] Heidegger, *The Fundamental Concepts of Metaphysics*, 363.

[132] This is a reference to Friedrich von Schelling's thesis that "Since I seek to ground my knowledge only *in itself*, I enquire no further as to the ultimate ground of this primary knowledge (self-consciousness), which, if it exists, must necessarily lie *outside* knowledge," *System of Transcendental Idealism*, trans. Peter Heath (Charlottesville: University Press of Virginia, 1997), 18. On Schelling's relation to Hegel, Derrida and Ronell see Willems, "The Hyperreal Territory of the Animal," 43-4.

Genius he draws a line from projection to the secret of literature, which is projection's generative power. Derrida's path winds around the word *genre*, which, in French (as well as in English), contains the initial phoneme *gé*, which is a part of such pregnant words as *génie*, *générosité*, and *généologie*. This is then phonetically linked by Derrida to the French *jet* or *jeter*, meaning *to throw*, which can be seen in the English *jetty*, *jet* and then finally to *projectile* and *projecting*.[133] The links can then be extended to *subject* and *object*, showing an inherent unity between *genes*, *subjects* and *generation*. What is important about this cascade is the connection between subject and generation. Generation is not something that the subject engages in, but it is rather a part of the subject itself. For Derrida, this self-reflexivity of the subject being the seat of its own generation is the secret of literature – its generative world-formation power: "The secret of literature is thus the secret itself. It is the secret place in which it establishes itself as the very possibility of the secret, the place it, literature as such, begins, the place of its genesis or of its genealogy, properly speaking."[134]

For Heidegger, a non-human being is not able to complete this self-reflexive turn; instead non-humans are always chasing their own tails. Heidegger provides a very concrete example of what he means through a description of a bee gathering either nectar rich in carbohydrates or pollen rich in protein:

> Poor in world implies poverty as opposed to richness; poverty implies less as opposed to more. The animal is poor in world, it somehow possesses less [...] The bee, for example, has its hive, its cells, the blossoms it seeks out, and the other bees of the swarm. The bee's world is limited to a specific domain and is strictly circumscribed [...] The worker bee is familiar with the blossoms it frequents, along

---

[133] Jacques Derrida, *Geneses, Genealogies, Genres, & Genius: The Secrets of the Archive*, trans. Beverley Bie Brahic (New York: Columbia University Press, 2006), 9.

[134] Ibid., 18. At the end of the novel Tommy tells Kathy a secret he had never told anyone, that after making a goal in football, he always imagined himself splashing through water afterwards (*NLMG* 280).

> with their colour and scent, but it does not know the stamens of these blossoms *as* stamens.[135]

The bee is unable to turn towards but is always encompassed by, or subservient to, its world. This is a reading of Jakob von Uexküll's *Umwelt*, otherwise known as a *function-circle*. As von Uexküll describes in his *Theoretical Biology*, the function circle of the animal consists of responses to stimuli, which then affect the outer world, which then influence the stimuli. Such a periodic circle is the *function-circle* of the animal: "For each individual animal, however, its function-circles constitute a world by themselves, within which it leads its existence in complete isolation."[136] For the animal, the world is always something that is crossed out: inaccessible *as a whole*; the human is able to access the world as a whole through language, which is the underpinning unthought of Heidegger here, as Derrida has shown. However, as Simon Critchley argues, Heidegger's description of crossed-out being is "an attempt to render Being invisible that simply makes it more visible."[137] Therefore, another unthought of Heidegger can be stated thus: his investment in developing the gap between the poverty of the non-human being and the human-being's being-in-the-world only makes poverty more visible, and thus, in a reflexive manner, enacts a destructive allegory of the human.

---

[135] Heidegger, *The Fundamental Concepts of Metaphysics*, 193.

[136] Jakob von Uexküll, *Theoretical Biology* (New York: Kegan Paul, Trench, Trubner & Co., 1926), 126. One of the most important contributions of von Uexküll is disregarding a superiority of the human's function circle when compared to the animals: both are seen through their "limitations."

[137] Simon Critchley, *Very Little – Almost Nothing: Death, Philosophy, Literature* (London: Routledge, 1997), 17. Or, as Floyd Merrell argues, "Within each organism, along the functional cycle or information-conveying loop, external signals enter and become internal signals, having been processed in the transition according to our particular capacities," *Sensing Corporeally: Toward a Posthuman Understanding* (Toronto: University of Toronto Press, 2003), 266.

2.8 The Poverty of Care

Another aspect of death that Heidegger puts on the side of poverty is experiencing the death of another. Kathy, in her role as a carer who travels around England being with and comforting clones recovering from donations, including those who are dying from a maximum fourth donation,[138] sets up not necessarily a challenge to Heidegger's position but a development of his unthought fundamental "with." The reason this "with" is important for a reading of *Never Let Me Go* is that it is another angle from which to approach the engine of allegory, of a reflexive sameness. As Jean-Luc Nancy states in "The Being-with of Being-there," "Heidegger does everything to affirm the essentiality of the *with*," although at the same time this thought remains undeveloped.[139] In fact, it is Heidegger's refusal to allow a being-with to surface that Winkler reads as an example of poverty existing within the world of Dasein.[140]

For Heidegger, being-towards-death is connected with an access to the authenticity [*Eigentlichkeit*], or the "ownness" [*Eigen*] of Dasein. Heidegger argues it is impossible for anyone to experience their own demise since they can only relate to the world through life, and life itself can never know death, which is another; it is actually the experience of this impossibility that is

---

[138] Although there is a hint of wonder as to what could lie beyond the fourth donation. Kathy's friend and eventual lover Tommy wonders: "'How maybe, after the fourth donation, even if you've technically completed, you're still conscious in some sort of way; how then you find there are more donations, plenty of them, on the other side of that line; how there are no more recovery centres, no carers, no friends; how there's nothing to do except watch your remaining donations until they switch you off. It's horror movie stuff [...]" (*NLMG* 274). This perhaps contradicts Mike Godwin's claim that "in Ishiguro's story, becoming a donor means you'll likely be dying sooner rather than later. There is no hint that donors, all of whom must donate four organs before they 'complete,' ever survive 'completion,'" "Remains of the DNA," *Reason* 37.5 (October 2005), 58.

[139] Jean-Luc Nancy, "The Being-there of Being-with," trans. Marie-Eve Morin, *Continental Philosophy Review* 41.1 (2008), 3.

[140] Winkler, "Heidegger and the Question of Man's Poverty in the World," 529.

mine.[141] As Françoise Dastur (who initiated the 7-page footnote in Derrida's *On Spirit*) argues:

> If no one can take over the burden of another's death, and in the strict sense die for him, it follows that dying is not merely an extrinsic property of existence, an "accident" of the substance "man", but, rather, an essential attribute of the latter. So the relation which the human being entertains with dying is integral to its very being and prior to all its other properties. This is what leads Heidegger to assert [...] that the certitude of one's going-to-die is the foundation of the certitude *Dasein* has of itself, such that it is not the *cogito sum*, the "I think, I am", that constitutes the true definition of *Dasein*'s being but, rather, *sum moribundus*, "I am dying", where only "*moribundus*", "destined for death", is what gives "*sum*", "I am", its meaning. [142]

However, Heidegger's position prompts Nancy to ask if being-towards-death is "the making *mine* of that which cannot be mine or the letting myself be disappropriated at and from the fullest point of mineness [...]"[143] Nancy's thought is important at this juncture because the tension between "one's own" and "being-with" follows the structure of the duality of Dasein's relationship to the everyday, meaning that within the flatness of the everyday there exists an impetus from which authentic being can come forth: flatness and authenticity are in no way exclusive:

> Heidegger confuses the everyday with the undifferentiated, the anonymous, and the statistical. These are no less important, but they can only constitute themselves in

---

[141] Heidegger, *Being and Time*, 301-2. Calarco argues: "*Dasein*'s death means that there can no longer be any relation to the phenomenon as such; in death, phenomenology reaches its limit. But, and this is Derrida's point, if death marks the end and the impossibility of the relation to the phenomenon as such, then it is precisely *this impossibility* that cannot appear as such. By definition, the disappearance of the as such is what refuses to appear as such," "On the Borders of Language and Death," 23.

[142] Françoise Dastur, *Death: An Essay on Finitude*, trans. John Llewelyn (London; Antlantic Highlands: Athlone, 1996), 49.

[143] Nancy, "The Being-there of Being-with," 3.

> relation to the differentiated singularity that the *everyday* already is by itself: each day, each time, day to day. One cannot affirm that the meaning of Being must express itself starting from everydayness and then begin by neglecting the general differentiation of the everyday, its constantly renewed rupture, its intimate discord, its polymorphy and its polyphony, its relief and its variety. A "day" is not simply a unit for counting; it is the turning of the world – each time singular. And days, indeed every day, could not be similar if they were not first different, difference itself. Likewise "people," or rather "peoples," given the irreducible strangeness that constitutes them as such, are themselves primarily the exposing of the singularity according to which existence exists, irreducibly and primarily – and an exposition of singularity that experience claims to communicate with, in the sense of "to" and "along with," the totality of beings.[144]

For Nancy there is a rupture or disturbance within the everyday that allows for difference. Heidegger describes this moment as that in which Dasein is fleeing [*Flucht*] the everyday,[145] although he does not develop a mechanism for this fleeing. For Nancy, the mechanism for this rupture is actually being-with itself, or community: "there has to be a *clinamen*. There has to be an inclination or an inclining from one toward the other, of one by the other, or from one to the other. Community is at least the *clinamen* of the 'individual.'"[146]

---

[144] Nancy, *Being Singular Plural*, 9.

[145] Heidegger, *Being and Time*, 229.

[146] Jean-Luc Nancy, *The Inoperative Community*, trans. Peter Connor, Lisa Garbus, Michael Holland and Simona Sawhney (Minneapolis: University of Minnesota Press, 1991), 3-4. Daniel Hoolsema, discussing *The Literary Absolute*, co-authored by Nancy and Lacoue-Labarthe, summarizes this position, showing how "a significant alteration of Heidegger's thinking, for whom the speaking or languaging of the essence of language, the silent contraction of difference [*der Unterschied*] that exposes Dasein to the gift of being, takes place in a single given event [*Eriegnis*]. In contrast, Lacoue-Labarthe and Nancy describe events always occurring multiply. Contra Heidegger, Lacoue-Labarthe and Nancy argue that, stricto sensu, there is no such thing as an event [*Ereignis*]; for them, there are only events. Single moments bring forth a plurality of events," "The Echo of an Impossible Future in *The Literary Absolute*," *MLN* 119.4 (2004), 854-5.

Community is the mechanism of this rupture because being-with something else can be an experience of contamination, of letting some of the outside in without disengaging either one or the other (inside or outside). This contaminated being-with requires "that the openings intersect each other in some way, that they cross, mix or let their properties interfere with one another, but without merging into a unique *Dasein* (or else the *mit* would be lost) [...]"[147]

Bruce Robbins' reading of the "commitment to proximity"[148] in *Never Let Me Go* maps out a territory of being-with in relation to Kathy's role as carer. In answering the question of why the students do not rebel against their fate as organ donors, Robins argues that "the primary answer to that question seems to be not the ideology of freedom but the ideology of the welfare state [...]"[149] Robbins' construction of the welfare state in novel, through which the clones participate as donors and carers for each other, centers around an increased identification between patient and carer through a feeling of being "like me" which is not generated through the kindness of the carer but rather through anger:

> If the representatives of the welfare state can be angry and at fault, then it is much easier to imagine working within the welfare state – being "like me" – as a potential terminus for the upwardly mobile juvenile offender of talent. It becomes possible to hypothesize such a thing as angry aspiration, a goal that would require maintaining rather than eliminating the anger that seems to block the passage upward.[150]

---

[147] Nancy, "The Being-with of Being-there," 4.

[148] Bruce Robbins, "Cruelty is Bad: Banality and Proximity in *Never Let Me Go*" *Novel: A Forum on Fiction* 40.3 (Summer 2007), 290. The version of Robbins' essay included in his book *Upward Mobility and the Common Good* does not include the introductory section from which this quote is taken. The title of the piece has also been revised to "Caring: Kazuo Ishiguro's *Never Let Me Go*," signaling a shift in focus for its inclusion in a book on literary representations of the welfare state.

[149] Ibid., 294.

[150] Ibid., 299.

What Robbins reads in Ishiguro is a vision of the welfare state not constructed on the closeness of care but on the distance of anger. This reading "allows us to consider the welfare state as a distanced, anger-bearing project in which the anger is a necessary part of a genuine concern for people's welfare."[151] While he does not draw out the philosophical implications of this statement, Robbins intuitively captures the copresencing of both distance and closeness (of being-with, or caring) in the novel.

The possibility of contamination or rupture within the narratee is at the heart of the previous discussion of the poverty of experience. There, the difference of the lie was needed in order to make present the contaminating power of allegory. However, this structure of contamination can also be seen in the ambiguity of Heidegger's uncanny "I" which experiences the utmost edge of being in being-towards-death (which can only be found in the extreme comportments of anxiety or profound boredom) which is at the same time that which is most Dasein's own. Maurice Blanchot makes a similar case in a parenthetical statement in *The Space of Literature*: "(Heidegger seems to dwell on this ambiguity when he speaks of death as the absolutely proper possibility, by which he means that death is the uttermost possibility, the most extreme thing that happens to the self, but also the 'ownmost,' the most personal event to befall the 'I,' the event where 'I' affirm myself the most and the most authentically.)"[152] This ambiguity of the "I" is indicative of opening a discussion of the possibility of authentic comportment through the experience of the death of an other, which Heidegger rightly (although in his case, negatively) sides with the everyday. Joseph Suglia provides an interesting interpretation of the death of the other in which one's own experience of facticity is based in the other's immortality:

> Although I cannot know my own death, I can experience mortality *via* the other person in its finite existence. Knowledge of the Other as a finite, existing being is at the

---

[151] Ibid., 301.

[152] Maurice Blanchot, *The Space of Literature*, trans. Ann Smock (Lincoln; London: University of Nebraska Press, 1989), 150.

> same time an experience of mourning. What is termed "death" does not refer to the futural non-existence of the self, but to the Other's infinite existence – an existence that contests the self by exposing it to an infinite alterity.[153]

However, the problem with Suglia's argument is that the *basis* of this exposure, whether to one's own impossibility or to the other's immortality, is still rooted in a linguistic "as such." Turning back to Heidegger at this point will help further the discussion, especially by focusing on his reading of care [*Sorge*]. For Heidegger, "Dasein's Being reveals itself as *care*."[154] Care is what Dasein is before any division: "Care, as a primordial structural totality, lies 'before' ['vor'] every factical 'attitude' and 'situation' of Dasein, and it does so existentially *a priori*; this means that it always lies *in* them [...] 'Theory' and 'practice' are possibilities of Being for an entity whose Being must be defined as 'care'."[155] As Alejandro Vallega argues: "being-in-the-world occurs as the event of and possibility for the disclosedness of all beings (*Lichtung*). This occurs out of dasein's 'care' (*Sorge*), out of dasein's being always already in the open with beings in an ontological engagement that gives the question of being its way of being. This care occurs out of dasein's finitude and temporality, i.e., dasein's essential 'being-toward-death.'"[156]

Another way to understand care is to understand what it is not. Care is not "will, wish, addiction, and urge [*Wille, Wunsch,*

---

[153] Joseph Suglia, *Hölderlin and Blanchot on Self-Sacrifice* (New York: Peter Lang, 2004), 76. It should be noted that Jonathan Dollimore calls the inability to experience one's own death a phrase of the "chop-logician": "It has been said that death is not an event in life, that I cannot 'experience' my own death. These are the phrases of the chop-logician: I do know death, and I experience it most acutely as the passing of time and of the death of others in time. Death is co-extensive with the span of the life it terminates – not as the permanent fear of dying, but as the trauma of ceaseless change and loss. To be mortal is to be subject to time," "Death's Incessant Motion," *The Limits of Death: Between Philosophy and Psychoanalysis*, ed. Joanne Morra, Mark Robson and Marquard Smith (Manchester: Manchester University Press, 2000), 80.

[154] Heidegger, *Being and Time*, 227.

[155] Ibid., 238.

[156] Vallega, *Heidegger and the Issue of Space*, 148-9.

Hang und Drang]."[157] Nor is it "concern" [*Besorgen*] or "solicitude" [*Fürsorge*].[158] However, as Nancy points out, "even in the negative mode" of care, "the *with* is affirmed as essential."[159] In *Never Let Me Go* Kathy, in her role as carer, sees to the physical, mental and contextual stability of donor clones during each donation of organs, at least until they complete. In another interpretation, Kathy, who as a clone is removed from the world of reproduction, is an integral part of the welfare state, or the world of *maintenance*, which is, according to Humberto Maturana and Francisco Varela, the definitive characteristic of a cognitive system.[160] As is shown in the next section, Kathy's position provides a reading of what is exemplified in Nancy's contamination of being-with. In other words, Kathy-as-clone is able to enact a reading of the human condition by always already being with the human through the difference of allegory. She is both care and a being-with others. She is able to be in such a "double-bind"[161] because she is in the middle position of poverty.

---

[157] Heidegger, *Being and Time*, 227. Ronell's *Crack Wars: Literature Addiction Mania* is about the capacitiy for addiction to be a fundamental attunement. Or, as she asks elsewhere: "Why is the body prepared for drugs?" *The ÜberReader*, 193.

[158] Heidegger, *Being and Time*, 237.

[159] Nancy, "The Being-with of Being-there," 6.

[160] Humberto Maturana and Francisco Varela, *Autopoiesis and Cognition: The Realization of the Living* (Dordrecht; Boston: D. Reidel Publishing Company, 1980), 13. In order for the clones to be autopoietic living machines they would, as components, also need to be responsible for the construction of their own components, although perhaps they are, in an extended manner, by maintaining the lives of the scientists that breed them: "*An autopoietic machine is a machine organized (defined as a unity) as a network of processes of production (transformation and destruction) of components that produces the components which:* (i) *through their interactions and transformations continuously regenerate and realize the network of processes (relations) that produced them; and* (ii) *constitute it (the machine) as a concrete unity in the space in which they (the components) exist by specifying the topological domain of its realization as such a network*," ibid., 76 (emphasis in original).

[161] Nancy, "The Being-with of Being-there," 6.

2.9 The Double-bind of Being

Kathy illustrates the "double-bind" of being in the first practical example of her job as a carer: an unnamed donor, upon hearing that she had been a student of Hailsham, asks to hear all about it.[162] However, it is not just curiosity that motivates the donor, but rather a desire to replace his memories with hers: "What he wanted was not just to hear about Hailsham, but to *remember* Hailsham, just like it had been his own childhood. He knew he was close to completing and so that's what he was doing [...] the line would blur between what were my memories and what were his" (*NLMG* 5). Before the donor completes he wants to replace, thereby reenacting the tension between symbol, which completes, and allegory, which replaces. Kathy as carer is actually the instrument for this tension, for the donor does not just want to hear a story, he wants his original replaced by a copy. What the donor wants is repositioning, a blurring of the lines. Such a repositioning is part of the allegory of the "what" in what is human, as Ted Toadvine discusses:

> a double-movement is required, which, on the one hand, opens a space for the positive description of the meaning of the animal's world as other than merely a modification of the world of the human subject, while, on the other hand – and this is perhaps the more complicated task – the human

---

[162] Ishiguro, before launching his career as a writer, worked as a social worker for the UK organization the Cyrenians, where he met his wife, Lewis, *Kazuo Ishiguro*, 3. The London Cyrenians Housing organization "is a not for profit, Registered Social Landlord and voluntary sector organisation providing care, support and housing to vulnerable adults offering a full continuum of services to a range of client groups from high care mental health through to floating support for young care leavers. LCH manages a number of supported housing projects in the Royal Borough of Kensington & Chelsea and the London Boroughs of Ealing, Hounslow and Hammersmith & Fulham," *London Cyrenians Housing*, Internet: http://www.londoncyrenians.org.uk, accessed March 24, 2009

as such must be reconceived as neither opposed to nor reducible to the animal.[163]

Toadvine's comments are important for drawing out that what allows Kathy to function as "double" is found both in Heidegger and in the unthought of Heidegger. Kathy and the unnamed donor are in a relationship of being-with, which Heidegger calls unauthentic, although their relationship also takes place at the moment of death, which can cause anxiety, a profound attunement of being. Kathy says of the donor: "He'd just come through his third donation, it hadn't gone well, and he must have known he wasn't going to make it. He could hardly breathe, but he looked towards me and said: 'Hailsham. I bet that was a beautiful place'" (ibid.). Kathy's substitutions come at the moment of the body's proximity to its soon-to-be non-being. Originally just there to help pass the time, "to keep his mind off it all" (ibid.), Kathy, through her role of carer, begins to raise questions of memory and self, since her implementation of memory in the donor happens in conjunction with her passing on of experience to the narratee: "There have been times over the years when I've tried to leave Hailsham behind, when I've told myself I shouldn't look back so much. But then there came a point when I just stopped resisting. It had to do with this particular donor I had once, in my third year as a carer [...]" (*NLMG* 5). Care is at the root of this passing-on because with care being-with is a priori. However, Kathy's coupling of substitution with completion foregrounds the difficulty in reading such a nonrelational conception of care.

2.10 Memory and Self

Kathy imbibes the unnamed donor with memories he never had; this "caretaking" foregrounds how memory is both that which

---

[163] Ted Toadvine, "How Not to be a Jellyfish: Human Exceptionalism and the Ontology of Reflection," *Phenomenology and the Non-Human Animal*, ed., Corinne Painter and Christian Lotz (Dordrecht: Springer, 2007), 41.

isthe basis for autobiographical identity and that which comes from outside the self. Stephen Bernstein says, of Kathy-as-narrator, that "Her medium is memory [...]"[164] As Ishiguro has stated, responding to a question about why memory has been such a recurring theme throughout his work, "I've always liked the texture of memory. I like it that a scene pulled from the narrator's memory is blurred at the edges, layered with all sorts of emotions, and open to manipulation. You're not just telling the reader: 'this-and-this happened.' You're also raising questions like: why has she remembered this event just at this point? How does she feel about it?"[165] Ishiguro seems to be making a connection to the "blurred lines" that Kathy spoke about regarding with the unnamed donor and the "edges" of a scene that is pulled out of memory. These blurred borders, according to Ishiguro, indicate both why this memory was chosen and the feelings associated with the event. In addition, Ishiguro is stating an opposition between a supposedly strictly communicative language and language that comes about and is spurned by memory. A way into an understanding of these connections is to look a bit closer at the language Ishiguro is using in this statement. When he describes the first kind of telling he says that "'this-and-this'" happens. Here Ishiguro is describing a from-one-to-the-other structure. In brief, this kind of language is transitive. In the second kind of telling, attention is turned *back* on to the teller; the speaking of the memory does not move on to something else, like in the first example, but it curls back, telling you more about the speaker, or at least raising questions about the person speaking: why are they doing it and how are they feeling. This second kind of telling is reflexive, which is a structure underpinning the various philosophical ramifications being drawn from Ishiguro's work.

Marie Mills has studied the recursive nature of memory by looking at the relationship between narrative identity and those who were losing that identity near the end of their lives – older people with dementia. According to Mills, a narrative identity "is supported by personal knowledge of one's individual

---

[164] Bernstein, "*Never Let Me Go,*" 139.

[165] *RadomHouse.com*, "A Conversation with Kazuo Ishiguro."

biography or life history."[166] Narrative identity thus presupposes two basic things: "Firstly, that one has accrued a life history and, secondly, that it is remembered."[167] What Mills found in her study was that not only was emotion a powerful ally to memory (the subject of the next chapter) but so was the presence and participation of the interviewer conducting the information-gathering for the study; the importance of the *interviewer* in regards to the *interview* is the crux of reflexivity in Mills' work. As also seen in Kathy's position with the unnamed carer described in the last section, in Mills' study the being-with aspect of interviewee and interviewer, or narrator and narrate/implied reader, was an unsuspected therapeutic aid for both the carer and the degenerating and dying patients:

> as informants became more cognitively impaired by their disease there was an awareness, on the part of the interviewer, that they had bequeathed their narrative to another. It is argued that the sharing of such a narrative, within dementia care, reinforces carer attitudes of respect, understanding and acceptance. In this sense, therefore, the personal narrative of dementia sufferers is never lost. It continues its existence in the form of a valuable resource which can be returned to them, either verbally or non-verbally, during subsequent interactions.[168]

While there is no intention here to compare Kathy's situation or that of the donors to sufferers of dementia, the *being-with* aspect of Mills' study is also important here. Kathy as carer is not only a only a good listener. She also participates in the creation of autobiographical identity by bequeathing her narrative to the donor, and then also, reflexively, acting as a kind of external hard drive for such a memory. In fact, such a participation is not only a part of the creation of memory, but also, as Alphonso Lingis argues, a part of being-with another's death: "We cannot think of the condemned human being without

---

[166] Marie Mills, "Narrative Identity and Dementia: A Study of Emotion and Narrative in Older People with Dementia," *Ageing and Society* 17 (1997), 673.

[167] Ibid., 673-4.

[168] Ibid., 695.

feeling a subterranean yearning to denude ourselves before that person and cover him or her with all we have of kisses and caresses. Erotic passion is the exultation of a moment of time without resources or goal, without past or future."[169] Lingis shows how, once again, being-with is a double-bind in that it has consequences for both parties. In the context of *Never Let Me Go*, both Kathy and the donor enact this double-bind of identity and memory by contaminating each other with their stories. Kathy interacts with the donor to that point where "the line would blur between what were my memories and what were his" (*NLMG* 6). And in fact, this blurring of the lines is not something foreign to the thinking surrounding narration as a part of autobiographical memory, but is rather an integral part of it. As Elaine Reese and Kate Farrant argue in "Social Origins of Reminiscing," "Reminiscing, or talking about the past with others, is a critical part of our autobiographical memories. Autobiographical memories are private and uniquely our own, but they are simultaneously public property because they usually involve other people. A primary function of reminiscing is social."[170] The self is social in the sense that talking about the

---

[169] Alphonso Lingis, "The Last Hours," *The Limits of Death: Between Philosophy and Psychoanalysis*, ed. Joanne Morra, Mark Robson and Marquard Smith (Manchester: Manchester University Press, 2000), 146. Havi Carel also argues for a reading of a being-with others, especially through an experience of death, as a fundamental attunement: "The death of another is also the other's ownmost, non-relational and not to be outstripped. Even if this death is *another's* ownmost, there is still a possibility, not explored in *Being and Time*, of exploring the death of another authentically *as the death of another*. [...] the death of another could also have the ontological significance of uncovering finitude. Although it is not mine, it still opens the possibility of understanding annihilation and loss […] I claim that the death of a loved one calls attention to finitude and limitation as well as my death," *Death in Freud and Heidegger*, 151.

[170] Elaine Reese and Kate Farrant, "Social Origins of Reminiscing," *Autobiographical Memory and the Construction of a Narrative Self: Developmental and Cultural Perspectives*, ed. Robyn Fivush and Catherine Haden (Mahwah: Lawrence Erlbaum Associates, 2003), 29. The tension between the "personal" and the "social" can also be seen in Heidegger's care: "While as human beings we cannot but 'care' about our being, fundamentally and in the sense of *Sorge* outlined in *Being and Time*, so that we cannot fundamentally be indifferent to it, there is nevertheless something about being itself, about its very event, its happening or unfolding, that strangely fails to touch us, that withdraws from us, that remains indifferent to us. We, as human beings, are those who stand and are held in the moment of being's decision, whether authentically

past with others is that which creates the narrative self, and a "blurring" occurs in the strain in maintaining outside and in, as Jerng says of *Never Let Me Go*: "narrative as a relational practice shifts our perspective from life 'taken as a whole' toward personhood as the capacity to relate."[171]

Memory-as-community can also be seen in the exchanges in which the students partook, where they would submit artwork of their own and then pick some from others: "If you think about it, being dependent on each other to produce the stuff that might become your private treasures – that's bound to do things to your relationships" (*NLMG* 16). These "things" done to relationships are the strains felt around the distinction of auto/biography, since every autobiography is also going to contain elements of biography (third-person descriptions of parents, friends and the famous, to begin with); conversely, it is impossible to erase the trace of the silent-narrator from biography.

However, there is a question in the novel regarding whether the students actually "have" a childhood at all. This is the focus of the experiment that was Hailsham – to be treated more humanely than almost any other institution at the time, prompting, at the end of the novel long after the school has been shut down, the ex-head of Hailsham to tell Kathy "we gave you your childhoods" (263). This question about actually "having" a childhood is raised through "the narrator's void of experience regarding infancy. Whereas even fictive autobiographies usually include some information about the birth and parentage of the subject, here we receive nothing, because there is simply no experience to mine."[172] Here McDonald reads what he calls (without explicit reference to Benjamin) this "poverty of

---

knowing or not," William McNeill, "The Time of *Contributions to Philosophy*," *Companion to Heidegger's* Contributions to Philosophy, ed. Charles Scott, Susan Schoenbohm, Daniela Vallega-Neu and Alejandro Vallega (Bloomington; Indianapolis: Indiana University Press, 2001), 134.

[171] Jerng, "Giving Form to Life," 387.

[172] McDonald, "Days of Past Future," 78. There are actually references to "the Infants," an admittedly rather hazy point of time in the past for the clones (*NLMG* 21; 45). On the relationship of the ability to "mine" memory, see Laurence A. Rickels, "Mine," *Terminals*, Internet: http://vv.arts.ucla.edu, accessed March 24, 2009. See also Laurence A. Rickels, "Devil Father Mine," *Lust for Life: On the Writings of Kathy Acker*, ed. Amy Scholder, Carla Harryman and Avital Ronell (London; New York: Verso, 2006).

experience"[173] as an actual engine for being-with in the implied reader's participation in the creation of Kathy's autobiographical self: "the reader is left to make his or her own assumptions about this unseen world, which of course reminds us of our own as it is extrapolated from contemporary moral landscapes."[174] In one sense McDonald reads Kathy's position of identity-giving to the unnamed donor as her ability to provide an allegory for the implied reader; in another the extrapolation he describes seems little more than an illustration of Wimsatt and Beardsley's affective fallacy, which is "a confusion between the poem and its *results* (what it *is* and what it *does*),"[175] meaning here the emotional response of the actual reader. However, McDonald does not take the implications of the contamination he describes to the next step: Kathy, in her flat, everyday poverty of experience, is, in a sense, the same as the implied reader. Instead, at the end of his essay, McDonald keeps things perhaps a bit too neatly separated: "The novel itself represents the symbolic field, where past things surface, and the reader and narrator exist at either side of this landscape, each looking for traces of lives lost."[176]

Instead, Kathy's disrupted position puts her in the perfect position of disrupter itself. As Nancy argued above, it is with the possibility of the rupture, the clinamen of difference, that a fundamental comportment is possible. This rupture is not, however, contrary to the economy of memory, but rather part and parcel of it. As Laurence A. Rickels argues in an essay on the possibility of a thinking machine, such a rupture would need to be built into a thinking mechanical device created from scratch: "The memories of machines should be able to feel this pain of the not-thought, the not-inscribed that still remains to be inscribed. Their rewinding must be a rewounding, too. How else

---

[173] McDonald, "Days of Past Future," 78.

[174] Ibid., 79. Michelle Scalise Sugiyama provides a reading of the evolutionary advantages provided by narrative in "Reverse-Engineering Narrative," *The Literary Animal: Evolution and the Nature of Narrative*, ed. Jonathan Gottschall and David Sloan (Evanston: Northwestern University Press, 2005).

[175] W. K. Wimsatt and Monroe Beardsley, "The Affective Fallacy," *The Verbal Icon*, W. K. Wimsatt (Lexington: University of Kentucky Press, 1967), 7.

[176] McDonald, "Days of Past Future," 82.

could these machines otherwise begin to think? We need machines that suffer from the being-stored, the storedom, of their many memories."[177] Or, as Mark Freeman argues in his essay "Rethinking the Fictive, Reclaiming the Real: Autobiography, Narrative Time and the Burden of Truth," *fiction* is often based on an over-narrow construction of the real based on a linear "clock time," meaning "the time of lines, instants, sequences – that is better applied to the world of *things* than to the world of *people*."[178] Freeman, discussing Michael S. Gazzaniga's *The Mind's Past* (1998), argues that it is not the over-riding structure of cohesiveness that makes humanity what it is, but rather the noise, disruptions and inconsistencies: "The interpreter, the last device in the information chain in our brain, reconstructs the brain events and in doing so makes telling errors of perception, memory, and judgment. The clue to how we are built is buried not just in our marvelously robust capacity for these functions, but also in the errors that are frequently made during reconstruction."[179] Or, as Slavoj Žižek puts it:

> what if failure comes first, what if the "subject" is nothing but the void, the gap, opened by the failure of reflection? What if all the figures of positive self-acquaintance are just so many secondary "fillers" of this primordial gap? Every recognition of the subject in an image or a signifying trait (in short: every identification) already betrays its core; every jubilant "That's me!" already contains the seed of "That's not me!" However, what if, far from consisting in some substantial kernel of identity, inaccessible to reflective recuperation, the subject (as distinct from substance) emerges in this very moment of the failure of identification?[180]

---

[177] Laurence A. Rickels, "Satan and Golem, inc.," *Parallax* 10.1 (2004), 56.

[178] Mark Freeman, "Rethinking the Fictive, Reclaiming the Real: Autobiography, Narrative Time and the Burden of Truth," *Narrative and Consciousness: Literature, Psychology, and the Brain*, Gary Fireman, Ted Mcvay Jr., Owen Flanagan, ed. (New York: Oxford University Press, 2003), 115.

[179] Ibid., 118.

[180] Slavoj Žižek, *The Parallax View* (Cambridge; London: The MIT Press, 2006), 244. Freeman states: "Does this mean that we are distorting our past or

The "failure first" approach is indicative of the importance of poverty for a reading of being-towards-death and authenticity: it is within the failure of the everyday that authenticity might be seen. The focus of the next chapter locates such failure not in the gaining of an experience of facticity but rather the failure-laden body of Tommy.

---

falsifying it or foisting meanings onto it that don't belong there by virtue of the fact that we are not retrieving it accurately? No, not necessarily. What we are doing is remembering and narrating, which means situating the experiences of the past – rewriting them – in accordance with and in relation to what has happened since, as understood and reunderstood from now, the moment of narration," "Rethinking the Fictive, Reclaiming the Real," 123. Greaney, in a discussion of Ilse Aichinger's work, makes a similar claim for the need for a failure of identification in memory in order to allow for the creation of identity: "A reading of Aichinger's texts shows how memories doe not always form identities, and a comparison with some theories of memory reveals that they do not sufficiently reflect on its alienating and productive force or on the provenance and implications of their concepts of identity. Instead of linking memory and identity, we have seen how memory appears in Aichinger's texts as an alienating relation to the unknown," "Estranging Memory in Ilse Aichinger," *The German Quarterly* 80.1 (Winter 2007), 54.

3. Being Poverty

The expression of this snake's face was hideous and fierce; the pupil consisted of a vertical slit in a mottled and coppery iris; the jaws were broad at the base, and the nose terminated in a triangular projection. I do not think I ever saw anything more ugly, excepting, perhaps, some of the vampire bats. I imagine this repulsive aspect originates from the features being placed in positions, with respect to each other, somewhat proportional to those of the human face; and thus we obtain a scale of hideousness.

- Charles Darwin[1]

This chapter focuses on the role of the body and emotions in making what is most human visible. The expression of emotions was the "feelings" element of Ishiguro's statement in the last chapter that Kathy's relationship to memory triggered the reflexive asking "why" and a questioning of the feelings she underwent due to these experiences. This chapter begins with a discussion of Charles Darwin and his study of emotions in humans and non-humans because Darwin was one of the first to "take emotions seriously." Then this chapter continues by reading the role emotions play in *Never Let Me Go*, especially in relation to the figure of Tommy. Darwin is important for a discussion of Tommy because of the way Darwin uses emotions to trace connections between human and non-human animals.[2] However, as can be seen in the epigraph for this chapter, taken from the 1845 *The Voyage of the Beagle*, at times the similarities between the two can be too close, and, like with Madame, feelings of disgust are produced. With his description of the snake's frightening expression, Darwin foreshadows Mori's

---

[1] Darwin, *From So Simple a Beginning*, 105.

[2] Although, as stated above, this in no way implies that the clones are "animals," but rather that Darwin's thought is useful in delineating the "other-than" human.

thought on the uncanny valley, discussed previously. To recap Mori's argument: the uncanny valley describes the gap that opens in a human's ability to relate to what is other-than-human. If the differences between the two are rather large, as between a human and a teddy bear, identification can be quite strong. However, there is a point at which the level of identification drops and horror takes its place. This happens when the similarity between the two entities is incredibly close, although some element is still found to be missing. It is when this single clinamen of the puzzle is absent that a potentially close identification turns into horror. This can be seen in the fearsome aspect of clowns, china dolls, and much humanoid CGI.[3] In this essay's epigraph, the similarity of the snake's face to a human's seems to lead Darwin down into such a hideous valley. However, by locating a discussion of emotions in the body, meaning outside the loaded location of the face, Darwin is able to focus on bringing to light the structure of such fear-of-similarity.

A focus on the body can be seen, for example, in the final words of Darwin's *The Descent of Man*: "Man still bears in his bodily frame the indelible stamp of his lowly origin."[4] While it is clear that not only the face but rather the whole body carries the marks of humanity's evolutionary journey, there seems to be good reason to try and think humanity's relation to other-than-humanity from a non-facial locus. Notwithstanding the uncanny valley, the face has had a rather varied recent history. Emmanuel Levinas, for example, has concentrated much of his work on relations to the other through the face. On the one hand, Levinas sees the face as a location of ethics. In a face-to-face confrontation with someone else, neighbor or enemy, we can see our own mortality reflected in their eyes. By seeing their face in the flesh, we are willing to be open to our responsibility both to

---

[3] At the First International Workshop on Shapes and Semantics held in 2006, Alejandra García-Rojas et al. presented a paper on the relative lack of quality in using motion-capture technology to recreate emotions in CGI scenarios. Instead they propose developing a specific ontology from within the domain of virtual worlds. See Alejandra García-Rojas et al, "Emotional Body Expression Parameters in Virtual Human Ontology," presented at the First International Workshop on Shapes and Semantics, Matsushima, Japan, 2006.

[4] Darwin, *From So Simple a Beginning*, 1248.

the similarities of ourselves in the other and to the other in ourselves. The neighbor becomes visible through the face, and the responsibility of seeing the difference and the similarity of our face and theirs is what constitutes ethics.[5] As Levinas observes in *Otherwise than Being*, "This *way* of the neighbor is a face."[6] On the other hand, such an openness is seen as having its boundaries for Levinas, as readings of his short 1975 essay "The Name of a Dog, or Natural Rights" show. In this essay Levinas states that Bobby, a dog which wandered into the camp where Levinas was interred during World War II, does not treat the humans it meets as a means to an end, and in that sense is "the last Kantian in Nazi Germany."[7] However, Levinas immediately qualifies this view, stating that Bobby is actually "without the brain needed to universalize maxims and drives" in a Kantian manner.[8] While Levinas' comments are more complex than there is space to examine here, it can be said that basically the inability to universalize is due to Bobby's lack of language.[9] As Cary Wolfe observes, while a thinking of the other can put what is taken to be "human" into question, there is still a reassuring difference between human and non-human being which is being asserted: "we retain the certainty that the animal remains the

---

[5] For elaboration see James Mensch, *Hiddenness and Alterity: Philosophical and Literary Sightings of the Unseen* (Pittsburgh: Duquesne University Press, 2005), 161-174.

[6] Emmanuel Levinas, *Otherwise than Being: Or Beyond Essence*, trans. Alphonso Lingis (Pittsburgh: Duquesne University Press, 1998), 88.

[7] Emmanuel Levinas, "The Name of a Dog, or Natural Rights," *Difficult Freedom: Essays in Judaism*, trans. Sean Hand (Baltimore: Johns Hopkins University Press, 1990), 153.

[8] Ibid.

[9] Much has been written on this moment in Levinas' thought. See, for example: H. Peter Steeves, "Lost Dog, or, Levinas Faces the Animal," *Figuring Animals: Essays on Animal Images in Art, Literature, Philosophy, and Popular Culture*, ed. Mary Pollock and Catherine Rainwater (New York; Hampshire: Palgrave, 2005); Lisa Guenther, "*Le flair animal*: Levinas and the Possibility of Animal Friendship," *PhaenEx* 2.2 (2007), 216-238; Karalyn Kendall, "The Face of the Dog: Levinasian Ethics and Human/Dog Co-evolution," *Queering the Non/Human*, ed. Noreen Giffney and Myra Hird (Hampshire: Ashgate, 2008); and John Llewelyn, "Am I Obsessed by Bobby? (Humanism of the Other Animal)," *Emmanuel Levinas: Critical Assessments of Leading Philosophers, Volume IV, Beyond Levinas*, ed. Claire Katz and Lara Trout (London: Taylor & Francis, 2004).

animal."[10] And Agamben locates the difference between human and non-human animals not in language but in speech.[11] Darwin's attention given to the body will lead to a reading of the way Tommy, in counter distinction to the other clones at Hailsham, is able to experience his facticity at a much earlier age than the other students. In some ways Tommy just does not "get it," as can be seen in the scene when deferrals are first discussed in the café outside Norfolk: two older veterans were talking about a former resident of the Cottages that Kathy, Ruth and Tommy did not know. Ruth would laugh vigorously at each reference she did not understand, Kathy would laugh out of politeness, and Tommy "seems to be understanding things even less than me and was letting out hesitant little half-laughs that lagged some way behind" (*NLMG* 148). However, Tommy excels in another area: his uncontrolled emotional outbursts which take place in his wild, flailing body.

---

[10] Wolfe, *Animal Rites*, 62.

[11] "It is a fact whose importance can never be overemphasized in understanding the structure of human language that if a child is not exposed to speech between the ages of two and twelve, his or her potential for language acquisition is definitively jeopardized. Contrary to ancient traditional beliefs, from this point of view man is not the 'animal possessing language', but instead the animal deprived of language and obliged, therefore, to receive it from outside himself," Agamben, "An Essay on the Destruction of Experience," 65. This gap between language and speech is essential for the appearance of the fable, as Agamben argues near the end of his essay: "This is why it is the fable, something which can only be narrated, and not the mystery, which must not be spoken of, which contains the truth of infancy as man's source of origin. For in the fairy tale man is freed from the mystery's obligation of silence by transforming it into enchantment: it is not participation in a cult of knowledge which renders him speechless, but bewitchment. The silence of the mystery is undergone as a rupture, plunging man back into the pure, mute language of nature; but as a spell, silence must eventually be shattered and conquered. This is why, in the fairy tale, man is struck dumb, and animals emerge from the pure language of nature in order to speak. Through the temporary confusion of the two spheres, it is the world of the *open mouth*, of the Indo-European root **bha* (from which the word fable is derived), which the fairy tale validates, against the world of the *closed mouth*, of the root **mu*," ibid., 70. J.M. Coetzee says: "Animals have only their silence left with which to confront us," *The Lives of Animals* (Princeton: Princeton University Press, 1999), 25.

3.1 Darwin's Emotions

By at times turning the investigation of emotion away from the face and onto the body "as a whole," meaning the non-intellectual, or visceral body, it is possible to foreground an experience that is not nonrelational but rather a kind of starting from scratch through the messy barbarism of the autonomic. As John Gray argues:

> Our conscious selves arise from processes in which conscious awareness plays only a small part. We resist this fact because it seems to deprive us of control of our lives. We think of our actions as the end-results of our thoughts. Yet much the greater part of everyone's life goes on without thinking. The sense of conscious agency may be an artefact of conflicts among our impulses. When we know what to do we are hardly conscious of doing it. That does not mean we are ruled by instinct or habit. It means we spend our lives coping with what comes along.[12]

It seems that for Darwin the uncanny valley of the "other's" face was sometimes hard to "cope with," as can be seen not only in his description of the hideous snake used as an epigraph to this chapter but also in his comments on how uncomfortable the "detestable expressions" of "mongrels" made him on his voyage aboard the *Beagle*.[13] However, as seen in Darwin's pioneering work on emotion, *The Expression of the Emotions in Man and Animals*, while the face does occupy a place of prominence, the body is given space in order to disrupt this dominant feature[14] and is actually what enables us to cope in the first place.

---

[12] John Gray, *Straw Dogs: Thoughts on Humans and Other Animals* (London: Granta, 2002), 70.

[13] Darwin, *From So Simple a Beginning*, 116.

[14] While it may seem "odd" to be using Darwin's study of emotions in the early 21st century, his book was far ahead of his times in that very little rigorous study was done on emotions in the years following, and, in many senses, some of the same basic techniques are still being used. Paul Ekman says, in 1999, "It is only in the last 30 years, nearly 100 years after Darwin wrote *The Expression of the Emotions in Man and Animals*, that psychologists finally focused their

First, it should be stated that *The Expression of the Emotions in Man and Animals* does have a thorough relationship with the face. This can be seen in the many photographs of facial expressions reproduced throughout the text.[15] In addition, Darwin had to decide whether the face or the body was more reliable, meaning, was face or body more difficult to control and "fake" emotions with? As Paul Ekman summarizes in "Darwin, Deception, and Facial Expressions," Darwin felt that "people can 'command' the movements of the body when angry (and presumably in any other emotion), and therefore bodily movement, unlike the reliable facial muscles, should be easy to conceal."[16] Ekman calls this the *"face>body leakage hypothesis"*[17] and it is a false assumption because with deception

---

attention on the question of whether expressions are universal or specific to each culture. Darwin's method of showing photographs and asking people to judge the emotion shown in the photograph has been the principle method," Paul Ekman, "Facial Expressions," *Handbook of Cognition and Emotion*, ed. Tim Dalgleish and Mick Power (New York: John Wiley and Sons, 1999), 303-4. See also Antonio Damasio's assessment below. In addition, as Ian McEwan describes, the "universality" of emotions that Darwin posited, due to the fact that they are products of evolution had "until fairly recently....been a reviled notion," "Literature, Science, and Human Nature," *The Literary Animal: Evolution and the Nature of Narrative*, ed. Jonathan Gottschall and David Sloan (Evanston: Northwestern University Press, 2005), 10.

[15] Although, as Alfred Russel Wallace – the "co- inventor" of the theory of natural selection – stated in an early review, "The book is admirably illustrated, both by woodcuts and by a number of photographs representing the most characteristic expressions," "*The Expression of the Emotions in Man and Animals*, By Charles Darwin, M.A., F.R.S., &c. London: Murray. 1872," *Quarterly Journal of Science* 3.37 (1873), 118, these images are actually the cause of much controversy surrounding Darwin's text since a number of them, used as illustrations of facial expressions, were actually photographs of mental patients suffering from a form of muscular dystrophy. These patients' facial muscles were electrically shocked into position through the process of faradization developed by Duchenne de Boulogne: "Duchenne used galvanic currents to innervate the zygomatic major (the main lifting muscle of the upper lips) and demonstrated that by varying the intensity of the current, the corresponding contraction produced different facial expressions from timid smiles to broad grins and the mimicry of loud laughter," Arthur Koestler, *Insight and Outlook: An Inquiry into the Common Foundations of Science Art, and Social Ethics* (New York: Macmillan, 1949), 11.

[16] Paul Ekman, "Darwin, Deception, and Facial Expression," *Annals New York Academy of Sciences* 1000 (2003), 207.

[17] Ibid.

"It is a more complex matter than one source, the face or the body, being a better source of leakage than the other."[18] However, Ekman does go on to argue that because humans receive very little input regarding emotions from another's body when they lie. This is because humans usually do very little to inhibit their body's actions; therefore, the body should be a more reliable indicator of a "true" emotional state. Ekman says: "Because most of us do not get much feedback from others about what our body movements are revealing, we do not learn the need to monitor these actions; and so, we hypothesized, when people lie, they usually do not fine-tune their body actions. If we are right, the body will be a good source of deception clues – exactly the opposite of what Darwin predicted."[19]

However, turning back to Darwin it can be seen that at points the body takes on great importance in *The Expression of the Emotions in Man and Animals*, as seen in his thinking on anger and joy. Here Darwin explores how the experiences of such emotions "naturally lead [...] to energetic movements"[20] of the body. Grief too may lead to wringing of the hands and other "energetic action of some kind."[21] Additionally, sound, which may eventually lead to language,[22] can also be the result of the movements of the autonomic nervous system: "when the sensorium is strongly excited, the muscles of the body are generally thrown into violent action; and as a consequence loud sounds are uttered, however silent the animal may generally be,

---

[18] Ibid.

[19] Ibid. It should be noted that Ekman rightly warns against collating deception with lying, saying that it is a mistake "to presume that concealed emotion is evidence that a person is lying about the topic of interest to the interviewer. We need to be careful to avoid what I have called Othello's error. He mistakenly assumed that Desdemona's expression of fear was the reaction of a woman caught in betrayal. He failed to understand that emotions do not tell you their cause. The fear of being disbelieved looks the same as the fear of being caught," ibid., 218.

[20] Darwin, *From So Simple a Beginning*, 1305.

[21] Ibid.

[22] Steven Mithen argues for the primacy of music over language in the history of the evolution of humans and their ancestors in *The Singing Neanderthals: The Origins of Music, Language, Mind and Body* (London: Weidenfeld and Nicholson, 2005).

and although the sounds may be of no use."[23] From agitation, or what Darwin calls, following the social evolutionist Herbert Spencer, an overflow of "nerve-force," swans' feathers ruffle, dogs' hair becomes erect, and a frog might "blow itself up from vanity and envy until it burst."[24] A more contemporary yet similar reading of the connection between movement, emotion and the generation of "the new" has been undertaken by Mark Hansen under the banner of "affectivity." Hansen argues that:

> Insofar as the sensorimotor nexus of the body opens it to its own indeterminacy, it is directly responsible for the body's constitutive excess over itself. In this respect, motion functions as the concrete trigger of affection as an active modality of bodily action. In what follows, I shall call this "affectivity": the capacity of the body to experience itself as "more than itself" and thus to deploy its sensorimotor power to create the unpredictable, the experimental, the new.[25]

In order to understand the ability of the body to be "more than itself" and cross the border of sensation into action the third of Darwin's three general principles of expression is essential. The first principle states that through habit, expressions are associated with certain states of mind.[26] The second principle is

---

[23] Darwin, *From So Simple a Beginning*, 1307, although it should be remembered that Darwin is arguing for a causal relationship and not an evolutionary one. As Ernst Mayr argues, one of Darwin's great leaps of thought was to move beyond the "Galilean-Cartesian philosophy that everything in nature is due to matter in motion [...] Darwin has liberated us from that philosophy which is so totally unsuitable for biology. Darwin's emphasis on variation, populations, chance, and pluralism started a new era is the philosophy of nature, an insight that can no longer be ignored even though there are still some philosophers who only read each other's writings or the literature of the physical sciences," Ernst Mayr, *Toward a New Philosophy of Biology: Observations of an Evolutionist* (Cambridge; London: Harvard University Press, 1988), 258. Here Mayr is taking aim at John Greene's 1957 *The Death of Adam.*

[24] Darwin, *From So Simple a Beginning*, 1319.

[25] Mark Hansen, *New Philosophy for New Media* (Cambridge: MIT Press, 2006), 7. For an important critique of Hansen's "affectivity," focusing on his excommunication of vision, see N. Katherine Hayles, *Electronic Literature: New Horizons for the Literary* (Notre Dame: University of Notre Dame Press, 2008), 102-120.

[26] This is "*The principle of serviceable associated Habits*," ibid., 1277.

that of antithesis, through which certain expressions result from being the opposite of an expression caused by the first principle (for example, an expression of relief is actually the opposite of an expression of tension).[27] The third principle states that certain expressions are due to the nervous system, stressing that they are actually independent of habit:

> When the sensorium is strongly excited, nerve-force is generated in excess, and is transmitted in certain definite directions, depending on the connection of the nerve-cells, and partly on habit: or the supply of nerve-force may, as it appears, be interrupted. Effects are thus produced which we recognize as expressive. This third principle may, for the sake of brevity, be called that of the direct action of the nervous system.[28]

In addition, Darwin stresses that the relationship between the body and emotions is a two-way street. It is not only that unintentional changes in the body landscape may signal changes in the interior state, *but the moving body is also often necessary a priori in order to experience emotions at all*: "Most of our emotions are so closely connected with their expression, that they hardly exist if the body remains passive – the nature of the expression depending in chief part on the nature of the actions which have been habitually performed under this particular state of the mind [...] So a man may intensely hate another, but until his bodily frame is affected, he cannot be said to be enraged."[29] Darwin restates this idea on the last pages of *Expressions*: "He who gives way to violent gestures will increase his rage; and he who remains passive when overwhelmed with grief loses his best chance of recovering elasticity of mind."[30]

---

[27] This is "*The principle of Antithesis*," ibid.

[28] This is "*The principle of actions due to the constitution of the Nervous System, independently from the first of the Will, and independently to a certain extent of Habit*," ibid.

[29] Ibid., 1400.

[30] Ibid., 1476. Laura Tanner, for example, argues for a physical component to mourning: "Given literature's reliance on words and images, literary representations of grief render the corporeal experience of loss with surprising frequency. Theoretical constructions of the mourning process, however, focus

While it may seem incongruent to use Darwin in an analysis of a literary text, in order to illustrate his theses throughout *Expressions* Darwin himself often gives recourse to literature. Following the quote above, for example, Darwin states that "Even the simulation of an emotion tends to arouse it in our minds,"[31] and he cites Hamlet's monologue from the end of act two, scene two, of Shakespeare's play as support:

> Is it not monstrous that this player here,
> But in a fiction, in a dream of passion,
> Could force his soul so to his own conceit,
> That, from her working, all his visage wann'd;
> Tears in his eyes, distraction in's aspect,
> A broken voice, and his whole function suiting
> With forms to his conceit? And all for nothing![32]

In addition to the many references to Shakespeare, Darwin also looks towards the literary works of Shelley, Coleridge, the Bible, Milton, Dickens, Hamerton, Spenser, Homer, Oliphant, Tennyson, Scott, Somerville, and Aesop. Darwin's thought may also be reflected and tested by looking at contemporary authors who have continued the discussion of the manner in which emotions may connect or relate humankind to other kinds of beings. For example, Philip K. Dick's 1968 *Do Androids Dream of Electric Sheep?* explores the ability of androids, humans, animals and their electric counterparts to feel interspecific empathy.[33] In another example, Mark Haddon's 2003 *The Curious Incident of the Dog in the Night-time* centers around the difficulties an autistic child has when trying to understand all but the most basic emotions of those around him.[34] Haddon's novel ends when the boy, Christopher, is seemingly able to move

---

almost exclusively on psychological definitions of recovery that assume a disembodied subjects," *Lost Bodies: Inhabiting the Borders of Life and Death* (Ithaca: Cornell University Press, 2006), 83-4.

[31] Darwin, *From So Simple a Beginning*, 1476.

[32] Qtd. in ibid.

[33] Philip K. Dick, *Do Androids Dream of Electric Sheep?* (New York: Del Rey Books, 1996).

[34] Mark Haddon, *The Curious Incident of the Dog in the Night-time* (New York: Vintage, 2003).

beyond a like/hate relationship with his father whom he comes to forgive for having killed a dog. However, it happens that both of these examples of emotional diction actually tend to focus on the face. In *Androids*, a test differentiates android and human by detecting autonomic variations of "capillary dilation in the facial area."[35] *The Curious Incident* features a number of illustrations included by the narrator, and both the first and last illustrations of the novel are playful "smiley faces" illustrating facial expressions.[36] However, in Ishiguro's *Never Let Me Go* a powerful reading of the body's relationship to experience is given through the traumatic and volatile corpus of Tommy. In Ishiguro's novel it is specifically the body and not the face that allows one of the main characters to penetrate the boundaries of what is and to begin to experience another world.[37]

3.2 Tommy's Body

At the beginning of the novel Tommy is first encountered through the difficulties he has fitting in with the other students. His problem lies in the way he expresses his emotions. For Tommy, the domain of the face does play a role, for it is there that he is just not able to get it right, as Kathy explains: "Tommy, who was in the stream coming down, had stopped dead on the stairs with a big open smile that immediately irritated me. A few years earlier maybe, if we ran into someone we were pleased to see, we'd put on that sort of look. But we were thirteen by then, and this was a boy running into a girl in a really public situation" (*NLMG* 13).[38] It is not that Tommy is

---

[35] Dick, *Do Androids Dream of Electric Sheep?*, 46.

[36] Haddon, *The Curious Incident of the Dog in the Night-time*, 2-3; 220.

[37] Lingis actually extends the face "down the whole length of the body" because it is the whole body which gesticulates, Alphonso Lingis, "Animal Body, Inhuman Face," *Zoontologies: The Question of the Animal*, ed. Cary Wolfe (Minneapolis; London: University of Minnesota Press, 2003), 180-1.

[38] In *The Remains of the Day* the attempts of the butler Stephens to express himself normally only serve to highlight his constructedness: "I put down my tray and seated myself – in an appropriate posture – on the armchair Mr Cardinal

less "natural" than the other students, but rather that he is less able to fake authenticity. Kathy says that when they were thirteen they would "put on" the look Tommy was "using" at the moment. However, the statement implies, it is not that now they would not put on any face, but rather their skill set has increased.

Tommy's lack of skill comes to the fore in the artwork the students have to make. Although Kathy gives few details, Tommy's drawing of "an elephant standing in some tall grass" (19) is seen as an obvious sign of his immaturity and lack of artistic merit. Although at first Tommy is able to pass his drawings off as "a feeble joke" (20), a problem arises when these drawings are taken as accurate reflections of Tommy's ability; the childish work is actually praised by Miss Geraldine, a guardian teaching art, as if it were a commendable effort: "That was how the resentment started" (ibid.).

Tommy expresses his resentment through his body rather than his words. Tommy's "resentful" body can be seen when he is being picked last for a game of football:

> Tommy burst into thunderous bellowing [...] Then he began to scream and shout, a nonsensical jumble of swear words and insults [...] He was just raving, flinging his limbs about, at the sky, at the wind, at the nearest fence post. Laura said he was maybe "rehearsing his Shakespeare." Someone else pointed out how each time he screamed something he'd raise one foot off the ground, point it outwards, "like a dog doing a pee." (9-10)

In his tantrum Tommy is associated with both Shakespeare and a urinating dog. Instead of reading this as a snide comment on Shakespeare (or the dog) this collocation indicates that Tommy is being more-than himself in these tantrums, both in the direction of extreme creativity (although the reference to Shakespeare is probably aimed at over-dramatic acting) and an animal nature. As such, this scene locates Tommy in the "middle" position of poverty. And this is not his only outburst as a young student:

---

was indicating," Ishiguro, *The Remains of the Day* (London: Faber and Faber, 1999), 231.

> There were more temper tantrums, like the time Tommy was supposed to have heaved over two desks in Room 14, spilling all the contents on the floor, while the rest of the class, having escaped on to the landing, barricaded the door to stop him coming out. There was the time Mr Christopher had had to pin back his arms to stop him attacking Reggie D. during football practice [...] (14)

The question that then presents itself is what was at the root of these tantrums? It was argued above that resentment towards being assumed that a lack of creativity was the best Tommy could do was the source. This can be confirmed in that a more "positive" expression of creativity is at the root of what allows him, eventually, to get the tantrums under control. Eventually Tommy has a talk with Miss Lucy, and: "'What she said was that if I didn't want to be creative, if I really didn't feel like it, that was perfectly all right. Nothing wrong with it, she said'" (23). It is after this discussion that Tommy calms down, at least until the end of the novel. However, there is another line of thought that is raised by Tommy's interaction with Miss Lucy in this scene, and that is of donations. In this same conversation she tells Tommy that she is upset because, as Tommy reports to Kathy, "'She said we weren't being taught enough, something like that'" (29). Kathy asks *about what*, and Tommy answers "'about *us*. What's going to happen to us one day. Donations and all that'" (ibid.). However, Kathy says they have already been taught *about that*, and they let the topic drop, although not without raising the connection between Tommy's tantrums, poverty (lack of creativity/soul) and a knowledge of one's facticity. The latter can be seen when Kathy states that it was after Tommy confided in her about his talk with Miss Lucy that "we started off our whole thing of wondering and asking questions about ourselves" (72).[39]

After this conversation with Miss Lucy, Tommy "matures" and is able to control his body; however, the status of his body-first relationship to facticity resurfaces on a car trip with Kathy

---

[39] Tommy also later regresses after Miss Lucy tells him that her previous statement, about it being okay that he was not creative, was wrong, and that the others had been right all along, that creativity really was important (105).

at the end of the book. At this point Kathy and Tommy have become lovers, although this relationship too is coming to a close since Tommy is near death because of his donations. It is after Tommy has asked Kathy to stop being his carer, so that she will not have to see his last stages of decay, that his body breaks out once more. Kathy pulls the car over and Tommy runs out into a field; Kathy follows: "Tommy's figure, raging, shouting, flinging his fists and kicking out [...] He tried to shake me off, but I kept holding on" (269). After this outburst, Kathy decides that the movements of Tommy's body have something to do with his knowledge about their fate. Tommy apologizes for his behavior, and he asks Kathy what she is thinking: "'I was thinking,' I said, 'about back then, at Hailsham, when you used to go bonkers like that, and we couldn't understand it. We couldn't understand how you could ever get like that. And I was just having this idea, just a thought really. I was thinking maybe the reason you used to get like that was because at some level you always *knew*'" (270). Tommy responds: "'But that's a funny idea. Maybe I did know, somewhere deep down. Something the rest of you didn't'" (ibid.). Keeping in mind Darwin's thought on how at times the movement of the body comes first and is in fact always already necessary for emotions to be experienced, a question may now be asked: How does Tommy's emotionally attuned body allow him to become aware of knowledge that remains hidden, at least on an explicit level, from the others at his school?

Paul Weiss' thought in *Being and Other Realities* will help on this count. Although Weiss criticizes Darwin for anthropomorphically taking humans as the measure and then seeing animals as differing from humans only in degree,[40] his thought on the body-emotion/emotion-body continuum is actually a combination of Darwin's first and third general principles of expression. Weiss argues that emotions spring from

---

[40] Paul Weiss, *Being and Other Realities* (Chicago; La Salle: Open Court, 1995), 48. Weiss restates his claim further on: "It is questionable whether even the most advanced of apes understands why it seeks to mate or to sleep. None knows that it has a grandparent or grandchild, or that what has always occurred might not occur again. Such apes are best understood, not by viewing them as truncated humans or as wholly humanized, but as occupants of nature, living in a part of it not entirely separable from the rest," (ibid., 131).

within the movement between body and person, although the dominance of either (in Darwin's language, habit or the nervous system) is in flux:

> The claim that, because one was fearful, one began to run, is not to be separated from the counterclaim that, because one runs, one becomes fearful. Sometimes we run mainly because we are afraid, and sometimes we are afraid mainly because we run. At neither time is either the fear or the running entirely cut off from the others. Emotions are the outcome of meetings of person and organism, with an emphasis sometimes on the one and sometimes on the other.[41]

What is important, but underdeveloped, in Weiss' thought here is that while maintaining a rigorous separation between the humanized world, nature and the cosmos, it is emotions that allow a being to access other types of reality, becoming an important part of what Weiss calls the Dumanic-Rational.[42] Briefly, Weiss' concept of the Dumanic-Rational is a permanently tangled mix between "vibrancies, the nondeducible, the unpredictable, and the vague"[43] and rationality. This combination allows one to know that there is a world beyond the humanized one because we are never wholly located in just the person or the organism: "Sometimes it is more accurate to say that our hearts beat faster because we are frightened, and sometimes that we are frightened because our hearts beat faster. The beating of the heart is here not simply the beating that some

---

[41] Ibid., 108. Without intending to oversimplify, this differentiation may also be thought along the lines of genotype/phenotype or proximate/ultimate causes.

[42] Martin Buber makes a similar statement regarding the need to experience the construction of the humanized world rather than the beginnings of some kind of consciousness: "It is not sensible to try to discover when and how a certain species of life, instead of being content like the rest with the perception of things and conditions, began to perceive its own perceiving as well. The only way is to consider, in all its paradox and actuality, the category of being characterized by the name of man, in order to experience its ground and its beginning," *The Knowledge of Man: A Philosophy of the Interhuman*, trans. Maurice Friedman and Ronald Smith (New York: Harper Torchbooks, 1965), 59.

[43] Weiss, *Being and Other Realities*, 170.

machine might record, but the beating of a heart in a person who is frightened."[44]

While Weiss begins to indicate how the body might go beyond itself, he actually seems to assume that we are conscious of our emotions all the time. In fact, he insists that what differentiates humans in their humanized world from animals in their natural one is that humans have a purpose or a goal they can set *as such*, in counter distinction to an animal's purposiveness, meaning its reactive engagement with the environment[45] (von Uexküll's *Umwelt*). Such a line of demarcation has been investigated here through a reading of the poverty of the self, meaning that traditional descriptions of a poverty of being have actually been paramount in the making-visible of the poverty of what has traditionally been called the human condition itself; as Krell puts it: "The animal cannot ask about the sun *as* sun, Heidegger repeats over again, as though this is what the human sun-worshipper ever does."[46] This thesis translates into this discussion of emotions in that in the realm of emotions we are often not conscious of what we do. As Antonio Damasio argues in *The Feeling of What Happens: Body, Emotion and the Making of Consciousness*, "It is through feelings, which are inwardly directed and private, that emotions, which are outwardly directed and public, begin their impact on the mind [...] There is, however, no evidence that we are conscious of *all* our feelings, and much to suggest that we are not,"[47] and the same is perhaps true for emotions.

Damasio develops his thesis through a discussion of what he calls the "good guy/bad guy experiment." In this experiment, the subject David, who has suffered extensive temporal lobe damage, has no ability to learn new facts, and therefore cannot recognize new acquaintances. However, Damasio learned that David was able to develop a preference between the doctors that

---

[44] Ibid., 221. Daniel Dennett has a similar point of view in *Consciousness Explained* (Boston; Toronto; London: Little, Brown and Company, 1991), 45.

[45] Weiss, *Being and Other Realities*, 148. Mayr specifically avoids such a distinction though his discussion of an organism's "programs," *Toward a New Philosophy of Biology*, 49.

[46] Krell, *Daimon Life*, 116.

[47] Antonio Damasio, *The Feeling of What Happens: Body, Emotion and the Making of Consciousness* (London: Vintage, 2000), 36.

treated him. Damasio's experiment consisted of sending David to three new doctors: one who treated him brusquely, one indifferently, and one kindly. When asked which doctor he would like to visit, David could not remember having met any of them before, but nevertheless he did consistently pick out the kind doctor as his preference.[48] Damasio argues that the body, in David's case, unconsciously participated in an emotional learning process. "I am not suggesting that *he* himself would have chosen to do so deliberately, but rather that his *organism*, given its available design and dispositions, would have homed in on such behavior. He would have developed a tropism for the good guy as well as an antitropism for the bad guy [...]"[49]

Damasio argues that Darwin's thought on the importance of emotion has been virtually ignored[50] and he seems to be influenced by Darwin in that Damasio thinks it is important how "emotions are *about* the life of an organism, its body to be precise, and their role is to assist the organism in maintaining life."[51] This helps explain the role of Tommy's body. Tommy's organism could "home in" on experience that the mind was unable to comprehend. As such, Tommy's body was the externalization of an unconscious reaction to facticity. Tommy's organism was able to develop a tropism for signals picked up from the school's staff about the future organ donations the clones were to make and to translate these signals into expression. Tommy is an example of Darwin's third general principle of expression, "that of the direct action of the nervous system."

However, the next question should be: Why is Tommy the locus of such experience which the others are seemingly denied? Perhaps the answer lies in the *unconscious* nature of his tantrums. The rest of the clones are surrounded by *trying*, meaning trying to be creative, or to have the right facial expression, for example. Tommy is a figure that fails at trying,

---

[48] Damasio, *The Feeling of What Happens*, 43-47.

[49] Ibid., 46. Damasio's use of the subjunctive in this quote is due to imagining what would have continued if the experiment had been carried on for a more extended period of time.

[50] Ibid., 39.

[51] Ibid., 51.

and so he has to rely on another kind of experience, one that he has not learned, meaning the tropisms his body was able to "unconsciously" acquire.

Unconscious expressions that come about in a body-first manner are perhaps one of the strongest avenues along which to connect with others, other knowledge, and other worlds. While keeping in mind, as Weiss argues, that what we experience is always and forever humanized, there are still bodily expressions that escape the master codes of our intelligence, and one of Darwin's great contributions is to trace a number of the coordinates of these expressions. It is autonomic expressions in both other humans and other-than-humans that allow such connections to be forged.[52] Such "purposeless" expressions can work as connectors between beings, as Darwin observes in *Expressions*: "Under a transport of Joy or vivid Pleasure, there is a strong tendency to various purposeless movements, and to the utterance of various sounds. We see this in our young children, in their loud laughter, clapping of hands, and jumping for joy; in the bounding and barking of a dog when going out to walk with his master; and in the frisking of a horse when turned out into an open field."[53]

While caution must be taken in seeing humans as the measure and then considering others as differing only in degree, the underlying argument here is that, as Damasio puts it, "the basic mechanisms underlying emotion do not require consciousness [...]"[54] It is this autonomic aspect of emotions that underlies their ability to transport a subject out and beyond its world. What should not be ignored in this process is that such

---

[52] This is in opposition to a statement by Lingis on the validity of visceral systems in the perception of others: "The moment this stream of behaviors breaks up into discordancy it begins to appear to me as a succession of mere spasms, and I lose the sense of there being an ego-identity immanent in them. And this body begins to appear to me as a pseudo-organism, a cadaver twitching due to local tensions, or a contraption, a department-store dummy, or robot gone haywire," *Phenomenological Explanations* (Dordrecht: Martinus Nijhoff Publishers, 1986), 87. My argument is that it is exactly the "local tensions" that allow for a perception of others. However, Lingis does argue for the validity of locality elsewhere, for example in regard to the Nazca lines of Peru in *Trust* (Minneapolis: University of Minnesota Press, 2004), 54-5.

[53] Darwin, *From So Simple a Beginning*, 1302-3.

[54] Damasio, *The Feeling of What Happens*, 42.

autonomic aspects do need to be observed, and tested, and named by a humanized subject. However, instead of working merely to criticize or limit the anthropomorphism found in someone like Darwin, perhaps a more radical question to ask is what makes anthropomorphism possible in the first place. Damasio offers a clue – movement: "The reason why you can anthropomorphize the chip [on a video screen] or an animal so effectively is simple: emotion, as the word indicates, is about movement, about externalized behavior, about certain orchestrations of reactions to a given cause, within a given environment."[55] Instead of reading a call to ethics in the human-only logos in the face of the other, perhaps it is the reflection of the Tommy-like autonomic paroxysms in the body's movements that allow for an experience of what is outside one's self.

3.3 Deterritorialization

The reason that Tommy's emotional experience is powerful is because it allows him to experience something that would be otherwise closed off to him; whether in the direction of Shakespeare or urinating dogs, what he is able to experience can be described as his facticity, meaning the "limits" of his own being. While Weiss calls this ability of experiencing "more" the Dumanic-Rational, a more familiar development is Gilles Deleuze and Félix Guattari's discussion under the banner of deterritorialization. For Deleuze and Guattari, deterritorialization is a removal from embedded patterns and an exploration of other instantiations that an object has the potentiality to become. Each instantiation is then another territorialization, which can then be deterritorialized again, moving even further from the "original" object or instantiation.[56] An early and well-known example that

---

[55] Ibid., 70.

[56] Gilles Deleuze and Félix Guattari, *A Thousand Plateaus: Capitalism and Schizophrenia*, trans. Brian Massumi (Minneapolis; London: University of Minnesota Press, 2005), 10. This pattern is the "rhizome."

Deleuze and Guattari provide for this in *A Thousand Plateaus* is of the relationship between an orchid and a wasp:

> An orchid deterritorializes by forming an image, a tracing of a wasp; but the wasp reterritorializes on that image. The wasp is nevertheless deterritorialized, becoming a piece of the orchid's reproductive apparatus. But it reterritorializes the orchid by transporting its pollen. Wasp and orchid, as heterogeneous elements, form a rhizome. It could be said that the orchid imitates the wasp, reproducing its image in a signifying fashion (mimesis, mimicry, lure, etc.). But this is true only on the level of the strata – a parallelism between two strata such that a plant organization on one imitates an animal organization on the other. At the same time, something else entirely is going on: not imitation at all but a capture of the code, surplus value of code, an increase in valence, a veritable becoming, a becoming-wasp of the orchid and a becoming-orchid of the wasp. Each of these becomings brings about the deterritorialization of one term and the reterritorialization of the other; the two becomings interlink and form relays in a circulation of intensities pushing the deterritorialization even further.[57]

Deterritorialization is not the creation of something new but rather "a capture of the code" or a making-visible of the "surplus value of the code" that is already a part of the object in question. The interaction of two elements can result in a "widening," of an increase of experience. What such becoming-others indicates is the greater "plane of consistency"[58] "beneath" such individual instantiations:

> The plane of consistency [...] is in no way an undifferentiated aggregate of unformed matters, but neither is it a chaos of formed matters of every kind. It is true that on the plane of consistency there are no longer forms or substances, content or expression, respective and relative deterritorializations. But beneath the forms and substances

[57] Ibid.

[58] Ibid., 70.

> of the strata the plane of consistency [...] *constructs continuums of intensity*: it creates continuity for intensities that it extracts from distinct forms and substances.[59]

What is important here is that deterritorialization is a movement from one intensity (or instantiation) to another along the plane of consistency. This can be seen in the interaction between the orchid and the wasp, each moving along the plane of consistency to explore the "surplus value of the code" that resides within them by interacting with each other. This movement can also be seen, for example, in the change of fossilization that soft tissue underwent around 500 million years ago, forming bone for the first time. Bone, however, still resides on the plane of consistency with its mineral past, making it the part of the animal body most easily petrified, thus allowing for a fossil record to exist.[60]

---

[59] Ibid. In mathematical terms, Deleuze and Guattari are referring to the plane space of Henri Poincaré where attractors would be intensities. See Manuel DeLanda, *Intensive Science and Virtual Philosophy* (London; New York: Continuum, 2004), 14-15. Gary Genosko develops the thought of deterritorialization through the critique Deleuze and Guattari offer regarding Konrad Lorenz's *On Aggression*, which argues for the coloring of certain poster-colored coral fish as a sign of aggression: "From this material Deleuze and Guattari extract their counter-reading that poster-colouring is not tied to a specific function (aggression) which they identify with transitoriness, but rather, with temporal constancy and spatial range: the day-time coloration of these fish (which changes during sleep) and the visibility of the colours at long distances," "A Bestiary of Territoriality and Expression: Poster Fish, Bower Birds, and Spiny Lobsters," *A Shock to Thought: Expressions After Deleuze and Guattari*, ed. Brian Massumi (London: Routledge, 2002), 49.

[60] Manuel DeLanda, *A Thousand Years of Nonlinear History* (New York: Zone Books, 2005), 26-7. Michel Serres offers another illustration of this plane, although he does not reference it explicitly as such, when he states that he no longer sees any difference between himself and a bee regarding "work": "Work flows from me like honey, like the spider's web. I don't know with what external order I nourished this second order; my body is transformer of itself, but also a transformer for this linguistic wax, a long secretion come from my five fingers; I work hard, I don't work at all; it comes easily, just like what an animal does when it follows its own instinct in doing this or that. I am a bee or a spider, a tree. I no longer can tell the difference between work and secretion," *The Parasite*, trans. Lawrence Schehr (Minneapolis; London: University of Minnesota Press, 2007), 86-7.

Deleuze and Guattari term the movement along the continuum of consistency "nomadic." In *A Thousand Plateaus* the concept of the nomad is set against a reading of the migrant: "The nomad is not at all the same as the migrant; for the migrant goes principally from one point to another, even if the second point is uncertain, unforeseen, or not well localized. But the nomad goes from point to point only as a consequence and as a factual necessity; in principle, points for him are relays along a trajectory."[61] However, it should be kept in mind that for Deleuze and Guatarri the territory is absolutely essential for deterritorialized nomadic being; they specify a nomadic relation *to* the territory: "The nomad has a territory; he follows customary paths; he goes from one point to another; he is not ignorant of points (water points, dwelling points, assembly points, etc.)."[62]

Ishiguro's novel also calls out the surplus of code within us already in the form of a making-visible of the poverty of the human condition. This poverty is within our instantiation already, and not along a different plane of being. This is the point of the clones in the novel being "so human," or even, as Ishiguro was quoted stating above, more-than human, although he coupled the more-than-human of the clones with their being drip-fed information regarding their factiticy. But it is exactly in

---

[61] Deleuze and Guattari, *A Thousand Plateaus*, 380.

[62] Ibid. In addition, Deleuze and Guattari develop a two-way street regarding the "movement" of the nomad: "the nomad is one who does not depart, does not want to depart, who clings to the smooth space left by the receding forest... Of course the nomad moves, but while seated, and he is only seated while moving," *A Thousand Plateaus*, 381. Jean Baudrillard makes a similar statement: "Animals maintain the nomadic way of life in the very heart of domesticity. Motionless, in their thousands, on the sandy slopes, the arid pasturelands. Yes, animals know no boundaries. The sterile, patriarchal expanses are their world. It is they who order the world of men," *Cool Memories*, trans. Chris Turner (London; New York: Verso, 1990), 28. This thought could also be construed as "Bakhtinian," if taken in a strict sense, since "It is in fact all to easy to deploy such characteristically Bakhtinian terms as *heteroglossia*, or *chronotope*, if only as incantations to dignify already existing analytical habits that have not been affected by Bakhtin's thought in any meaningful way. What is difficult about Bakhtin is the demand that his was of thinking makes on our way of thinking, the demand to change the basic categories that most of us use to organize thought itself," Katerina Clark and Michael Holquist, *Mikhail Bakhtin* (Cambridge; London: Harvard University Press, 1984), 8.

the clones' "weakness" that they make "us" visible. Or put another way, it is the clones' all-too-obvious resemblance to us that makes us visible. In a sense *Never Let Me Go* follows Alain Badiou's critique of what he sees as an underdeveloped aspect of the plane of consistency in which the human is seen as already divided itself: for Badiou humans are "the univocity of the actual as a pure multiple,"[63] or as developed above along with Nancy, they are being-singular-plural.[64] However, by focusing on the "surplus value of the code" already installed, Deleuze and Guattari's model does prove a valuable means for understanding the ability of the human to make visible an aspect of itself usually ascribed to poverty. The plane of consistency and poverty are related in their immanence, or put in other words, in their self-reflexivity. As Žižek argues, self-reflexivity is the "fundamental paradox" of the plane of consistency: "the implication of his [Deleuze's] absolute immanentism, of his rejection of any transcendence, is precisely that an effect can transcend its cause, or – another aspect of the same problematic – that relations are external to the objects that relate to each other [...]"[65] Žižek continues: "The Deleuzian excess of relations is thus the space of freedom as that of *reflexive* relations, of relating to relations – the excess over the linear network of causal relations, the way the subject relates to its conditions and

---

[63] Alain Badiou, *Deleuze: The Clamor of Being*, trans. Louise Burchill (Minneapolis; London: University of Minnesota Press, 2000), 52. However, Daniel Smith argues that the difference between Deleuze and Badiou lies elsewhere: "it is enough to establish the point that the *differend* between Badiou and Deleuze concerns, not the distinction between the One and the Multiple, as Badiou argues, but rather the more profound distinction between two types of multiplicity, which correspond to the distinction between axiomatics and problematics (or 'major' and 'minor' science)," "Badiou and Deleuze on the Ontology of Mathematics," *Think Again: Alain Badiou and the Future of Philosophy*, ed. Peter Hallward (London; New York, Continuum, 2004), 88.

[64] Calarco argues: "There is not *one* difference that separates 'The Human' from 'The Animal' with respect to death any more than there is a *single* experience of death common to all animals as such or all humans as such. Such would be the conclusion reached by way of the 'logic' of *différance*, which insists on multiplication and complication where essentialist gestures have homogenized, reduced, or screened out important differences," "On the Borders of Language and Death," 24.

[65] Slavoj Žižek, *Organs Without Bodies: On Deleuze and Consequences* (New York; London: Routledge, 2004), 111.

causes (assuming or rejecting them)."[66] Such a movement foregrounds the structure of relation itself, one of the most powerful aspects of Ishiguro's novel: "To think of Ishiguro's novel in terms of the capacity to relate ultimately disrupts the opposition between clone and human on which narratives of clones' individuation rely."[67] Or, as Veyret argues: "Each novel from Ishiguro contains both the creation and the end of a world."[68]

3.4 Qualifying for Deterritorialization

One of the ways that the plane of consistency is made visible is through Tommy's emotional outbursts. This happens because emotions allow him to move beyond the logocentricity of the face and into the experience of the body, which is also a way for him to experience a removal from his own territory, a deterritorialization, and experience that which is "proper" to him, his own facticity, or the non-being of his being. However, as Deleuze and Guattari argue, each deterritorialization involves a reterritorialization, and Tommy is soon back in the world of Hailsham, stuck with the others in the everyday struggles of student life. It is only at the end of the novel that Tommy's visceral paroxysms make a return, allowing once again for the appearance of an awareness of his own death to come forth,

---

[66] Ibid., 112. Žižek echoes Espen Aarseth's classic reading of a nonlinear literature in which a whole is no longer assumed to exist somewhere beneath the fragmented parts. See Espen Aarseth, "Nonlinearity and Literary Theory," *Hyper/Text/Theory*, ed. George Landow (Baltimore: Johns Hopkins University Press, 1994). However, *Never Let Me Go* is not nonlinear, at least in the way Aarseth argues it. For example, in the scene where Kathy tells the story of the Judy Bridgewater tape, the story jumps around from the sales to smoking to a student asking a teacher about smoking and then being "tortured" (a scene presented earlier, but without context), then a discussion about why no one asked about why they were too special to smoke and then a line break before the topic of the tape is taken up again. This is not nonlinear because although jumbled, there is a linear order assumed to be running underneath the events.

[67] Jerng, "Giving Form to Life," 390.

[68] Veyret, *Kazuo Ishiguro*, 136 (translation mine).

allowing Tommy to again become a "*flesh-witness*."[69] However, before Tommy's emotional outbursts return, he and Kathy, who have become lovers, decide to try for a "deferral." There have been rumors of deferrals floating around the lives of the clones (at least with those who did not attend Hailsham), but it is on a trip to the lost corner of Norfolk that the topic becomes explicit. On this trip Rodney, the older boy who had spotted the "possible" model for Ruth, and his partner Chrissie ask Ruth, Kathy and Tommy about the possibility of a "deferral," meaning that there were rumors that a couple, if they could *prove* that they were really in love, could apply to have their time as a donor deferred a year or two, allowing them to live in the Cottages together. Chrissie describes what she believes to be true:

> "It wasn't easy, but just sometimes they'd let you do it. So long as you could convince them. So long as you *qualified*." [...] "What they said," Chrissie continued, "was that if you were a boy and a girl, and you were in love with each other, really, properly in love, and if you could show it, then the people who run Hailsham, they sorted it out for you. They sorted it out so you could have a few years together before you began your donations." [...] "Three years just to themselves, because they could prove they were properly in love." (*NLMG* 150-1)

The clones have a plan for escape; but this is not a fleeing across borders, or a way "outside" of themselves, but it is rather the *passing of a test*. While tests are often seen as means through which prevailing power structures can reinforce codes through positive backwash (when the expectations of a test are brought into a classroom in order to prepare students for that test), *disruptive* elements within testing have been developed by Ronell in *The Test Drive*, in which the final chapter is entitled "Testing Your Love." However, an initial epigraph to Ronell's book encapsulates the disruptive thread running throughout the text: "Even in its most hallucinatory conditions of satisfaction,

[69] Toker and Chertoff, "Reader Response and the Recycling of Topoi in Kazuo Ishiguro's *Never Let Me Go*," 173.

the ego senses that something may be missing; it becomes insecure and must start up the machinery of testing."[70] Testing is one manner of covering up a lack of security, or put another way – passing the test is a manner of keeping poverty at bay, although when viewed another way, testing is also that which makes such poverty visible, and as such disrupts a number of "given" human traits:

> Their desire to live, one of the many topics they [the clones] silently place out of bounds in order to be able to carry on, takes the form of a belief in the possibility of a deferment for those who can "prove" that they are in love. This myth piggybacks on a myth that sustained them in their earlier childhood, when they were told that they could demonstrate their uniqueness through their artwork, their "creativity," as it is repeatedly called.[71]

Seaman, in the quote above, connects the "myth" of deferrals to that of creativity. Both of these myths "sustained" the students, which means that as lies they function to actually make the students "better humans." Tommy's response to the myth of creativity is a physical outburst. His response is the same to the myth of deferrals, but only after it is explained to Kathy and Tommy that they never have existed. What Tommy highlights in both of these situations is, as Summers-Bremner describes below, that whereas "giving ourselves to fiction" is a realization of humanity, when this fiction is taken away what remains is facticity:

> The discomfort we find at the end of *Never Let Me Go* arises partly because this exchange of lacks has placed us in the position of harbouring the inhuman – the stand-in for the unavailable perspective of the animal – specifically as the symptom of our death. In giving ourselves to the fiction, we have identified with Kathy as though she were like we are,

---

[70] Avital Ronell, *The Test Drive* (Urbana; Chicago: University of Illinois Press, 2005), n.p.

[71] Seaman, "Becoming More (than) Human," 266.

> only to find that her not being so is related to our greatest human lack.[72]

While Summers-Bremner comes very close to stating my main argument, she diverges from it in her use of the term "related" in the last sentence. Summers-Bremner states that through a close identification with Kathy we find that she differs from "us" in some crucial manner. It is this difference that is *related* to our lack. Instead, I would offer that this difference is what *makes* this lack *visible*. While perhaps seeming like a minor difference at first, *related* sets up the coordinates of affinity, while *making visible* is meant to foreground the work that an other such as Kathy does for us.

The making visible of poverty is brought about through the tests the clones face in England's lost corner, which include: asking about the possibility of proving your love in the hope of deferral; proving Rodney's guess that he has found Ruth's "possible" (also testing whether there are any "possibles" at all); testing the loyalty of the students to pre-established rules of behavior, to which only Kathy is inclined to follow;[73] testing whether people recognize who or rather what they are on the streets of a city (they do not); and finally, a test of the bond between Tommy and Ruth (who are currently a couple) when pitted against that of Tommy and Kathy, as they search for and eventually find a copy of the tape containing the song "Never Let Me Go" which Kathy no longer had since it had gone missing in Hailsham. This is a lot of testing, and it will be seen that so much testing cannot but cast a large net of doubt:

> For the reader, the clones' experiences and responses to those experiences regularly confirm their humanity, but within the posthuman world of the narrative, their humanity must be proven. For the clones – as they believed it is for the supposedly more "real" humans – to be human is to have

---

[72] Summers-Bremner, "'Poor Creatures,'" 158.

[73] For example, in the café outside Norfolk, Chrissie and Robbie are deciding whether to visit a carer, which is not permitted. Kathy reminds the others that they are not supposed to visit this carer, and Ruth says: "'Kathy *hates* to be naughty. So we'd better not go and visit him'" (*NLMG* 148).

> an interior self that is able to express what it feels, and that feels love in particular. The clones who are the central figures of the novel are shown, through the narrative, to meet that requirement as fully as any humans. However, the more "real" and biologically enhanced humans are revealed to be lacking in the humanity expressed in so many ways by their scientific offspring.[74]

However, what Seaman does not directly state is that it is *because* the clones "meet" the requirements of what is human *that* the lack of such requirements in "us" becomes visible. Or to put it in other words: "The act of obtaining knowledge of the real is a light that always somewhere casts shadows."[75]

This quote from Ronell actually points to the real reason that Madame cried when she saw Kathy dancing to "Never Let Me Go" and holding the pillow: it was because Kathy simultaneously stood for the need to keep the horrors of human cloning in the dark and the bright and cruel light of science that blazes on the disease-free "normals," as Miss Emily explains in the final confrontation between her, Madame, Kathy and Tommy. Miss Emily describes the days before Hailsham: "'Before that, all clones – or *students*, as we preferred to call you – existed only to supply medical science. In the early days, after the war, that's largely all you were to most people. Shadowy objects in test tubes'" (*NLMG* 256).[76] But the goal of Hailsham was to change that, to show that the students had souls, that they were capable of *experience*. The making-visible of the clones' ability to experience through their ability to produce art for Madame's Gallery seems to follow a connection between art and humanity seen at least since Aristotle's *Metaphysics*, as here described by Agamben:

---

[74] Seaman, "Becoming More (than) Human," 266. Britzman makes a similar argument: "these 'students,' as Ishiguro names them, are real and invoke horror because they can never be separated from their function and our cruelty," "On Being a Slow Reader," 308.

[75] Ronell, *The Test Drive*, 45.

[76] In addition, in the scene where the students scare Madame at Hailsham Kathy says "it was like we'd walked from the sun right into the chilly shade" (35). Also, Kathy describes the last years at Hailsham, when their purpose had become clear to them, as "like day moving into night" (76).

> Aristotle also says that animals have impressions and memory (*φαντασίαι καὶ μνήμη*) but not experience, while man is capable of *ἐμπειρία* and, thanks to it, has art and science (*ἐπιστήμη καὶ τέχνη*). Experience, Aristotle adds, looks very similar to art, but differs from it in substantial ways: "For to have a judgment that when Callias was ill of this disease this did him good, and similarly in the case of Socrates and in many individual cases, is a matter of experience; but to judge that it has done good to all persons of a certain constitution, marked off in one class, when they were ill of this disease [...], this is a matter of art [*τέχνη*]."[77]

The problematic aspect of the Gallery project was precisely in its conjunction of art and experience, for to admit that the students had souls meant to deny life-saving treatments for those for whom soul-possession was supposedly a no-brainer: "How can you ask a world that has come to regard cancer as curable, how can you ask such a world to put away that cure, to go back to the dark days?" (*NLMG* 257). The students were set up to fail their test in humanity: the stakes were simply too high. However, even though Madame explains that the death of the clones as organ donors has made cancer curable, it must be remembered that it is still impossible for the clones to die *for us*. They can extend our lives, save us from a disease, but what the clones cannot do is to die instead of us; for as Derrida reminds us, death always awaits:

---

[77] Giorgio Agamben, *Man Without Content*, trans. Georgia Albert (Stanford: Stanford University Press, 1999), 74. Alan Bourassa puts it thus: "Human or non-human? Our own creation or a gift that obsesses us? We might think of language as we would think of an apparition out of the darkness of an empty road. Is it a fellow wanderer? Does it share my nature and is it haunted by the silence and mystery of the darkness? Does it fear and ward off the imminent reality of the outside? Is it powerless to fight the spirit that possesses it? And can I speak to it? Gain comfort in a shared humanness? Or is this figure itself a secretion of the darkness? A ghost sent to haunt and possess me? Even if it shows compassion for my plight, will its infinite power over me always make it a stranger?" "Literature, Language, and the Non-human," *A Shock to Thought: Expressions After Deleuze and Guattari*, ed. Brian Massumi (London: Routledge, 2002), 62

> Death's dative (dying *for* the other, giving one's life *to* the other) does not signify a substitution (*for* is not *pro* in the sense of "in the place of the other"). If something radically impossible is to be conceived of – and everything derives its sense from this impossibility – it is indeed dying *for the other* in the sense of dying *in the place of* the other. I can give the other everything except immortality, except this *dying for her* to the extent of dying in the place of her and so freeing her from her own death. I can die for the other in a situation where my death gives him a little longer to live, I can save someone by throwing myself in the water or fire in order to temporarily snatch him from the jaws of death, I can give her my heart in the literal or figurative sense in order to assure her of a certain longevity. But I cannot die in her place, I cannot give her my life in exchange for her death. Only a mortal can give, as we said earlier. That should now be adjusted to read: and that mortal can only give to what is mortal since he can give everything except immortality, everything except salvation as immortality.[78]

What is essential to take away from Derrida's passage here is the inserted side comment that while it is impossible to die for another, "everything derives its sense from this impossibility." A foregrounding of this impossibility in the guise of poverty is one of the philosophical ramifications of *Never Let Me Go*. Still, while "in the dark" is where the organ-hosts are kept, away from the front pages of the news, the dark is also where humanity would plunge without the cancer-curing organs provided by student donations. Miss Emily says: "'For a long time you were kept in the shadows [...]'" (258) and "'they wanted you back in the shadows'" (259). Kathy and the other clones are about light,

---

[78] Jacques Derrida, *The Gift of Death*, trans. David Willis (Chicago; London: The University of Chicago Press, 1996), 43. The gift, for Derrida, "should overrun the border, to be sure, toward the measureless and the excessive; but it should also suspend its relation to the border and even its transgressive relation to the separable lien or trait of a border," *Given Time: I. Counterfeit Money*, trans. Peggy Kamuf (Chicago; London: The University of Chicago Press, 1994), 91. For a reading of *The Gift of Death* along with *The Unconsoled* which focuses on the importance of non-human others in helping the human (Ryder) do its work, see Stanton, *Cosmopolitan* Fictions, 13-4.

but only in the sense of making darkness visible. Kathy wants to know the truth, which also means that she wants to do what she is *supposed* to do, which is circumscribed by the "they." As Ishiguro has stated, ""Not only do they not want to escape, but they feel a sense of duty [...] They want to be good donors, just like we all want to be good postmen or writers or whatever. I think that's what I find touching and admirable and sad about people in general."[79] Again, Ishiguro focuses on facticity as an acceptance of poverty. Kathy's experience is that of shining light on darkness not to dispel it but to make it come forth. As Mark Jerng puts it:

> It is not that Ishiguro fails to portray these clones as human; rather, he writes a story that reverses the narrative trajectory of individuation. Ishiguro does not reveal the human as unfolding and developing from a given inert potentiality. This is a much more disturbing story because it withholds the reader's desire for emancipation: the clones do not rebel and thus "become human." Rather, they learn to make sense of their lives as clones. In this way, *Never Let Me Go* disrupts the narrative of individuation and the values placed on the mysteriousness of birth, the "giftedness" of life, and wholeness. The novel takes up the question that challenges our privileged narratives of humanness: how is a life that is not "born" in the usual sense given form and dignity? By disrupting the narrative trajectory of individuation, Ishiguro gives us the imaginative potential of shifting our expectations of the form of humanity.[80]

---

[79] Qtd. in Jeff Giles, "Like Lambs to Slaughter," *Newsweek* 145.15 (2005), 82.

[80] Jerng, "Giving Form to Life," 382-3.

3.5 Making Shadows Visible

Making darkness visible can be seen in Japanese novelist Jun'ichirō Tanizaki's long essay *In Praise of Shadows*, mentioned in a previous footnote. Ishiguro rightly warns that one should not compare two writers merely because they hail from the same country (Ishiguro's family immigrated to England from Japan when he was five[81]), and he is especially wary of comparisons to Tanizaki: "Tanizaki wrote in a lot of different styles and he wrote for a long, long time. Tanizaki actually went into his eighties, and he produced an enormous amount of books as he went through lots of different stages. I can't really see that anybody would particularly compare me to any Japanese writer if it weren't for the fact that I have this Japanese name."[82] Nonetheless, Tanizaki is valuable here not because of any kind of "Japaneseness," but rather because of his calling for a return to shadows in literature, something which colors both Miss Emily's reaction to the song "Never Let Me Go" and Ronell's connection between testing and darkness.

Tanizaki's impetus for his essay is building his house, which he wishes to build as traditionally as possible, although he does desire electric lights, plumbing and other modern conveniences. This leads him to a discussion of the differences between architecture in the East and West:

> I understand that in the Gothic cathedral of the West, the roof is thrust up and up so as to place its pinnacle as high in the heavens as possible – and that herein is thought to lie its special beauty. In the temples of Japan, on the other hand, a roof of heavy tiles is first laid out, and in the deep, spacious shadows created by the eaves the rest of the structure is built.[83]

---

[81] Lewis, *Kazuo Ishiguro*, 1.

[82] Vorda and Herzinger, "An Interview with Kazuo Ishiguro," 81. For an overview of race and ethnicity in Ishiguro's work (up through *The Unconsoled*), see Sheng-mei Ma, "Kazuo Ishiguro's Persistent Dream for Postethnicity: Performance in Whiteface," *Post Identity* 2.1 (1999), 71-88.

[83] Tanizaki, *In Praise of Shadows*, 17.

Tanizaki is arguing for a space carved around shadows, rather than light, for if Ronell is correct, any attempt at construction using only light (the light of reason, for example) is only an attempt at distracting from the shadows underneath.[84] As quoted above, this is why Miss Emily wept when she saw Kathy dancing; not because Kathy would be unable to have children, but:

> "I was weeping for an altogether different reason. When I watched you dancing that day, I saw something else. I saw a new world coming rapidly. More scientific, efficient, yes. More cures for the old sicknesses. Very good. But a harsh, cruel world. And I saw a little girl, her eyes tightly closed, holding to her breast the old kind world, one that she knew in her heart could not remain, and she was holding it and pleading, never to let her go." (*NLMG* 266-7)

Miss Emily's statements beg the questions: What is it that is supposed to remain within Kathy? What is it that she will not let go? What Kathy will not let go seems to be the shadows, the darkness, disruption, noise: poverty. Tanizaki argues for the beauty of shadows, for the beauty of the whiteness of a smile of a woman who lacquers her teeth black.[85] Then Tanizaki, in the

---

[84] Also the central thesis of Max Horkheimer and Theodor Adorno's *Dialectic of Enlightenmen: Philosophical Fragments*, trans. Edmund Jephcott (Stanford: Stanford University Press, 2002).

[85] "The woman of old was made to hide the red of her mouth under green-black lipstick, to put shimmering ornaments in her hair; and so the last trace of color was taken from her rich skin. I know of nothing whiter than the face of a young girl in the wavering shadow of a lantern, her teeth now and then as she smiles shining a lacquered black through lips like elfin fires. It is whiter than the whitest white woman I can imagine," Tanizaki, *In Praise of Shadows*, 33. It should be remembered that Tanizaki was arguing for an aesthetic that he thought was rapidly disappearing from Japan: "It is important to emphasize that for Tanizaki the world of shadows was no longer a dominant and realistic presence, as he saw the pull toward technology as relentless and unavoidable. The world of shadows was therefore, for him an aesthetic and cultural choice that had to be articulated intellectually as an abstraction. Yet Tanizaki strained to express the ineffable, seeking to restore a tangible emotional identity that time and change threatened to banish," Tetsuo Najita and H. D. Harootunian, "Japan's Revolt against the West," *Modern Japanese Thought*, ed. Bob Tadashi Wakabayashi (Cambridge: Cambridge University Press, 1998), 251.

last pages of his essay, sees a place for the sheltering and care for such shadows in literature:

> I have thought there might still be somewhere, possibly in literature or the arts, where something could be saved. I would call back at least for this literature this world of shadows we are losing. In the mansion of literature I would have the eaves deep and the walls dark, I would push back into the shadows the things that come forward too clearly, I would strip away the useless decoration. I do not ask that this be done everywhere, but perhaps we may be allowed at least one mansion where we can turn off the electric lights and see what it is like without them.[86]

In this last passage Tanizaki seems to have given up on hoping for a mansion carved from shadows, and is not meagerly hoping for a mansion, which he names literature, to at least contain some of the darkness that remains. In *Never Let Me Go*, the context for these shadows is the test because it is what could propel Kathy and Tommy from out of the shadows, although only into a recognition that would allow them a middle ground of a possible three-year deferral at the Cottages. However, although Kathy and Tommy are skeptical about there being any test to pass at all, they still want to prove their love in the hope of a deferral, for Tommy's fourth and surely final donation is approaching. When Miss Emily asks them if this is the reason why they are there, Kathy thinks: "If she'd asked this in a certain way, like the whole idea was completely crazy, then I'm sure I'd have felt pretty devastated. But she hadn't quite said it like that. She'd asked it almost like it was a test question she knew the answer to; as if, even, she'd taken other couples through an identical routine many times before" (*NLMG* 247). The possible many times before that Kathy indicates points towards a mechanism for keeping the darkness visible, and that is repetition, or not letting go.

---

[86] Tanizaki, *In Praise of Shadows*, 42.

3.6 Not Letting Go

In the "Testing Your Love" chapter of *The Test Drive*, Ronell maps out the upward motion, the "break *up*,"[87] of Nietzsche and Wagner. Ronell's commentary is important here because she shows how the test of true love, which Kathy and Tommy desire to take in order to be rewarded their deferral, is a test not meant to be passed. In fact it is the position opened up by Nietzsche "from which misunderstanding has become a philosophically rigorous way toward thinking."[88] As indicated in the quote at the end of the last section, this is a test that has been given before; the answer is known, and the outcome decided: it is "sure" that Tommy and Kathy are in love, *and* it is "sure" that they will not get their deferral.[89] This is a tragic ending in which the clones are kept in the shadows, but as all else in the novel, the story works on the level of an allegory of "the human condition." Ronell's work on Nietzsche here will help develop the coordinates of this allegory.

Nietzsche's being enamored of Wagner started when he first heard *Tristan* as a student,[90] and it was Wagner who proved so essential for jump-starting Nietzsche's early work: "It was Wagner's presence that convinced Nietzsche that greatness and genuine creation were still possible, and it was Wagner who inspired him with the persistent longing first to equal and then to outdo his friend."[91] However, Ronell focuses on Nietzsche's later break with Wagner, which is important because it also included a holding on to Wagner's importance: "For Nietzsche, saying 'thank you' involves the experience of letting go without disavowing that history which has run its course. Thanking

---

[87] Ronell, *The Test Drive*, 293.

[88] Avital Ronell, "Hitting the Streets: *Ecce Fama*," *Finitude's Score: Essays for the End of the Millennium* (Lincoln; London: University of Nebraska Press, 1994), 66.

[89] This "sure" is taken up in the next section.

[90] Walter Arnold Kaufmann, *Nietzsche: Philosopher, Psychologist, Antichrist* (Princeton: Princeton University Press, 1974), 30.

[91] Ibid.

sends it on its way, thus allowing it to have arrived."[92] This break is in one sense that which allows, recalling Benjamin's reading of a new barbarianism, for one to "start from scratch, detach."[93] However, this break is not "complete," but rather from within the act of thanking *for* there develops a distance *from*. By holding this place of both being turned *towards* and turned *away from* it is "as if in the act of thanking he [Nietzsche] were continually testing himself."[94] Nietzsche's position can be seen in a passage on the *amor fati* from *The Gay Science* in which he invokes the "yes" that is both a turning away from and a turning towards: "I want to lead no war against the ugly. I do not want to accuse, I do not want to accuse the accusers even once. Let *looking away* be my only denial! And, all in all and on the whole: I want someday to be only a Yes-sayer!"[95] The importance of Nietzsche's position is that he "posits himself as the test site, putting himself continually at risk, obeying the provisional logic of the test."[96] Ronell is drawing out the importance of not letting go, of putting one's self "continually" at risk. What interests Ronell is that Nietzsche loved Wagner *and* that he broke with him.[97] This break, which is one of thanks, is also "an engagement, a commitment – a vow that does not restrict itself to the acknowledgement of a fact but that firmly

[92] Ronell, *The Test Drive*, 281. Ronell later states: "When letting go (a dreadful gift) occurs or arrives or has happened without arriving, thanks are given to mark an almost historical ability to split off from a powerful, a once necessary convergence of forces that held you to the tyranny of promise," ibid., 284. Kaufmann says: "Even after his break with Wagner, Nietzsche frankly admitted how much he owed to the early inspiration of this friendship – and one may safely follow his judgment in this instance," *Nietzsche*, 30.

[93] Ronell, *The Test Drive*, 282.

[94] Ibid.

[95] Friedrich Nietzsche, *The Gay Science*, trans. Walter Kaufmann (New York: Vintage Books, 1974), 276.

[96] Ronell, *The Test Drive*, 282. Earlier in the same text Ronell reads the Zen kōan as another test site in which the question is more important than the answer: "Once the question had been posed, the puzzle formulated, the student was expected to hold fast to it. However, the kōan resisted such a hold. It was meant to summon up terrific doubt and brought practitioners to the edge of endurance," ibid., 112. For elaboration see Brian Willems, "Avital Ronell: The Work of Survival," *artUS* 23 (2008), 25.

[97] Ronell, *The Test Drive*, 285.

invokes a responsibility."[98] It is a break that will not let go because "it requires the affirmation of breakage by submitting itself to the test of the eternal return."[99] This "*zweideutige*, double-binding"[100] horizon of the break is not really a break at all, but a relationship to the break, "over and over renewing the commitment to the break."[101] In the language being developed here, Nietzsche *makes the break visible* through a constant renewal, an over-renewal of its conditions. However, even this moment of making-visible is shrouded in darkness, for, as Greaney argues, this eternal return "never appears as something that Zarathustra masters well enough to spell out [...] Zarathustra never offers a straightforward, discursive lesson of the word that is putatively his. The eternal return always takes the form of a parable, a vision, a parody, or, as Avital Ronell suggests, a rumor."[102] This ambiguity that Greaney describes as part of "parable" and "parody" is the "lie" that was seen to be necessary in Benjamin's fable in order for experience to be passed on.

3.7 The Eternal Return of the Test

This experience of eternal return, of the scrambling of question and answer, points to the *drive* in the title of Ronell's work, meaning it points to the calling of a disruption which "leaves the very notion of place in suspense,"[103] where, "nearly every social encounter involves a secret testing system on which one is bound to do poorly."[104] And poorly is what Tommy and Kathy

---

[98] Ibid., 292.

[99] Ibid.

[100] Ibid.

[101] Ibid., 293.

[102] Greaney, *Untimely Beggar*, 79. Or, as Nietzsche says at the end of his preface to *Human, All Too Human*, "one *remains* a philosopher only by – being silent," Friedrich Nietzsche, *Human, All Too Human: A Book for Free Spirits*, trans. Marion Faber and Stephen Lehmann (Lincoln; London: University of Nebraska Press, 1986), 11. On Ronell and rumor, see "Street-Talk."

[103] Ronell, *The Test Drive*, 127.

[104] Ronell, *Stupidity*, 47.

do, since actually *proving* that you are sure you are in love is not really why they came to ask about the deferral, as Miss Emily indicates:

> "Sure?" It was the first time she'd spoken for ages and we both jolted back a bit in surprise. "You say you're *sure*? Sure that you're in love? How can you know it? You think love is so simple? So you are in love. Deeply in love. Is that what you're saying to me?" [...] "You believe this? That you're deeply in love? And therefore you've come to me for this...this deferral? Why? Why did you come to me?" (*NLMG* 247)

Miss Emily states that Kathy and Tommy came to her for a deferral, and it is only *after* she states this answer that she then asks the question of why they came. As such she indicates that they are there for a different reason. Kathy and Tommy are there to show that there is really no test to begin with, and that there are no deferrals to dole out. The reason they are there is to make the empty structure of the test visible. This structure of the test is not only the structure of the "deferral" test, but also of the "soul" test for which the Gallery was created. These two tests are connected in this final confrontation with Miss Emily and Madame because Tommy has started to make art. Tommy first shares this fact with Kathy when they, along with Chrissie and Rodney, are in Norfolk. Although he is still dating Ruth, Tommy tells Kathy that he has started working on drawings, since, as a guardian had once told Tommy, "they *revealed what you were like inside*. She said *they revealed your soul*. [...] *they need something to go on*" (173). Something to go on when "they" judge you at the end. But Kathy thinks there are other ways to undergo the test: "'Maybe they've got all sorts of ways to judge,' I said after a moment. 'Maybe the art's just one out of all kinds of different ways'" (174).

Kathy's comment, like Miss Emily's above, indicates that the "kind" of test is not what is at stake. Perhaps the real test is not one that either Kathy or Tommy take, but rather one that they are: clones that have come about because of advances in technology. As Bernard Stiegler has argued, the rate of technological revolutions has slowly increased, so that now we are at the point where there is no stability between revolutions, but rather we see only one revolution after another, with no stability in between.[105] This continual eruption is akin to the relationship between technology and testing as read by Ronell:

> In a way, technology ensures its evolving perpetuation by quietly positing as its sole purpose an infinite series of testing events severed from any empirical function. Thus an elliptical circuit has been established between testing and the real: a circuit so radically installed – it is irreversible – cancels the essential difference between the test and what was assumed to be real.[106]

This continually spinning technological revolution "leaves," as Ronell was quoted claiming above, "the very notion of place in suspense." Such a suspense is what the fantasizing about Norfolk was all about for Kathy and Tommy, it was where "it was possible to forget for whole stretches of time who we really were" (*NLMG* 140); it was a "cosy state of suspension" (ibid.). This state of suspense is the double-bind of the novel, which is also thematized in the drawings that Tommy works on both during his time with Ruth, and later, when he picks up drawing again while he is with Kathy; these drawings are of animals, but tiny electric animals. They are small, because of the paper

---

[105] Bernard Stiegler, *Technics and Time, 1: The Fault of Epimetheus*, trans. Richard Beardsworth and George Collins (Stanford: Stanford University Press, 1998), 37-43. This argument is based on the thought of Bertrand Gille. Sloterdijk offers a similar argument: "If there is man, then that is because a technology has made him evolve out of the prehuman. It is that which authentically brings about humans. Therefore humans encounter nothing strange when they expose themselves to further creation and manipulation, and they do nothing perverse when they change themselves autotechnologically, given that such interventions and assistance happen on such a high level of insight into the biological and social nature of man that they become effective as authentic, intelligent and successful coproductions with evolutionary potential," "Anthropo-Technology," *NPQ* 21.4 (Fall 2004), 43. Sloterdijk's reading of "manipulation" seems to echo N. Katherine Hayles' developement of "flickering signifiers" in *How We Became Posthuman: Virtual Bodies in Cybernetics, Literature, and Informatics* (Chicago; London: University of Chicago Press, 1999), 25-49.

[106] Ronell, *The Test Drive*, 163.

Tommy is using, but they are also dense, and they have to be viewed from up close: it is in the intersection of being small and close that they come to life:

> "If you make them tiny, and you have to because the pages are only about this big, then everything changes. It's like they come to life by themselves. Then you have to draw in all these different details for them. You have to think about how they'd protect themselves, how they'd reach things. Honest, Kath, it's nothing like anything I ever did at Hailsham." (176)

Tommy sets up an economy of proximity with his animals: first *you make* them tiny. Then, once you get close, proximity encourages being-with: hospitality.[107] There is no claim to ontological primordialness here: the animals are still in the realm of simile, it is "like" they come to life. But within this "like" participation is demanded, and *you have* to get involved. You have to care, because you are being-with. But Kathy has trouble getting excited:

> So I was taken aback at how densely detailed each one was. In fact, it took a moment to see they were animals at all. The first impression was like one you'd get if you took the back off a radio set: tiny canals, weaving tendons, miniature screws and wheels were all drawn with obsessive precision, and only when you held the page away could you see it was some kind of armadillo, say, or a bird. (184-5)[108]

Tommy's drawings, which are supposed to be the location of his soul, proof of his human-defining love is actually the electric, the fake. This location is outside the Edenic origin mythos of capital-H Humanity.[109] Instead, there is a devotion

---

[107] On hospitality and autobiography, see E. S. Burt, "Hospitality in Autobiography: Levinas Chez de Quincey," *ELH* 71 (2004).

[108] It should also be noted that Kathy need to hold the page *away* from her to see the whole picture, thus reinforcing the structure of proximity and distance developed previously.

[109] Donna Haraway sees a similar role for the cyborg: "The cyborg would not recognize the Garden of Eden; it is not made of mud and cannot dream of

from within the coordinates of the soul-test to that which has no soul: the proof of personhood lies in poverty. Even Kathy has to admit that "For all their busy, metallic features, there was something sweet, even vulnerable about each of them" (*NLMG* 185).

The devotedness to poverty of Kathy can be seen at the end of the novel, after she and Tommy have found out that there is no test to be passed at Madame's. It is on the way home from this encounter that Tommy has a recurrence of his now almost-forgotten fits, and the meaning to the song "Never Let Me Go" is emphasized: Kathy is going to hold on to the experience of facticity, meaning, she is never going to let Tommy go. Tommy has his fit in the middle of a muddy field, and Kathy holds him tight: "it seemed we were holding onto each other because that was the only way to stop us being swept away into the night [...]" (269). Kathy is there, with the visceral, holding on tight in the same way both Kathy and Tommy are devoted to what they are *supposed to do*, meaning to donate their organs, showing how an assumed freedom of choice is but neglecting the recognition of the function-circle around you.[110] As Tommy says, "'After all, it's what we're *supposed* to be doing, isn't it?" (223).

In the final scene of the book, after Tommy has completed after his fourth donation, Kathy makes her way back to Norfolk. However, in order to remain inside the "lostness" of the place,

---

returning to dust. Perhaps that is why I want to see if cyborgs can subvert the apocalypse of returning to nuclear dust in the manic compulsion to name the Enemy. Cyborgs are not reverent; they do not remember the cosmos. They are wary of holism, but needy for connection – they seem to have a natural feel for united front politics, but without the vanguard party. The main trouble with cyborgs, of course, is that they are the illegitimate offspring of militarism and patriarchal capitalism, not to mention state socialism. But illegitimate offspring are often exceedingly unfaithful to their origins. Their fathers, after all, are inessential," "A Cyborg Manifesto," 152.

[110] Kwame Anthony Appiah provides a refreshing look at the butler Stevens from *The Remains of the Day* in which he is also seen as enacting a kind of freedom by doing what he is supposed to do: "Mr. Stevens serves as a good example of the moral power of individuality because he exemplifies it even though he doesn't himself believe in liberty, equality, and fraternity. Even someone as illiberal as Mr. Stevens, that is, demonstrates the power of individuality as an ideal," "Liberalism, Individuality, and Identity," *Critical Inquiry* 27.2 (Winter 2001), 315-6.

she parks in an unknown territory, keeping her space in flux: "At one stage I found myself on a road I'd never been on, and for about half an hour I didn't know where I was and didn't care. I went past field after flat, featureless field, with virtually no change except when occasionally a flock of birds, hearing my engine, flew up out of the furrows" (281). It is in this lost, deterritorialized space, open on to a flock of birds and the noise of an engine, that Kathy is able to cry, to experience her facticity, the result of which is another territorialization along the plane of consistency: Kathy turns back and starts her life as a donor; she "turned back to the car, to drive off to wherever it was I was supposed to be" (ibid., 282).

This reading of *Never Let Me Go* has developed an allegory of "the human condition" which reflexively disrupts the coordinates of that condition along a three-pronged axis: First, by rescheduling a traditionally human-only-facticity in other-than-humans the novel foregrounds not the necessity of a second-order level of consciousness within the non-human but rather the poverty of the so-called human condition itself. By showing the structure of familiarity within strangeness, *Never Let Me Go* draws forth the unthought linguistic nature of nonrelation and develops a hermeneutics of the told/not told from which the ontological difference between human being and other-than-human being is put at risk. Second, making the unthought of nonrelation visible was taken up through the philosophical ramifications of poverty. This making-visible was traced through an awakening of fundamental attunement from within the everyday. The engine for this awakening was found within the recursive nature of poverty itself, which was seen as an essential element of both memory and autobiographical narration. Third, the poverty of the human condition was developed through an exegesis of the body as a location of experience. Unconscious expressions and visceral paroxysms were read as pathways to the dual-structure of deterritorialization and reterritorialization. This argument is not that of "beyond" but rather "along"; in other words, the title of Ishiguro's novel was taken in a literal sense by developing a not-letting-go of the human condition through an exegesis of poverty itself: a continued renewal of the relationship to the "break" between human and other-than-human was seen as what is actually most human.

Bibliography

Aarseth, Espen. "Nonlinearity and Literary Theory." *Hyper/Text/Theory*. Edited by George Landow. Baltimore: Johns Hopkins University Press, 1994.

Adams, Tim. "'For Me, England is a Mythical Place.'" *The Observer* (Feb 20 2005): 17.

Adorno, Theodor. *Aesthetic Theory*. Translated by Robert Hullot-Kentor. Minneapolis: University of Minnesota Press, 1997.

Agamben, Giorgio. "Bartleby, or On Contingency." *Potentialities: Collected Essays in Philosophy*. Translated by Daniel Heller-Roazen. Stanford: Stanford University Press, 1999.

_____. "Infancy and History: An Essay on the Destruction of Experience." Translated by Liz Heron. *Infancy and History: The Destruction of Experience*. London; New York: Verso, 2007.

_____. *Man Without Content*. Translated by Georgia Albert. Stanford: Stanford University Press, 1999.

_____. *Remnants of Auschwitz: The Witness and the Archive*. Translated by Daniel Heller-Roazen. New York: Zone Books, 2002.

_____. *The Open: Man and Animal*. Translated by Kevin Attell. Stanford: Stanford University Press, 2004.

Allen, Brooke. "The Damned and the Beautiful." *New Leader* (March/April 2005): 25-27.

Alweiss, Lilian. "Heidegger and 'the Concept of Time.'" *History of the Human Sciences* 15.117 (2002): 117-132.

Appiah, Kwame Anthony. "Liberalism, Individuality, and Identity." *Critical Inquiry* 27.2 (Winter 2001): 305-332.

Arendt, Hannah. "A Reply to Eric Voegelin." *The Portable Hannah Arendt*. Edited by Peter Baehr. London: Penguin, 2003.

Aycock, Alan. "Derrida/Fort-Da: Deconstructing Play." *Postmodern Culture* 3.2 (January 1993). Internet: http://www.iath.virginia.edu/pmc/textonly/issue.193/aycock.193 [Accessed March 24, 2009].

Badiou, Alain. *Deleuze: The Clamor of Being*. Translated by Louise Burchill. Minneapolis; London: University of Minnesota Press, 2000.

_____. *Ethics: An Essay on the Understanding of Evil*. Translated by Peter Hallward. London; New York: Verso, 2001.

Barthes, Roland. "The Death of the Author." *Image, Music, Text*. Translated by Stephan Heath. New York: Hill and Wang, 1999.

Baudrillard, Jean. *Cool Memories*. Translated by Chris Turner. London; New York: Verso: 1990.

Benjamin, Walter. "Experience and Poverty." Translated by Rodney Livingstone. *Selected Writings: Volume 2, 1927-1934*. Edited by Michael Jennings, Howard Eiland and Gary Smith. Cambridge; London: The Belknap Press of Harvard University Press, 1999.

_____. *The Origin of German Tragic Drama.* Translated by John Osborne. London; New York: Verso, 1998.

_____. "The Storyteller: Reflections on the Works of Nikolai Leskov." *Illuminations: Essays and Reflections*. Translated by Harry Zohn. Edited by Hannah Arendt. New York: Schocken Books, 1969.

Bernard, Rollin. "Keeping Up with the Cloneses: Issues in Human Cloning." *The Journal of Ethics* 3 (1999): 51-71.

Bernstein, Stephen. "*Never Let Me Go.*" *The Review of Contemporary Fiction* 25.1 (2005): 139.

Bhabha, Homi. "Unpacking My Library Again." *The Journal of the Midwest Modern Language Association* 28.1 (Spring 1995): 5-18.

Blanchot, Maurice. *The Space of Literature*. Translated by Ann Smock. Lincoln; London: University of Nebraska Press, 1989.

_____. *Thomas the Obscure*. Translated by Robert Lamberton. *The Station Hill Blanchot Reader: Fiction and Literary Essays*. Edited by George Quasha. Barrytown: Station Hill, 1999.

Block, Allison. "Ishiguro, Kazuo. *Never Let Me Go*." *Booklist* (Jan 1 & 15, 2005): 783-4.

Bourassa, Alan. "Literature, Language, and the Non-human." *A Shock to Thought: Expressions After Deleuze and Guattari*. Edited by Brian Massumi. London: Routledge, 2002.

Bradford, Richard. *The Novel Now: Contemporary British Fiction*. Malden: Blackwell, 2007.

Bradley, Malcolm. *The Modern British Novel*. London: Secker and Warburg, 1993.

Britzman, Deborah. "On Being a Slow Reader: Psychoanalytic Reading Problems in Ishiguro's *Never Let Me Go*." *Changing English* 13.3 (December 2006): 307-318.

Buber, Martin. *The Knowledge of Man: A Philosophy of the Interhuman.* Translated by Maruice Friedman and Ronald Smith. New York: Harper Torchbooks, 1965.

Burley, Justine. "A Braver, Newer World." *Nature* 435.26 (2005): 427.

Burt, E. S. "Hospitality in Autobiography: Levinas Chez de Quincey." *ELH* 71 (2004): 867-897.

Burton, Rob. *Artists of the Floating World: Contemporary Writings between Cultures*. Lanham: University Press of America, 2007.

Butcher, James. "A Wonderful Donation." *Lancet* 365 (2005): 1299-1300.

Butler, Judith. *Bodies That Matter: On the Discursive Limits of "Sex."* New York; London: Routledge, 1993.

Calarco, Matthew. "On the Borders of Language and Death: Derrida and the Question of the Animal." *Angelaki* 7.2 (2002): 17-25.

Carel, Havi. *Life and Death in Freud and Heidegger*. Amsterdam: Rodopi, 2006.

Carrigan, Henry. "Ishiguro, Kazuo. *Never Let Me Go*." *Library Journal* (January 2005): 98.

Cicero. *On the Immortality of the Soul, or* Quaestinonum Tusculanarum*, volume I.* Annover: Flagg, Gould, and Newman, 1833.

Cixous, Hélène. "Fiction and Its Phantoms: A Reading of Freud's *Das Unheimliche* (The 'Uncanny')." *New Literary History* 7.3 (Spring 1976): 525-548; 619-645.

Clark, Katerina and Michael Holquist. *Mikhail Bakhtin*. Cambridge; London: Harvard University Press, 1984.

Coetzee, J. M. *The Lives of Animals*. Princeton: Princeton University Press, 1999.

Connor, Stephen. *The English Novel in History: 1950-1995*. London; New York: Routledge, 1996.

Crapanzano, Vincent. *Imaginative Horizons: An Essay in Literary-Philosophical Anthropology*. Chicago; London: The University of Chicago Press, 2004.

Critchley, Simon. *Very Little – Almost Nothing: Death, Philosophy, Literature*. London: Routledge, 1997.

Culler, Jonathan. *Structuralist Poetics: Structuralism, Linguistics, and the Study of Literature*. Ithaca: Cornell University Press, 1976.

Damasio, Antonio. *The Feeling of What Happens: Body, Emotion and the Making of Consciousness*. London: Vintage, 2000.

Darwin, Charles. *From So Simple a Beginning: The Four Great Books of Charles Darwin*. Edited by Edward Wilson. New York: W. W. Norton & Co., Inc., 2006.

Dastur, Françoise. *Death: An Essay on Finitude*. Translated by John Llewelyn. London; Antlantic Highlands: Athlone, 1996.

Davidson, Michael. *Concerto for the Left Hand: Disability and the Defamiliar Body*. Ann Arbor: University of Michigan Press, 2008.

Davis, Steven. "The Path of a Thinking, Poetizing Building: The Strange Uncanniness of Human Being on Earth." *Heidegger and the Earth: Issues in Environmental Philosophy*. Edited by Ladelle McWhorter. Kirksville: Truman State University Press, 1992.

Deb, Siddhartha. "Lost Corner." *New Statesman* (March 7 2007): 55.

Deigh, John. *Emotions, Values, and the Law*. Oxford: Oxford University Press, 2008.

DeLanda, Manuel. *Intensive Science and Virtual Philosophy*. London; New York: Continuum, 2004.

_____. *A Thousand Years of Nonlinear History*. New York: Zone Books, 2005.

Deleuze, Gilles. *The Fold: Leibniz and the Baroque*. Translated by Tom Conley. Minneapolis: University of Minnesota Press, 1993.

Deleuze, Gilles and Félix Guattari. *A Thousand Plateaus: Capitalism and Schizophrenia*. Translated by Brian Massumi. Minneapolis; London: University of Minnesota Press, 2005.

de Man, Paul. *Aesthetic Ideology*. Edited by Andzrej Warminski. Minneapolis: University of Minnesota Press, 1997.

_____. *Allegories of Reading: Figural Language in Rousseau, Nietzsche, Rilke and Proust*. New Haven; London: Yale University Press, 1979.

_____. *Blindness and Insight: Essays in the Rhetoric of Contemporary Criticism*. Minneapolis: University of Minnesota Press, 2006.

de Montaigne, Michel. "That to Study Philosophy is to Learn to Die." *The Works of Montaigne*. Edited by William Hazlitt. London: John Templeman, 1842.

Dennett, Daniel. *Consciousness Explained.* Boston; Toronto; London: Little, Brown and Company, 1991.

Derrida, Jacques. *Aporias*. Translated by Thomas Dutoit. Stanford: Stanford University Press, 1993.

_____. *Geneses, Genealogies, Genres, & Genius: The Secrets of the Archive*. Translated by Beverley Bie Brahic. New York: Columbia University Press, 2006.

_____. *The Gift of Death*. Translated by David Willis. Chicago; London: The University of Chicago Press, 1996.

_____. *Given Time: I. Counterfeit Money*. Translated by Peggy Kamuf. Chicago; London: The University of Chicago Press, 1994.

_____. *Of Spirit: Heidegger and the Question*. Translated by Geoffrey Bennington and Rachel Bowlby. Chicago; London: University of Chicago Press, 1991.

_____. *The Postcard: From Socrates to Freud and Beyond.* Translated by Alan Bass. Chicago; London: The University of Chicago Press, 1987.

Dick, Philip K. *Do Androids Dream of Electric Sheep?* New York: Del Rey Books, 1996.

Dollimore, Jonathan. "Death's Incessant Motion." *The Limits of Death: Between Philosophy and Psychoanalysis*. Edited by Joanne Morra, Mark Robson and Marquard Smith. Manchester: Manchester University Press, 2000.

Dreyfus, Hubert. *Being-in-the-world: A Commentary on Heidegger's* Being and Time, *Division I.* Cambridge: MIT Press, 1991.

Düttmann, Alexander García. "Making Poverty Visible -- Three Theses." *Parrhesia* 4 (2008): 1-10.

Ekman, Paul. "Darwin, Deception, and Facial Expression." *Annals New York Academy of Sciences* 1000 (2003): 205-221.

_____. "Facial Expressions." *Handbook of Cognition and Emotion.* Edited by Tim Dalgleish and Mick Power. New York: John Wiley and Sons, 1999.

Elden, Stuart. "Heidegger's Animals." *Continental Philosophy Review* 39 (2006):273-291.

Eliot, George. *Daniel Deronda.* London: Penguin, 2003.

Eliot, T. S. *Collected Poems: 1902-1963.* Orlando: Harcourt, Brace and Company, 1991.

Fish, Stanley. "How Ordinary is Ordinary Language?" *Is There a Text in this Class?* Cambridge: Harvard University Press, 1980.

Fluet, Lisa. "Introduction: Antisocial Goods." *Novel: A Forum on Fiction* 40.3 (2007): 207-215.

Flusser, Vilém. "What is Communication?" *Writings.* Translated by Erik Eisel. Edited by Andreas Ströhl. Minneapolis; London: University of Minnesota Press, 2002.

Forster, E. M. *Aspects of the Novel.* Orlando: Harcourt, 1985.

Forsythe, Ruth. "The Cultural Displacement and the Mother-Daughter Relationship in Kazuo Ishiguro's *A Pale View of Hills.*" *The West Virginia University Philological Papers* 52 (2005): 99-108.

Foucault, Michel. *The History of Sexuality, Vol. 1: An Introduction*. Translated by Robert Hurley. New York: Vintage Books, 1978.

Freeman, John. "Never Let Me Go: A Profile of Kazuo Ishiguro." *Conversations with Kazuo Ishiguro*. Edited by Brian Shaffer and Cynthia Wong. Jackson: University Press of Mississippi, 2008.

Freeman, Mark. "Rethinking the Fictive, Reclaiming the Real: Autobiography, Narrative Time and the Burden of Truth." *Narrative and Consciousness: Literature, Psychology, and the Brain*. Edited by Gary Fireman, Ted Mcvay Jr. and Owen Flanagan. New York: Oxford University Press, 2003.

Freud, Sigmund. *Beyond the Pleasure Principle*. Translated by James Strachey. New York; London: W. W. Norton and Company, 1989.

_____. "The Uncanny." *Art and Literature*. Edited by Albert Dickenson. London: Penguin, 1990.

Friedrichsen, G. W. S., R. W. Burchfield and C. T. Onions. *The Oxford Dictionary of English Etymology*. Oxford: Oxford University Press, 1966.

Fynsk, Christopher. *Heidegger: Thought and Historicity*. Ithaca: Cornell University Press, 1993.

_____. *Infant Figures: The Death of the "Infans" and Other Scenes of Origin*. Stanford: Stanford University Press, 2000.

_____. *Language and Relation: ...that there is language*. Stanford: Stanford University Press, 1996.

Gallix, François. "Kazuo Ishiguro: The Sorbonne Lecture." *Conversations with Kazuo Ishiguro*. Edited by Brian Shaffer and Cynthia Wong. Jackson: University Press of Mississippi, 2008.

García-Rojas, Alejandra, et al. "Emotional Body Expression Parameters in Virtual Human Ontology." Presented at the First International Workshop on Shapes and Semantics, Matsushima, Japan, 2006.

Genette, Gérard. *Narrative Discourse Revisited.* Translated by Jane Lewin. Ithaca: Cornell University Press, 1988.

Genosko, Gary. "A Bestiary of Territoriality and Expression: Poster Fish, Bower Birds, and Spiny Lobsters." *A Shock to Thought: Expressions After Deleuze and Guattari.* Edited by Brian Massumi. London: Routledge, 2002.

Giannet, Stanley. "The Human-Animal Divide: Interdisciplinary Ethical Reflections." *Journal of Evolutionary Psychology* 24 (2003): 9-13.

Giles, Jeff. "Like Lambs to Slaughter." *Newsweek* 145.15 (2005): 82.

Godwin, Mike. "Remains of the DNA." *Reason* 37.5 (October 2005): 57-9.

Gordon, David. *Imagining the End of Life in Post-Enlightenment Poetry: Voices Against the Void.* Gainesville: University Press of Florida, 2005.

Gray, John. *Straw Dogs: Thoughts on Humans and Other Animals*. London: Granta, 2002.

Greaney, Patrick. "Estranging Memory in Ilse Aichinger." *The German Quarterly* 80.1 (Winter 2007): 42-58.

_____. "Language and Form: Hölderlin's Errancy." *MLN* 113.3 (1998): 537-560.

_____. *Untimely Beggar: Poverty and Power from Baudelaire to Benjamin.* Minneapolis; London: University of Minnesota Press, 2008.

Guenther, Lisa. "*Le flair animal*: Levinas and the Possibility of Animal Friendship." *PhaenEx* 2.2 (2007): 216-238.

Haddon, Mark. *The Curious Incident of the Dog in the Night-time*. New York: Vintage, 2003.

Haker, Hille. "Narrative Bioethik: Ethik des biomedizinischen Erzählens." *Narrative Ethik: Das Gute und das Böse erzählen*. Edited by Karen Joisten. Berlin: Akademie Verlag, 2007.

Hansen, Mark. *New Philosophy for New Media*. Cambridge: MIT Press, 2006.

Hanssen, Beatrice. *Walter Benjamin's Other History: Of Stones, Animals, Human Beings, and Angels*. Berkeley: University of California Press, 2000.

Haraway, Donna. "A Cyborg Manifesto: Science, Technology, and Socialist-Feminism in the Late Twentieth Century." *Simians, Cyborgs and Women: The Reinvention of Nature*. New York; Routledge, 1991.

Harris, John. *On Cloning*. New York: Routledge, 2004.

Hayles, N. Katherine. *Electronic Literature: New Horizons for the Literary*. Notre Dame: University of Notre Dame Press, 2008.

_____. *How We Became Posthuman: Virtual Bodies in Cybernetics, Literature, and Informatics*. Chicago; London: University of Chicago Press, 1999.

Heidegger, Martin. "Die Armut." *Heidegger Studies* 10 (1994): 5-11.

_____. *Being and Time*. Translated by Joan Stambaugh. Albany: State University of New York Press, 1996.

_____. "Hölderlin and the Essence of Poetry." *Elucidations of Hölderlin's Poetry*. Translated by Keith Hoeller. Amhurst: Humanity Books, 2000.

_____. *The Fundamental Concepts of Metaphysics: World, Finitude, Solitude*. Translated by William McNeill and Nicholas Walker. Bloomington; Indianapolis: Indiana University Press, 1995.

_____. "Letter on Humanism." *Basic Writings*. Edited by David Farrell Krell. New York: HarperCollins, 1993.

_____. *Ontology: The Hermeneutics of Facticity*. Translated by John van Buren. Bloomington: Indiana University Press, 1999.

_____. *La Pauvreté (Die Armut)*. Translated by Philippe Lacoue-Labarthe. Strasbourg Cedex: Presses Universitaires de Strasbourg, 2004.

Hill, Tobias. "England's Dreaming." *The Times, Weekend Review* (Feb 26 2005): 6.

Hofmann, Albert. *LSD: My Problem Child*. Sarasota: Multidiciplinary Association for Psychedelic Studies, 2005.

Hoffmann, E. T. A. "The Sandman." *The Best Tales of Hoffmann*. Edited by E. F. Bleiler. New York: Dover, 1967.

Hoolsema, Daniel. "The Echo of an Impossible Future in *The Literary Absolute*." *MLN* 119.4 (2004): 845-868.

Horkheimer, Max and Theodor Adorno. *Dialectic of Enlightenmen: Philosophical Fragments*. Translated by Edmund Jephcott. Stanford: Stanford University Press, 2002.

Ingersoll, Earl. "Taking Off into the Realm of Metaphor: Kazuo Ishiguro's *Never Let Me Go*." *Studies in the Humanities* 34.1 (2007): 40-59.

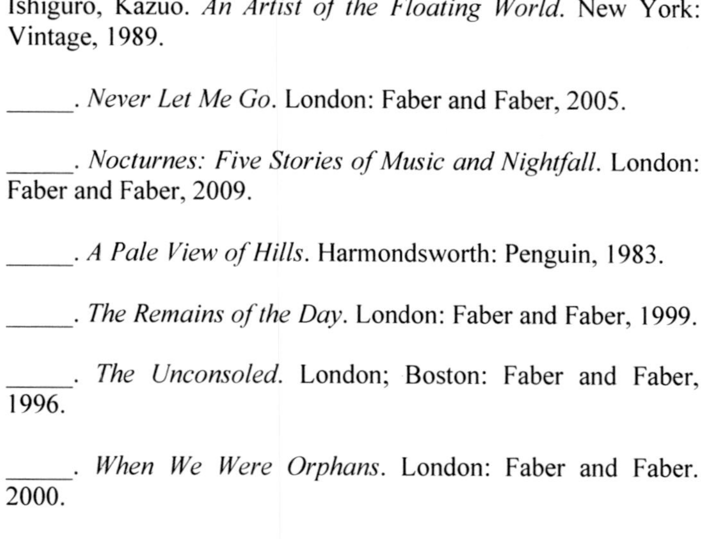

Ishiguro, Kazuo. *An Artist of the Floating World.* New York: Vintage, 1989.

_____. *Never Let Me Go*. London: Faber and Faber, 2005.

_____. *Nocturnes: Five Stories of Music and Nightfall.* London: Faber and Faber, 2009.

_____. *A Pale View of Hills*. Harmondsworth: Penguin, 1983.

_____. *The Remains of the Day*. London: Faber and Faber, 1999.

_____. *The Unconsoled.* London; Boston: Faber and Faber, 1996.

_____. *When We Were Orphans*. London: Faber and Faber. 2000.

Ishiguro, Kazuo and Kenzaburo Oe. "The Novelist in Today's World: A Conversation." *Conversations with Kazuo Ishiguro.* Edited by Brian Shaffer and Cynthia Wong. Jackson: University Press of Mississippi, 2008.

Jackson, Rosemary. *Fantasy: The Literature of Subversion.* London: Routledge, 2001.

Janik, Del Ivan. "No End of History: Evidence from the Contemporary English Novel." *Twentieth Century Literature* 41.2 (Summer 1995): 160-189.

Jentsch, Ernst. "On the Psychology of the Uncanny." *Angelaki: A New Journal in Philosophy, Literature, and the Social Sciences* 2.1 (1996): 7-17.

Jerng, Mark. "Giving Form to Life: Cloning and Narrative Expectations of the Human." *Partial Answers: Journal of Literature and the History of Ideas* 6.2 (2008): 369-393.

Kac, Eduardo. *Telepresence & Bio Art: Networking Humans, Rabbits, & Robots*. Ann Arbor: University of Michigan Press, 2005.

Kakutani, Michiko. "Sealed in a World That's Not As It Seems." *New York Times* Section E (April 4 2005): 1.

Kaufmann, Walter Arnold. *Nietzsche: Philosopher, Psychologist, Antichrist*. Princeton: Princeton University Press, 1974.

Kauppinen, Jari. "Death as Limit of Phenomenology: The Notion of Death from Husserl to Derrida." *Analecta Husserliana* 66 (2000): 323-348.

Kendall, Karalyn. "The Face of the Dog: Levinasian Ethics and Human/Dog Co-evolution." *Queering the Non/Human*. Edited by Noreen Giffney and Myra Hird. Hampshire: Ashgate, 2008.

Kippen, David. "Ishiguro Imagines Love among Clones." *San Francisco Chronicle* Section E (April 14 2005): 1.

Kittler, Friedrich. *Gramophone, Film, Typewriter*. Translated by Geoffrey Winthrop-Young and Michael Wutz. Stanford: Stanford University Press, 1999.

Klein, Melanie. *Envy and Gratitude: A Study of Unconscious Sources*. London: Routledge, 2003.

Koestler, Arthur. *Insight and Outlook: An Inquiry into the Common Foundations of Science Art, and Social Ethics*. New York: Macmillan, 1949.

Kofman, Sarah. *Nietzsche and Metaphor*. Translated by Duncan Large. London: Athlone Press, 1993.

Kracauer, Siegfried. "Bordom," *The Mass Ornament: Weimar Essays*. Translated by Thomas Levin. Cambridge; London: Harvard University Press, 1995.

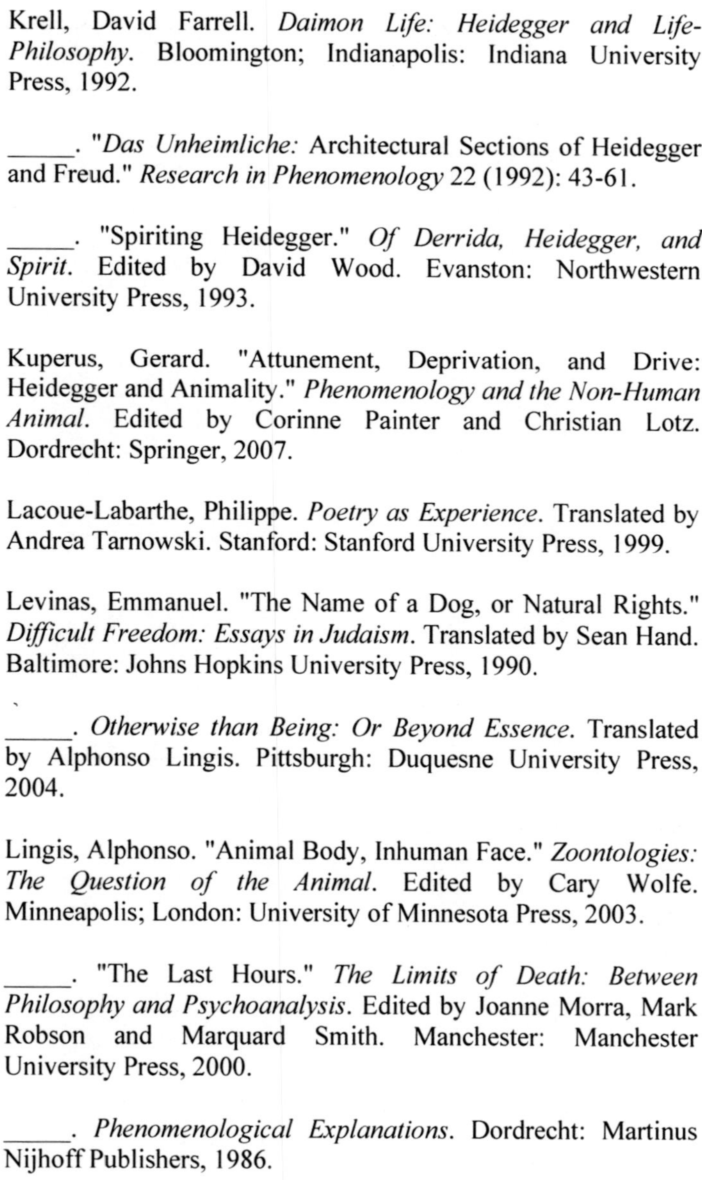

Krell, David Farrell. *Daimon Life: Heidegger and Life-Philosophy*. Bloomington; Indianapolis: Indiana University Press, 1992.

_____. "*Das Unheimliche:* Architectural Sections of Heidegger and Freud." *Research in Phenomenology* 22 (1992): 43-61.

_____. "Spiriting Heidegger." *Of Derrida, Heidegger, and Spirit*. Edited by David Wood. Evanston: Northwestern University Press, 1993.

Kuperus, Gerard. "Attunement, Deprivation, and Drive: Heidegger and Animality." *Phenomenology and the Non-Human Animal*. Edited by Corinne Painter and Christian Lotz. Dordrecht: Springer, 2007.

Lacoue-Labarthe, Philippe. *Poetry as Experience*. Translated by Andrea Tarnowski. Stanford: Stanford University Press, 1999.

Levinas, Emmanuel. "The Name of a Dog, or Natural Rights." *Difficult Freedom: Essays in Judaism*. Translated by Sean Hand. Baltimore: Johns Hopkins University Press, 1990.

_____. *Otherwise than Being: Or Beyond Essence*. Translated by Alphonso Lingis. Pittsburgh: Duquesne University Press, 2004.

Lingis, Alphonso. "Animal Body, Inhuman Face." *Zoontologies: The Question of the Animal*. Edited by Cary Wolfe. Minneapolis; London: University of Minnesota Press, 2003.

_____. "The Last Hours." *The Limits of Death: Between Philosophy and Psychoanalysis*. Edited by Joanne Morra, Mark Robson and Marquard Smith. Manchester: Manchester University Press, 2000.

_____. *Phenomenological Explanations*. Dordrecht: Martinus Nijhoff Publishers, 1986.

_____. *Trust*. Minneapolis: University of Minnesota Press, 2004.

Lippit, Akira Mizuta. *Electric Animals: Toward a Rhetoric of Wildlife*. Minneapolis: University of Minnesota Press, 2000.

Llewelyn, John. "Am I Obsessed by Bobby? (Humanism of the Other Animal)." *Emmanuel Levinas: Critical Assessments of Leading Philosophers, Volume IV, Beyond Levinas*. Edited by Claire Katz and Lara Trout. London: Taylor & Francis, 2004.

London Cyrenians Housing. Internet: http://www.london-cyrenians.org.uk [Accessed March 24, 2009].

Ma, Sheng-mei. "Kazuo Ishiguro's Persistent Dream for Postethnicity: Performance in Whiteface." *Post Identity* 2.1 (1999): 71-88.

Marion, Jean-Luc. *God Without Being*. Translated by Thomas Carlson. Chicago; London: University of Chicago Press, 1995.

Mason, Gregory. "An Interview with Kazuo Ishiguro." *Conversations with Kazuo Ishiguro*. Edited by Brian Shaffer and Cynthia Wong. Jackson: University Press of Mississippi, 2008.

Maturana, Humberto and Francisco Varela. *Autopoiesis and Cognition: The Realization of the Living*. Dordrecht; Boston: D. Reidel Publishing Company, 1980.

Mayr, Ernst. *Toward a New Philosophy of Biology: Observations of an Evolutionist*. Cambridge; London: Harvard University Press, 1988.

McDonald, Keith. "Days of Past Futures: Kazuo Ishiguro's *Never Let Me Go* As 'Speculative Memoir.'" *Biography* 30.1 (Winter 2007): 74-83.

McEwan, Ian. "Literature, Science, and Human Nature." *The Literary Animal: Evolution and the Nature of Narrative*. Edited by Jonathan Gottschall and David Sloan. Evanston: Northwestern University Press, 2005.

McGee, Glenn. "A Pragmatic Approach to Human Cloning." *The Cloning Sourcebook*. Edited by Arlene Judith Klotzko. New York: Oxford University Press, 2001.

McNeill, William. "The Time of *Contributions to Philosophy*." *Companion to Heidegger's* Contributions to Philosophy. Edited by Charles Scott, Susan Schoenbohm, Daniela Vallega-Neu and Alejandro Vallega. Bloomington; Indianapolis: Indiana University Press, 2001.

Mead, Emily. "Future Present." *Publishers Weekly* (Jan 21 2005): 47.

Menand, Louis. "There's Something about Kathy: Ishiguro's Quasi-Science-Fiction Novel." *New Yorker* 81.6 (2005): 78.

Mensch, James. *Hiddenness and Alterity: Philosophical and Literary Sightings of the Unseen*. Pittsburgh: Duquesne University Press, 2005.

Merrell, Floyd. *Sensing Corporeally: Toward a Posthuman Understanding*. Toronto: University of Toronto Press, 2003.

Messud, Claire. "Love's Body." *The Nation* (May 16 2005): 28-31.

Miller, Michael. "A Joyful Path to *Dasein*?" *New Blackfriars* 86.1004 (2005): 379-388.

Mills, Marie. "Narrative Identity and Dementia: A Study of Emotion and Narrative in Older People with Dementia." *Ageing and Society* 17 (1997): 673-698.

Mithen, Steven. *The Singing Neanderthals: The Origins of Music, Language, Mind and Body*. London: Weidenfeld and Nicholson, 2005.

Moore, Michael Scott and Michael Sontheimer. "*Spiegel* Interview with Kazuo Ishiguro." *Spiegel Online*. Internet: http://www.spiegel.de [Accessed March 24, 2009].

Mori, Masahiro. "The Uncanny Valley." Translated by Karl MacDorman and Takashi Minato. *Energy* 7.4 (1970): 33-35.

Mouzakitis, Angelos. "Radical Finitude Meets Infinity: Levinas's Gestures to Heidegger's Fundamental Ontology." *Thesis Eleven* 90.1 (2007): 61-78.

Munno, Antonio. "*Never Let Me Go*," *General Practitioner* (February 2007): 69.

Najita, Tetsuo and H. D. Harootunian. "Japan's Revolt against the West." *Modern Japanese Thought*. Edited by Bob Tadashi Wakabayashi. Cambridge: Cambridge University Press, 1998.

Nancy, Jean-Luc. *Being Singular Plural*. Translated by Robert Richardson and Anne O'Byrne. Stanford: Stanford University Press, 2000.

_____. "The Being-there of Being-with." Translated by Marie-Eve Morin. *Continental Philosophy Review* 41.1 (2008): 1-15.

_____. *The Inoperative Community*. Translated by Peter Connor, Lisa Garbus, Michael Holland and Simona Sawhney. Minneapolis: University of Minnesota Press, 1991.

National Bioethics Advisory Commission. "Cloning Human Beings." Internet: http://bioethics.georgetown.edu [Accessed March 24, 2009].

Nelson, Eric. "Heidegger and the Ethics of Factiticty." *Rethinking Facticity*. Edited by François Raffoul and Eric Nelson. Albany: State University of New York Press, 2008.

Nietzsche, Friedrich. *The Gay Science*. Translated by Walter Kaufmann. New York: Vintage Books, 1974.

_____. *Human, All Too Human: A Book for Free Spirits.* Translated by Marion Faber and Stephen Lehmann. Lincoln; London: University of Nebraska Press, 1986.

Pascal, Blaise. *Pensées*. Translated by A. J. Krailsheimer. London: Penguin, 1966.

Pégon, Claire. *L'Art de la Fugue chez K. Ishiguro*. Toulouse: Presses Universitaires du Mirail, 2004.

Peirce, Charles. *Peirce on Signs: Writings on Semiotic by Charles Sanders Peirce*. Chapel Hill: The University of North Carolina Press, 1991.

Petry, Mike. *Narratives of Memory and Identity: The Novels of Kazuo Ishiguro*. Frankfurt am Main: Peter Lang, 1999.

Plato. *Phaedo* Translated by G. M. A. Grube. Indianapolis: Hackett Publishing Company, Inc., 1977.

Porée, Marc. *Kazuo Ishiguro: The Remains of the Day*. Paris: CNED - Didier Érudition, 1999.

Puchner, Martin. "When We Were Clones: On Kazuo Ishiguro." *Raritan* XXVII (Spring 2008): 34-49.

RandomHouse.com. "A Conversation with Kazuo Ishiguro." (2005). Internet: http://www.randomhouse.com [Accessed March 24, 2009].

Rayment-Pickard, Hugh. *Impossible God: Derrida's Theology*. Hants; Burlington: Ashgate, 2003.

Reese, Elaine and Kate Farrant. "Social Origins of Reminiscing." *Autobiographical Memory and the Construction of a Narrative Self: Developmental and Cultural Perspectives*. Edited by Robyn Fivush and Catherine Haden. Mahwah: Lawrence Erlbaum Associates, 2003.

Reitano, Natalie. "The Good Wound: Memory and Community in *The Unconsoled.*" *Texas Studies in Literature and Language* 49.4 (Winter 2007): 361-386.

Rickels, Laurence A. "Devil Father Mine." *Lust for Life: On the Writings of Kathy Acker*. Edited by Amy Scholder, Carla Harryman and Avital Ronell. London; New York: Verso, 2006.

_____. "Mine." *Terminals*. Internet: http://vv.arts.ucla.edu [Accessed March 24, 2009].

_____. "Satan and Golem, inc." *Parallax* 10.1 (2004): 49-57.

Robbins, Bruce. *Upward Mobility and the Common Good: Toward a Literary History of the Welfare State*. Princeton: Princeton University Press, 2007.

Robinson, Richard. "Nowhere, in Particular: Kazuo Ishiguro's *The Unconsoled* and Central Europe." *Critical Quarterly* 48.4 (2006): 107-130.

Ronell, Avital. *Crack Wars: Literature Addiction Mania*. Lincoln; London: University of Nebraska Press, 1992.

_____. "Hitting the Streets: *Ecce Fama*." *Finitude's Score: Essays for the End of the Millennium*. Lincoln; London: University of Nebraska Press, 1994.

_____. *Stupidity*. Urbana; Chicago: University of Illinois Press, 2002.

_____. *The Test Drive*. Urbana; Chicago: University of Illinois Press, 2005.

_____. *The ÜberReader*. Edited by Diane Davis. Urbana; Chicago: University of Illinois Press, 2008.

Rorty, Richard. "Consolation Prize." *Village Voice Literary Suppliment* (October 1995): 13.

Royle, Nicholas. *The Uncanny*. Manchester: Manchester University Press, 2003.

Rushdie, Salman. "Kazuo Ishiguro." *Imaginary Homelands: Essays and Criticism 1981-1991*. New York; London: Penguin, 1992.

Sayers, Valerie. "Spare Parts." *Commonweal* (July 15 2005): 27-28.

Scanlan, Margaret. "The Recuperation of History in British and Irish Fiction." *A Companion to the British and Irish Novel: 1945-2000*. Edited by Brian Shaffer. Mladen: Blackwell, 2005.

Schirmacher, Wolfgang. "*Homo Generator*: The Challenge of Gene Technology." *Technology and Responsibility*. Edited by Paul Durbin. Dordrecht; Boston: D. Reidel Publishing Company, 1987.

Schopenhauer, Arthur. *The World as Will and Representation, vol. 1*. Translated by E. F. J. Payne. Mineola: Dover, 1966.

Screech, M. A. "Good Madness in Christendom." *The Anatomy of Madness: Essays in the History of Psychiatry, volume 1, People and Ideas*. Edited by W. F. Bynum, Roy Porter and Michael Shepherd. Oxford: Taylor and Francis, 2004.

Scheerbart, Paul. *The Gray Cloth*. Translated by John Stewart. Cambridge: MIT Press, 2001.

Schneider, Rebecca. "Hello Dolly Well Hello Dolly: The Double and its Theatre." *Psychoanalysis and Performance*. Edited by Patrick Campbell and Adrian Kear. New York: Routledge, 2001.

Seaman, Myra. "Becoming More (than) Human: Affective Posthumanisms, Past and Future." *Journal of Narrative Theory* 37.2 (2007): 246-275.

Serres, Michel. *The Parasite*. Translated by Lawrence Schehr. Minneapolis; London: University of Minnesota Press, 2007.

Shaffer, Brian. *Understanding Kazuo Ishiguro*. Columbia: University of South Carolina Press, 1998.

Sheets-Johnstone, Maxine. "Consciousness: A Natural History." *Synthesis Philosophica* 44.2 (2007): 283-299.

Sim, Wai-chew. *Globalization and Dislocation in the Novels of Kazuo Ishiguro*. Lewiston; Ceredigion: Edwin Mellen Press, 2006.

Simic, Charles. "Notes on Poetry and Philosophy." *New Literary History* 21.1 (1989): 215-221.

Sloterdijk, Peter. "Anthropo-Technology." *NPQ* 21.4 (2004): 40-47.

Smith, Daniel. "Badiou and Deleuze on the Ontology of Mathematics." *Think Again: Alain Badiou and the Future of Philosophy*. Edited by Peter Hallward. London; New York, Continuum, 2004.

Stanton, Katherine. *Cosmopolitan Fictions: Ethics, Politics, and Global Change in the Words of Kazuo Ishiguro, Michael Ondaatje, Jamaica Kincaid, and J. M. Coetzee*. New York; London: Routledge, 2006.

Steeves, H. Peter. "Lost Dog, or, Levinas Faces the Animal." *Figuring Animals: Essays on Animal Images in Art, Literature, Philosophy and Popular Culture*. Edited by Mary Pollock and Catherine Rainwater. New York; Hampshire: Palgrave-Macmillan, 2005.

Sterling, Bruce. *Shaping Things*. Cambridge: MIT Press, 2005.

Stiegler, Bernard. *Technics and Time, 1: The Fault of Epimetheus*. Translated by Richard Beardsworth and George Collins. Stanford: Stanford University Press, 1998.

Sugiyama, Michelle Scalise. "Reverse-Engineering Narrative." *The Literary Animal: Evolution and the Nature of Narrative*. Edited by Jonathan Gottschall and David Sloan. Evanston: Northwestern University Press, 2005.

Suglia, Joseph. *Hölderlin and Blanchot on Self-Sacrifice*. New York: Peter Lang, 2004.

Summers-Bremner, Eluned. "'Poor Creatures': Ishiguro's and Coetzee's Imaginary Animals." *Mosaic* 39.4 (December 2006): 145-160.

Swain, Don. "Don Swain Interviews Kazuo Ishiguro." *Conversations with Kazuo Ishiguro*. Edited by Brian Shaffer and Cynthia Wong. Jackson: University Press of Mississippi, 2008.

Tanizaki, Jun'ichirō. *In Praise of Shadows*. Translated by Thomas Harper and Edward Seidensticker. Stony Creek: Leete's Island Books, 1977.

_____. *The Makioka Sisters*. Translated by Edward Seidensticker. New York: Grosset and Dunlap, 1966.

Tanner, Laura. *Lost Bodies: Inhabiting the Borders of Life and Death*. Ithaca: Cornell University Press, 2006.

Terestchenko, Michel. "Servility and Destructiveness in Kazuo Ishiguro's *The Remains of the Day*." *Partial Answers: Journal of Literature and the History of Ideas* 5.1 (2007): 77-89.

Thomson, Iain. "Can I Die?: Derrida on Heidegger on Death." *Philosophy Today* 49.1 (Spring 1999): 29-42.

Toadvine, Ted. "How Not to be a Jellyfish: Human Exceptionalism and the Ontology of Reflection."

Phenomenology and the Non-Human Animal. Edited by Corinne Painter and Christian Lotz. Dordrecht: Springer, 2007.

Todorov, Tzvetan. *The Fantastic: A Structural Approach to a Literary Genre*. Translated by Richard Howard. Ithaca: Cornell University Press, 1975.

Toker, Leona and Daniel Chertoff. "Reader Response and the Recycling of Topoi in Kazuo Ishiguro's *Never Let Me Go*." *Partial Answers: Journal of Literature and the History of Ideas* 6.1 (2008): 163-180.

Vallega, Alejandro. *Heidegger and the Issue of Space: Thinking on Exilic Grounds*. University Park: The Pennsylvania State University Press, 2003.

Verdonk, Peter. *Stylistics*. Oxford: Oxford University Press, 2002.

Veyret, Paul. *Kazuo Ishiguro: L'encre de la mémorie*. Pessac: Presses Universitaires de Bordeaux, 2005.

von Schelling, Friedrich. *System of Transcendental Idealism*. Translated by Peter Heath. Charlottesville: University Press of Virginia, 1997.

von Uexküll, Jakob. *Theoretical Biology*. Translated by Doris Mackinnon. New York: Kegan Paul, Trench, Trubner & Co., 1926.

Vorda, Allan and Kim Herzinger. "An Interview with Kazuo Ishiguro." *Conversations with Kazuo Ishiguro*. Edited by Brian Shaffer and Cynthia Wong. Jackson: University Press of Mississippi, 2008.

Vorhaus, Daniel. "Review of Kazuo Ishiguro, *Never Let Me Go*." *The American Journal of Bioethics* 7.2 (2007): 99-100.

Wallace, Alfred Russel. "*The Expression of the Emotions in Man and Animals*, By Charles Darwin, M.A., F.R.S., &c. London: Murray, 1872." *Quarterly Journal of Science* 3.37 (1873): 113-118.

Warren, James. *Facing Death: Epicurus and His Critics*. Oxford: Clarendon Press, 2004.

Weber, Samuel. *The Legend of Freud, Expanded Edition*. Stanford: Stanford University Press, 2000.

_____. "Stages and Plots: Theatricality after September 11, 2001, a Discussion with Simon Morgan Wortham and Gary Hall." *Theatricality as Medium*. New York: Fordham University Press, 2004.

Weiss, Paul. *Being and Other Realities*. Chicago; La Salle: Open Court, 1995.

Willems, Brian. "Avital Ronell: The Work of Survival." *artUS* 23 (2008): 22-25.

_____. *Hopkins and Heidegger*. London; New York: Continuum, 2009.

_____. "The Hyperreal Territory of Animals." *Poiesis* 10 (Summer 2008): 40-52.

Wimsatt, W. K. and Monroe Beardsley. "The Affective Fallacy." *The Verbal Icon*. Lexington: University of Kentucky Press, 1967.

Winkler, Rafael. "Heidegger and the Question of Man's Poverty in World." *International Journal of Philosophical Studies* 15.4 (2007): 521-539.

Wolfe, Cary. *Animal Rites: American Culture, the Discourse of Species, and Posthumanist Theory*. Chicago; London: University of Chicago Press, 2003.

Wong, Cynthia. *Kazuo Ishiguro, Second Edition.* Tavistock: Northcote House Publishers Ltd., 2005.

_____. "The Shame of Memory: Blanchot's Self-Dispossession in Ishiguro's *A Pale View of Hills*." *CLIO* 24.2 (1995): 127-45.

Wong, Cynthia and Grace Crummett. "A Conversation about Life and Art with Kazuo Ishiguro." *Conversations with Kazuo Ishiguro*. Edited by Brian Shaffer and Cynthia Wong. Jackson: University Press of Mississippi, 2008.

Wood, James. *How Fiction Works*. New York: Farrar, Straus and Giroux, 2008.

_____. "The Human Difference." *The New Republic* (May 16 2005): 36-39.

_____. "Ishiguro in the Underworld." *Guardian* (May 5 1995): 5.

_____. "The Unconsoled: *When We Were Orphans* by Kazuo Ishiguro." *The New Republic* (Oct 16 2000): 43-8.

Wrathall, Mark. "Social Constraints on Conversational Content: Heidegger on *Rede* and *Gerede*." *Heidegger Reexamined: Volume 1, Dasein, Authenticity and Death.* Edited by Hubert Dreyfus and Mark Wrathall. New York; London: Routledge, 2002.

Wroe, Nicholas. "Profile: Living Memories: Kazuo Ishiguro." *The Guardian Saturday Pages* (Feb 19 2005): 20.

Žižek, Slavoj. *Organs Without Bodies: On Deleuze and Consequences*. New York; London: Routledge, 2004.

_____. *The Parallax View*. Cambridge; London: The MIT Press, 2006.

Zupančić, Alenka. *Ethics of the Real: Kant, Lacan*. London; New York: Verso, 2000.

Index

*Items in **bold** refer to a chapter or section of a chapter*

Think Media: EGS Media Philosophy Series

Wolfgang Schirmacher, editor

The Ethics of Uncertainty: Aporetic Openings. Michael Anker

Trans/actions: Art, Film and Death. Bruce Alistair Barber

Trauma, Hysteria, Philosophy. Hannes Charen and Sarah Kamens

Literature as Pure Mediality: Kafka and the Scene of Writing.
Paul DeNicola

Deleuze and the Sign. Christopher M. Drohan

Imaginality: Conversant and Eschaton. A. Staley Groves

Hospitality in the age of media representation. by Christian Hänggi

The Organic Organisation: freedom, creativity and the search for fulfilment. Nicholas Ind

Media Courage: impossible pedagogy in an artificial community.
Fred Isseks

Mirrors triptych technology: Remediation and Translation Figures.
Diana Silberman Keller

Sonic Soma: Sound, Body and the Origins of the Alphabet.
Elise Kermani

The Art of the Transpersonal Self: Transformation as Aesthetic and Energetic Practice. Norbert Koppensteiner

Can Computers Create Art? James Morris

Propaganda of the Dead: Terrorism and Revolution. Mark Reilly.

The Novel Imagery: Aesthetic Response as Feral Laboratory. Dawan Stanford.

Community without Identity: The Ontology and Politics of Heidegger.
Tony See

other books available from Atropos Press

Teletheory. Gregory L. Ulmer

Philosophy of Culture-Kulturphilosophie: Schopenhauer and Tradition. Edited by Wolfgang Schirmacher.

Grey Ecology. Paul Virilio
Edited with introduction by Hubertus von Amelunxen. Translated by Drew Burk

Talking Cheddo: Liberating PanAfrikanism. Menkowra Manga Clem Marshall

The Tupperware Blitzkrieg. Anthony Metivier

Che Guevara and the Economic Debate in Cuba. Luiz Bernardo Pericás

Follow Us or Die. Vincent W.J. van Gerven Oei and Jonas Staal

Just Living: Philosophy in Artificial Life. Collected Works Volume 1.
Wolfgang Schirmacher

Lightning Source UK Ltd.
Milton Keynes UK
UKOW04f1843140715

255190UK00001B/25/P